THE PSYCHOLOGY OF FAMILY LAW

PSYCHOLOGY AND THE LAW
General Editor: Linda J. Demaine

The Psychology of Tort Law
Jennifer K. Robbennolt and Valerie P. Hans

The Psychological Foundations of Evidence Law
Michael J. Saks and Barbara A. Spellman

The Psychology of Family Law
Eve M. Brank

The Psychology of Family Law

Eve M. Brank

With a Preface by Linda J. Demaine

NEW YORK UNIVERSITY PRESS

New York

NEW YORK UNIVERSITY PRESS
New York
www.nyupress.org

Library of Congress Cataloging-in-Publication Data
Names: Brank, Eve M., author.
Title: The psychology of family law / Eve M. Brank.
Description: New York : New York University Press, 2019. | Series: Psychology and the law | Includes bibliographical references and index.
Identifiers: LCCN 2018026986| ISBN 9781479865413 (cl : alk. paper) | ISBN 9781479824755 (pb : alk. paper)
Subjects: LCSH: Domestic relations. | Domestic relations—Psychological aspects.
Classification: LCC K670 .B73 2018 | DDC 346.01/5—dc23
LC record available at https://lccn.loc.gov/2018026986

New York University Press books are printed on acid-free paper, and their binding materials are chosen for strength and durability. We strive to use environmentally responsible suppliers and materials to the greatest extent possible in publishing our books.
Manufactured in the United States of America
10 9 8 7 6 5 4 3 2 1
Also available as an ebook

CONTENTS

PREFACE

LINDA J. DEMAINE

The NYU Press Psychology of Law book series addresses an intriguing state of affairs in legal scholarship. Although law and legal process are inherently psychological in nature, traditionally, relatively few law professors, judges, or legal practitioners have drawn on empirical psychological research to inform their perspectives and decisions. In recent years, the legal community has increasingly recognized that both substantive law and legal procedure rest on a multitude of testable assumptions about human behavior that can be informed by psychological research. Without formal training in psychology, however, it can be challenging for legal experts to identify relevant and informative psychological research, evaluate its methodological rigor, and interpret the empirical results. Consequently, in the absence of trusted resources to translate findings from psychological studies and apply them to core legal issues, psychology's potential to inform legal doctrine and practice will remain unfulfilled. Lawyers, in particular, will lack the tools that would enable them to better understand the law's effects on human behavior and how the law might be better constructed to achieve its goals.

Three important exceptions to psychology's peripheral status in legal scholarship are eyewitness testimony, false confessions, and jury decision making. In each of these realms, insights from psychological research have entered legal discussions and debates, resulting in marked improvements in the legal system's functioning. These exceptions, which developed precisely because lawyers communicated the fundamental legal issues to psychologists and psychologists introduced lawyers to informative research findings, demonstrate the potential of psychology to inform the law.

The Psychology of Law book series is intended to help make the exceptions to the rule by expanding and strengthening the intersection of law and psychology. To achieve this goal, the series applies psychology to subjects covered in the core law school curriculum. The books are designed to facilitate exchanges between lawyers and psychologists about these fundamental legal issues by introducing lawyers to the most pertinent research methods and findings and introducing psychologists to the central and generally complex legal issues. The books are valuable assets for law professors who desire to incorporate psychological science into their classes. To facilitate their adoption in law classrooms, the books map on to popular casebooks and are relatively brief and practical. The books are also prime resources for participants in psychology-law graduate programs, professors who teach undergraduate law and psychology courses, and mainstream psychologists who study legal issues. The books' expansive coverage of psychological research on core legal topics and their identification of areas in need of further research will provide these audiences with current knowledge and a roadmap to inspire further research. Finally, the books will be useful to legal practitioners whose work in particular areas of law can benefit from an understanding of psychology. All volumes are authored by eminent scholars who are conversant in both psychology and the law and possess the expertise necessary to identify and articulate legal issues of import, apply psychological theory and research findings to them, and identify areas of future research for psychologists.

In *The Psychology of Family Law*, Eve Brank considers the intersection of psychological theory and research with both long-established and developing family law doctrine. Brank begins with the observation that family law governs some of our most intimate human relationships, including spouses, lovers, and parents and children. Family law intrudes, in a sense, on the privacy generally inherent in these relationships, and so should be carefully calibrated and wisely applied to balance the sometimes competing interests of the individuals and society. From this perspective, Brank explores key psychological aspects and legal parameters of the marital relationship. These include the basis for, and consequences of, legal limitations on who may marry (including age requirements and incest prohibitions), the rights and duties that attach to persons in marital relationships sanctioned by the state (from financial benefits and liabilities to medical decision making to evidentiary privileges in court), and legal oversight of the dissolution of marriage (such as waiting periods, asset distribution, and spousal support). Brank also addresses complicated legal and psychological issues that can arise when individuals and couples desire to create a family—assisted reproductive technology, surrogate pregnancy, and adoption—or, conversely, wish to avoid reproduction or parenthood. To round out this coverage of marriage, procreation, and parenthood, she discusses the law and psychology of dissolving the marital relationship when children are involved. Brank also enters the darker side of intimate human relations, examining three areas of abuse and neglect that present difficult issues of social policy and have been the subject of focused psychological study: intimate partner violence, child maltreatment, and elder maltreatment. She addresses the psychological precursors to, and consequences of, these forms of abuse and neglect, and the legal system's responses. Throughout the book, Brank identifies family law doctrines that align with psychological research findings or depart therefrom, providing legal scholars, legal practitioners, and psychological experts valuable yet often overlooked insights into the discipline and fodder for future theory development and empirical study.

Introduction

The Door to the Family Home

Picture your front door. Do you see grand wood or smudged glass? Can you hear that door groan as it opens? Or do you feel the tug as it sticks in the summer humidity? Is it a door painted a bright, loud red or stained to match the wraparound front porch? Can you smell the neighbor's dinner in the next-door apartment? Is there a holiday wreath? A welcome mat? An eviction notice? Do you readily turn the knob, knowing that the door rarely is locked? Or do you only reach for the knob after unlocking several deadbolts? As your door begins to open, what do you see? When you picture your home, is it your childhood home that you see, or is it where you live now? Is it a set of worn stairs leading to your childhood room that you shared with your big brother? Is it an expansive great room with light pouring in from skylights and east-facing windows? Is it a narrow hallway leading to the rest of the apartment? Is it cold and dark or light and warm? What family awaits you inside the home? Is it your partner and his children? A grandmother and some cousins? Your Alaskan husky and a kitten? Your dad? Two moms? Your foster parents and foster siblings? Your elderly dad and your wife? A mom and a dad and one sibling?

For me, the door is sometimes metal, sometimes wood, and sometimes glass. Some are grand while others have seen better days. The home inside is a combination of rooms and hallways from all the different houses I have called home. The family inside is not only a combination of my current family—me, my supportive husband, and my wise-beyond-her-years teenage daughter—but also the generations of me. I see my grandparents, aunts, uncles, parents, sister, brothers-in-law, sister-in-law, and all my beloved nieces and nephews. My definition of *family* will always be influenced by these people whom I call my family.

The lens through which I see the world is shaped and polished by each one of them. I expect that is true for you, too.

We all approach family law from the vantage point of personal experience. There is no other area of law that shapes us in such intimate ways at key turns in our lives. No matter your social experience with your parents, it is a biological certainty that genetically you have at least two parents. And, no matter the social structure of your family, the law was involved in some way like it is involved in all social structures. For some, the law may have positively intervened; for others, it may have negatively interfered. Still others may not have recognized the role of law in their family—but it was there.

I was met with some doubt when I first started discussing this book with colleagues and generally anyone who would listen to me talk about my "book deal." *Is there enough to say for a whole book? Maybe you should write a law review article on the topic first or a column for your department newsletter. After all, how much can you say about the role of psychology in family law?* Most people took a very narrow view of the topic and thought I was planning to write an entire book about therapy sessions for couples and children going through a divorce. In no way diminishing the role of psychological therapy during divorce, that topic is but a small illustration of the myriad ways in which psychological theory and research stand to help us understand and critique family law. For both psychology and family law there is a great deal more to them than the superficial topics that provide chatter with your airplane seat companion. The current text provides a first look at how psychology and family law are inextricably linked yet distinct. Psychology and law seem like they would naturally fit together because they both focus on human behaviors and solve human problems.[1] But psychology is based on empiricism whereas the law is based on precedent. In other words, psychology is descriptive whereas the law is prescriptive,[2] and those core difference mean the two systems' goals can and will clash.

When I teach about family law and juvenile law, I analogize government intrusion on family privacy and decision making to that of entering a door to the family home. Just as each of us has a different picture of a physical door and home, there are also differences in how much that door is opened to government involvement. Consider two families. The first family includes a married couple and one child. The child is 12 years old; neither the parents nor the child has had any legal infractions—in fact, no known family members have ever had more of a criminal record than a speeding ticket. This family lives in a home they purchased in a quiet neighborhood. The second family includes a divorcing couple with one biological child and one foster child. Both children have been arrested, and the foster child is currently on probation. The father recently moved out and is living with his father (the paternal grandfather), who is a registered sex offender. The mother and two children live in a rented apartment. Although the mother is a legal U.S. citizen, her parents are undocumented immigrants who live with the mother during the winter when they are not able to find work.

Now imagine the metaphorical door to the family home for these two families. The door represents how much government or legal oversight there is in family decisions. For the first family, the door is merely cracked open. The law is barely a factor in the decisions that the family makes. No judge, probation officer, or caseworker will examine the size of the child's room or dictate how many children are permitted to share a bedroom. If this family decides to take an impromptu road trip across three state lines, there will be no one to call except a neighbor to watch their pets and water their plants. If the child in the first family brings home a report card with a few more Ds than As, the parents will have the power, within reason, to decide how to motivate their child to be a better student. Of course, the door can be pushed wide open if that child goes to school with bruises and broken bones from parents attempting to "motivate" better grades, but requiring more studying or taking away privileges is within the parents' power. Although the law determines how many days of school the child can miss before truancy becomes an issue, the parents have a great deal of latitude when deciding whether their child stays home from school a few days.

Contrast family one's barely cracked open door to that of family two's wide-open door. Although the law is consistent for both families, the second family's door is open because of their situation. For example, the law defines minimal standards for both families, and they are both held to the same standard of school attendance. However, unlike family one, the law is likely the main factor family two considers in their decisions. School absences could take on a new meaning because of impending child custody agreements or probation requirements. Consider the analogy of leaving your front door cracked open versus wide open. Before long, the outside is in the house permeating every surface. Sometimes outside is the smell of fresh jasmine, and other times, it is ice. The second family's approach to child-rearing is similarly affected by the sometimes cracked, but often wide-open, door for government involvement into their family home.

The metaphorical door to the family home makes family law a uniquely personal and psychologically relevant area of the law. Everyone has a different experience with how wide the door was open and how much the law was a part of their family decision making. How wide that door opens has long-term impacts on the psychological well-being of both the individual family members and the family unit. It also determines how we, as adults, approach basic questions about family law.

The Law and Psychology of Families

How does a person decide whom to marry? Can you marry your cousin? Who gets to decide if you can marry your cousin? Does a prenuptial agreement undermine the contractual and emotional promises of marriage? What basis do you need to get a divorce? How should property be divided when a couple divorces? Can an unmarried person adopt? How much should a noncustodial parent pay in child support? When does corporal punishment become abuse? Should grandparents have visitation rights with their grandchildren? What surname should a child receive? Should a husband be able to sue his wife for her tortious acts?

Each one of these questions can be answered either legally or psychologically. Often the two disciplines are in general agreement, with their answers intertwined in such a way that they are virtually impossible to separate. Other times, as you will read throughout this book, the law proscribes certain behaviors that psychology would encourage or encourages certain behaviors that psychological research suggests are counterproductive. In addition to the juxtaposition of psychology and law, the fragmentation of family law should also be obvious. The preceding list of questions represents a staggering number of both legal and psychological topics, even though it only begins to touch on the issues addressed by family law doctrine.[3] Family law attorneys and judges need to understand a vast array of psychological topics to adequately handle family law matters, from child development to substance abuse and mental illness.[4] Moreover, according to a recent Pew Research Center survey, a vast majority of respondents (76%) said family was the most important element in their life. Another 22% said it was one of the most important elements.[5] These results demonstrate that when family matters appear before the courts, the courts' focus is on a topic, the family, which is often the most important element in someone's life. It is undeniable that the psychological underpinnings and effects are immense.

Family Law Theory—or Lack Thereof

Law school professors Kelly Weisberg and Susan Frelich Appleton, in their family law casebook, explain it this way: "Modern Family Law offers valuable interdisciplinary perspectives. Family law has been heavily influenced by work in the fields of family history, psychology, sociology, social work, medicine, and philosophy . . . family law is not just analyzed and applied—it is experienced."[6] Many other areas of law tend to garner centralizing theories.[7] For example, the law of torts focuses on the circumstances surrounding when a person or an entity is to be held civilly liable for harming another person or entity.[8] Holistic doctrinal explanations fall short for family law. Instead, centralized principles, concepts, or themes are provided as doctrinal structure. Some scholars structure the discipline around the battle between privacy and state power.[9] Law professor Vivian Hamilton describes conjugality, privacy, contract, and *parens patriae* as the four main principles in family law.[10] Another law professor, Brian Bix, expands this list to ten overarching principles, ranging from federalism to the primary notion of the family.[11] For the current book's purposes, a number of Bix's principles are particularly relevant psychologically. For example, Bix explains the tension between *ex post* and *ex ante* decision making that pulls between making decisions that are best and most just for the current parties versus creating the best incentives and policies for future parties.[12] This, of course, summons the psychological principles of motivation and conditioning. Another example is that of discretionary versus nondiscretionary decisions, exemplified by the best interest standard versus strict child support guidelines.[13]

As noted earlier, despite the diversity of issues encompassed within family law, the two main topics everyone thinks of when they think of family law and psychology are divorce and counseling. Although this book addresses those two topics, it goes well beyond them to demonstrate the wide reach of psychological study within family law.

Beyond Divorce

Without a doubt, the topic of divorce overshadows much of the family law curriculum, especially courses on family law practice. In a quick survey of the family law texts on my own bookshelf, material focused on topics related to divorce generally composes one-third to more than one-half of the chapters. These chapters address topics such as the act of divorce, division of property, alimony, child custody, child support, and alternative dispute resolution.[14] And the focus is on litigated appellate cases.[15] Divorce is certainly an important topic, and like the textbooks, it comprises a great deal of family law attorneys' time. But family law doctrine and practice are much broader ranging than litigated divorce, and understanding these other topics is essential to an informed perspective on the field.

The current text goes beyond divorce to address those issues that arise before a wedding, such as dating and barriers to marriage. There is a chapter on staying married and avoiding divorce. An additional chapter describes reproductive issues. Finally, there is another chapter that addresses domestic violence including intimate partner, child, and older adult abuse—topics often addressed in different courses and texts such as domestic violence, children and the law, or elder law.

Beyond Counseling

Legal professionals may not be clear on the different types of psychologists and the types of expertise they could bring to family law issues.[16] Indeed the public mostly sees psychologists as only clinicians or counselors who address mental health issues.[17] Yet, similar to family law, psychology is a diverse field. In fact, the American Psychological Association (APA) has 54 distinct divisions that each focus on either a subdiscipline of psychology or a specific topic area within psychology.[18]

These divisions range from general psychology[19] to the advancement of pharmacotherapy.[20] The APA is the largest scientific and professional organization for psychology in the United States, with more than 120,000 members, and it reflects the wide variety of issues addressed by psychological theory and research.[21]

This diversity is also mirrored in most university psychology departments, which offer separate programs or tracks available for faculty affiliation and graduate student training. In addition, psychologists are frequently found in other departments at universities and collaborate with many different people across campuses. Recently, psychology's wide reach has led to it being characterized as a "hub science."[22] A hub science is one that is central to a variety of theorizing and research. Other hub disciplines include mathematics, physics, chemistry, earth sciences, medicine, and the social sciences.[23] It is thus clear that psychology is a science that goes well beyond counseling sessions. Psychology at its core wants to know how and why people make decisions and how and why they perceive, think, feel, and act.[24] All different kinds of psychologists and psychological research can speak to virtually every area within the law.

Unfortunately, although law psychology exists as an interdisciplinary field, it has not realized its birthright of influence on the law.[25] One reason law psychology has not had the intended impact may be because the emphasis of the discipline has been too narrow in scope.[26] Most law-psychology research and writing is focused on jury decision making and eyewitnesses.[27] Despite repeated calls for broadening the discipline,[28] very little attention branches beyond the safety of a few select areas. This book and the series of which it is a part seek to make an impact in that void. There is much to be gained in the law from interdisciplinary ventures and empirical psychology examinations.[29] And there is much to be gained in psychology by understanding the legal issues that raise empirical questions.

The Natural "Marriage" of Psychology and Family Law

Although family law is diverse and does not fit into a neat theoretical objective statement as do many other areas of law, one consistent theme is present in family law—human behavior. As law professor Brian

Bix notes, "[w]hen courts, legislators, or commentators argue for legal change in family law—or when they argue for status quo, for resisting change—they often do so on the basis of an express or implied claim about the effect a proposed change would have on human behavior."[30] Bix continues: "These are empirical claims about the world, and they are in principle subject to experimental support or refutation. However, the fact is that in family law (and likely in many other areas of law), the social science data relevant to law and law reform is scarce, and what data there is, is frequently controversial and subject to challenge."[31] Bix then provides the example of custody or divorce rules and a desire to have one such rule over another because we believe that a particular rule will serve the long-term benefit of most family members better than another rule. We focus on the individual and social well-being and attempt to use that in our process of selecting what rules would be best. But we must be careful to not let our own biases rather than empirical data shape these decisions.[32]

It is important to note that there are risks with relying too heavily and uncritically on empirical data and conclusions. Family law scholar Clare Huntington provides an in-depth critique of blindly accepting empirical data to change family law.[33] Not only is it unethical to use stringent experimental methods such as random assignment in most family law contexts; it is also extremely difficult to be able to adequately test complex family law issues, such as love and acceptance with empirical science. Huntington also highlights the risks of empirical sciences neglecting marginalized groups while also allowing a value-based judgment to look neutral. At the same time, there are promise and utility because empirical science provides a balance against politicizing family law policy. As such, Huntington describes the need for legal scholars to serve as gatekeepers to best utilize empirical science in family law. In her framework, she advocates for those gatekeepers to determine when there is a consensus about values being considered and then to be sophisticated and skeptical in that empirical evidence.[34] When there is no consensus, Huntington argues that empirical evidence is less useful. Of course, it is possible that empirical evidence could serve to build consensus.

Despite the lack of unifying theory for family law and some risks of empiricizing family law, this book focuses on the premise that empirical research in family law—or, to borrow from our physician friends, "evidence-based"[35] family law—can lead to better outcomes in many situations. Like other texts in the current series, this book examines and includes a variety of psychological theories stemming from both applied and basic research. Many of the subdisciplines of psychology are represented—with social, developmental, clinical, and counseling among the most often referenced areas. At times, the research presented is basic science and seemingly unrelated or far too simple to be applied to the weighty issues of family law, but this is done to provide a starting point or a spark from which future researchers can think about integrating known basic science tenets into complex and thorny family law issues. Additionally, other related areas of social science are relied on when appropriate because this interdisciplinary focus provides a broad foundation on which future psychology research can be based.

The current book has four main ambitions: (1) to explain the current state of family law, (2) to demonstrate the relevance of psychological research to family law topics, (3) to describe the existing research on those topics, and (4) to outline areas for future research, offering specific research questions in some instances. This book focuses on current U.S. society, but often our conceptions of family and the laws surrounding it are only historical or cultural constructions. The very notion of a nuclear family is a modern phenomenon born out of class development.[36] Therefore, the chapters that follow generally provide a historical and cultural context for each topic. As legal scholar Deborah Anthony noted in an article about surnames, "[t]he law—especially family law—serves the function of channeling people into certain socially preferred institutions and practices, while discouraging those that are viewed as less acceptable."[37] But getting married, staying married, and having children within a marriage are no longer norms. The general institution of marriage is in flux. Historically, marriage meant a way to have, support, and protect children. Today, many of those requirements can be achieved without marriage. Although the legal distinction of men's duty to support and women's duty of service is largely a historical relic, are there psychological vestiges that remain in the form of stereotypic expectations?[38] Because of historical trends and changes, our grandfather's family law is not the same family law we study and practice today. Today's family law serves to channel people into different institutions and practices from what it did merely a few decades earlier.[39]

In their 2011 book on modern marriage, law professors Joanna Grossman and Lawrence Friedman inquire, "If behavior changes, can legal change be far behind?"[40] Grossman and Friedman conclude that legal change is inevitable. The chapters that follow in the current book explore that notion by examining the historical behaviors and individual choices that laid the foundation for the evolution of family law from its origin to its current state. The book also asks the complement of Grossman and Friedman's question by examining the resulting behaviors (or lack thereof) associated with changes in family law.

Conclusion

Grossman and Friedman begin their book by noting that "[e]verybody, in every society, is born into a family. Even a newborn baby, unwanted, abandoned as soon as it is born . . . will eventually end up in somebody's family."[41] They go on to say that human beings are "social animals, family animals. The family is the fundamental unit of society."[42] Indeed, family law, like no other area of law, is intimately linked to personal experience, because every individual has personal experience with family law. Not only does everyone have a history with family law, but the topics on which the area of family law touches are also those that are most deeply personal and private. Despite the magnitude of the area, there is no clear unifying theory or holistic doctrine from which to guide examination, especially when the goal is to focus on more than simply divorce or counseling. The only constant this book has is the desire to bring empirical research to aid in answering the legal questions. And, as Carl Schneider and Lee Teitelbaum, two legal scholars, note, "every corner of family law is drenched with empirical questions on whose answers good policy depends. Those questions are massively ignored."[43] This book acknowledges these questions and shines a light on them.

The next chapter addresses the way in which the law has attempted to restrict some people from getting married and what the underlying psychological reasons for such restrictions may be.

1

Barriers to Marriage

Kathy Landin, writer for thefw.com, provides a story (with pictures) of the "15 weirdest marriages."[1] The marriages are between people and animals,[2] people and themselves,[3] and people and inanimate objects, such as the Eiffel Tower[4] and a roller coaster.[5] Amy Wolfe fell in love with a roller coaster. She taped pictures of the ride on her bedroom ceiling and carried in her pocket nuts and bolts from it.[6] To Ms. Wolfe, her marriage to the 1001 Nachts in Knoebels Amusement Park feels natural and similar to any other marriage.[7] Notably, her marriage and the other marriages mentioned earlier did not occur in the United States and are not legally binding. They do, however, demonstrate for some a more expansive informal definition of marriage than historically conceived within the law.[8]

Traditionally, there has been a set of formal requirements for a marriage. The most basic requirements of a valid marriage are a license and a wedding ceremony between two competent individuals conducted by an officiant.[9] Aside from age requirements, the legal standard for competency to marry is quite low. A person must only understand the concept of marriage. A person under conservatorship or deemed legally incompetent for other purposes may still be able to marry.[10]

Today in the United States, individual states hold the power of marriage regulation and deciding who can and cannot get married;[11] there is technically no uniform national-level family law doctrine. Supreme Court Justice Hugo Black said that "the power to make rules . . . is for the legislatures, not the life-tenured justices."[12] Yet, despite the Supreme Court's insistence on state control,[13] its holdings continue to shape and change state law.[14] The Supreme Court's reasoning for involvement is generally one of protecting family privacy from state interference.[15] Interestingly, one rationale for vesting family law within the states was to permit states to experiment and base their laws on local social conditions.[16] True experimentation has been lacking; instead, most laws and court opinions about marriage barriers are based on legislative or judicial intuition.[17]

Past Barriers

Physical and Mental Conditions

Well into the 20th century, U.S. states placed restrictions on who could marry because of their mental or physical conditions.[18] Insomuch as marriage was the route to reproduction, states forbade individuals who did not have a sound mind from marrying as a way to restrict those individuals from procreating.[19] For example, cognitive and physical conditions such as being "a common drunkard, habitual criminal, epileptic, imbecile, feeble-minded person, idiot or insane person" prohibited individuals from marriage in Washington State.[20] Even by the 1950s, 17 states restricted marital access from people with epilepsy.[21] Washington and other states furthered their eugenics crusade by restricting marital access from those with tuberculosis and venereal diseases. These laws required medical exams to certify the betrothed were free from contagions such as gonorrhea or syphilis. States have removed these health test requirements but some only as recently as the turn of the 21st century.[22]

Mental capacity restrictions still remain insomuch as they relate to a person's competency to enter into a contractual relationship.[23] Otherwise, the general restrictions of marriage for the mentally ill are gone. But, again, those restrictions have only recently lifted.[24] Similarly, for individuals with developmental disabilities, the question now is not whether they will pass on their developmental disability if they have offspring but whether they can comprehend and function within the marital agreement.[25] In less than a century, the United States has moved from sterilization and restricting developmentally disabled adults from marriage to statutes assuming their marriages are valid.[26] Today, developmental disabilities do not preclude marriage or parenting, and that change can largely be attributed to the work of the social science and medical communities, which have been able to establish safeguards and interventions that allow those with developmental disabilities to thrive in marriage relationships.[27]

Race

Mildred Jeter and Richard Loving could have never known when they started their teen romance in 1951 that they would eventually change U.S. marriage law. The young couple grew up near each other in Virginia where, despite a state law barring interracial marriage,[28] their rural community displayed little tension and segregation between the White and Black communities.[29] Although unique to U.S. law,[30] the state of Virginia was not alone in its anti-miscegenation law—15 other states had similar prohibitions.[31] At the same time, many cities were becoming less segregated,[32] the public was increasingly more supportive of desegregation,[33] and research suggested that intermarriage was on the rise.[34] Scholars noted that allowing interracial marriages could potentially reduce the "status gap" between Black and White Americans through such vehicles as familial wealth inheritance, job connections, and social networks.[35] As such, individual decisions about who to marry could have ripple effects for bringing greater equality within society beyond what legal desegregation could do alone. In other words, the will of the people and the changes in public attitudes laid the foundation for changes in the law.

Indeed, the individual decisions of Richard and Mildred Loving started a chain of events that eventually broke down interracial marriage barriers. Five weeks after they were married, the local sheriff stormed their bedroom, telling them that their marriage certificate hanging on their bedroom wall was "no good."[36] The couple pled guilty to the charge of violating the Racial Integrity Act and received suspended sentences conditioned on their leaving Virginia and not returning together for 25 years.[37] On appeal, the U.S. Supreme Court held that the law had "no legitimate overriding purpose independent of invidious racial discrimination"[38] and as such violated the Equal Protection Clause. The Supreme Court went on to say that the "freedom to marry has long been recognized as one of the vital personal rights essential to the orderly pursuit of happiness by free men."[39] This was the first time the U.S. Supreme Court had invalidated a state marriage regulation based on the U.S. Constitution.

Shortly after the Supreme Court decision in *Loving*, 182 White and Black Michigan high school students answered a survey about their opinions of interracial marriages.[40] Overall, 33% of the students were favorable toward interracial marriage, with proportionally more Black students (64.7%) than White students (28.7%) voicing support. These high school students' responses represented what seemed like a general trend toward more acceptance of interracial marriages. Indeed, Gallup has been asking about these attitudes since 1958, and responses have consistently shown more support for marriages between Whites and Blacks over time.[41] In 1958, the approval rate was 4%, compared to 87% in 2013 (Blacks' approval at 96% and Whites' approval at 84%).

Despite the Supreme Court acceptance and apparent public endorsement of interracial marriages, such unions represent less than 10% of all U.S. marriages.[42] Some clever empirical research may help to explain this apparent disconnect. Rather than ask respondents whether they supported interracial marriages in the abstract, more general sense, the General Social Survey added questions that ask respondents whether they supported their close relatives marrying outside their race.[43] Across a 12-year period, from 2000 to 2012, attitudes did not significantly change; however, there were noticeable racial differences. Approximately half of the Black respondents approved of a close relative marrying a White person, while only about 25% of Whites similarly approved. As compared to general approval of interracial marriage, these lower approval ratings provide a potential explanation for the lower rates of interracial marriage.

Same Sex

The fundamental right to marry from *Loving*[44] rested on the Equal Protection Clause of the Fourteenth Amendment because the Virginia statute arbitrarily forbade the couple from exercising their fundamental liberty to marry. The Court went on to say that marriage is a "basic civil right."[45] Later cases concerning marriage like that of *Griswold v. Connecticut* in 1965 relied on a right to privacy, under the Due Process Clause of the Fourteenth Amendment.[46] Although the Court has noted that not every state restriction on marriage must be subjected to the strict scrutiny test, those restrictions that interfere *directly and substantially* with the right to marry should be.[47] Restrictions that merely deter or burden will be evaluated with the rational basis test,[48] which means that the restrictions must only be rationally related to a legitimate government interest. This legal distinction in scrutiny applied raises the question of whether restrictions more directly and substantially interfere with one subset of the population than another.

The U.S. Supreme Court answered those questions as they relate to same-sex couples in the 2015 case of *Obergefell v. Hodges.*[49] The five-justice majority held that the right to marry is a fundamental right guaranteed by both the Due Process and Equal Protection Clauses of the Fourteenth Amendment. Their landmark decision overturned *Baker v. Nelson* (1972) from more than 40 years prior.

In the spring of 1970, two male University of Minnesota students had applied for and were denied a marriage license by a county clerk located in Minneapolis. The only basis for denying Richard Baker and James McConnell their marriage license was the fact that both were the same sex.[50] They filed suit on the grounds that Minnesota law had no explicit requirement that couples be of opposite sexes. They also contended that if the Minnesota court construed the law as requiring such, then the law violated the U.S. Constitution because it imposed on First, Eighth, Ninth, and Fourteenth Amendment rights. After the trial court dismissed the case, Baker and McConnell appealed to the Minnesota Supreme Court, which affirmed the lower court, noting that marriage was intended to be between a man and a woman. Baker and McConnell took their case to the U.S. Supreme Court claiming Ninth and Fourteenth Amendment violations.[51] The U.S. Supreme Court provided a one-sentence dismissal that indicated that there was no substantial federal question.[52]

For the next four decades, the Court continued to address issues related to same-sex relationships with unfavorable legal results for people in same-sex relationships. In 1986, the Court held in *Bowers v. Hardwick* that Georgia's statute criminalizing sodomy was constitutional.[53] Ten years later, the Court struck down a Colorado provision preventing homosexuals from being placed in a protected class.[54] A few years later, a Hawaii court held that the state did not possess a compelling state interest in banning same-sex marriages.[55] Yet, what seemed like a victory of same-sex marriages in Hawaii was short-lived. Soon after the case, the legislature in Hawaii enacted a state constitutional amendment effectively banning same-sex marriages, and the people of Hawaii voted to ratify it.[56] Additionally, many other states passed similar legislation and the U.S. Congress enacted the Defense of Marriage Act (DOMA), which defined marriage as between a man and a woman and allowed states to not recognize same-sex marriages granted in other states.[57]

Despite the legislative bans, cases continued to make their way through the court systems. The Supreme Court in Vermont ruled to extend heterosexual marriage rights to same-sex couples,[58] with the Vermont legislature subsequently approving civil unions in 2000 and then legalizing same-sex marriages several years later in 2009.[59] In *Lawrence v. Texas*,[60] the U.S. Supreme Court also struck down as unconstitutional state laws banning homosexual sodomy—thus reversing its earlier decision in *Bowers*. In the same year as *Lawrence*, Massachusetts became the first state to allow same-sex couples to legally marry, holding that not allowing same-sex marriages would violate the state's constitutional guarantee of individual liberty and equality.[61] In 2008, California became the second state to make same-sex marriages legal,[62] and in 2009, the Iowa Supreme Court followed suit.[63] Other states allowed only same-sex unions that permitted the same rights as marriages but did not go as far as to require those unions be called marriages.[64]

Seventeen years after the enactment of DOMA, the Supreme Court held in *U.S. v. Windsor*[65] that defining marriage as a union only between a man and a woman was unconstitutional. Decided on the same day, *Hollingsworth v. Perry*[66] ruled that same-sex opponents did not have standing to oppose the California court decision. The California court had held unconstitutional a voter initiative that imposed an opposite-sex limitation on marriages.[67] The *Hollingsworth* decision effectively reinstated the same-sex right to marriage in California.

Two years after *Windsor* and *Hollingsworth*, the five-justice majority for *Obergefell* began their opinion by recognizing the underlying battle between ideologies. On one side, the respondents argued that a marriage is meant to be between two people of the opposite sex and that anything contrary to that arrangement would demean the institution of marriage.[68] On the other side, same-sex couples desire to be married not to devalue the institution but because they hold the institution in such high regard.

The American Psychological Association (APA) joined with a number of other organizations in weighing in on the *Obergefell* case through a 41-page *amicus curiae* brief that detailed decades of empirical research and other scholarly attention to the topic of same-sex marriages.[69] The brief's foundational arguments focused on the following seven principles:

> 1) Homosexuality is a normal expression of human sexuality, is generally not chosen, and is highly resistant to change; 2) Gay men and lesbians form stable, committed relationships that are equivalent to heterosexual relationships in essential respects; 3) The institution of marriage offers

> social, psychological, and health benefits that are denied to same-sex couples who cannot legally marry; 4) Many same-sex couples raise children; 5) The factors that affect the adjustment of children are not dependent on parental gender or sexual orientation; 6) There is no scientific basis for concluding that same-sex couples are any less fit or capable parents than heterosexual couples, or that their children are any less psychologically healthy and well adjusted; 7) Denying the status of marriage to same-sex couples stigmatizes them.[70]

The Court held in *Obergefell* that the Fourteenth Amendment requires states to permit and recognize marriages between same-sex couples. The Court reasoned that the right to marry is a constitutionally protected right and it detailed four reasons why that right should extend to same-sex couples, with some reasons clearly influenced by the APA *amicus* brief: First, marital choice is inherent in individual autonomy. Second, marriage uniquely binds two individuals in a way no other association can. Third, marriage serves as a protection for the children of that marriage so that their parents' relationship is seen as the same as opposite-sex parents with the same stability and benefits. Fourth, marriage is a "keystone of the Nation's social order."[71] The majority opinion also recognized the evolution of marriage from one of arrangement between families to the couple voluntarily contracting with each other and from women viewed as property to becoming equal partners with men. They explained that allowing same-sex couples to marry is a similar evolution that will strengthen the institution of marriage.

Current Barriers

Today, there are only four substantive legal barriers to marriage—age (i.e., minors cannot marry without parental consent), incest, bigamy/polygamy, and fraud/duress.[72]

Age as a Barrier

State laws regulate the requisite age for marriage. Although different states have different age minimum and parental consent requirements, in general, the minimum age for marriage without parental consent is

18.[73] From 16 to 18 years of age, consent is often required from parents, the court and the parents, or the court in the parents' stead.[74] There is plenty of evidence that young marriages are generally difficult and related to a number of negative factors, such as lower income and increased divorce rates compared to those who marry later in life.[75]

Are those negative factors the result of the earlier marriage or because society and the law discourage early marriages? And why do we as a society allow someone to get married before they can legally buy alcohol? Historically, people entering marriages did so much younger than they do today.[76] Was there something developmentally different about adolescents in the previous millennia? Perhaps. Numerical age and a reliance on it are modern cultural phenomena.[77] Our current society hails 40 as the new 20 and 60 as the new 40.[78] Maybe 30 is the new 12, an age at which someone could get married in the 1800s.[79] Certainly life expectancy has increased over the past century, which among other effects has allowed the period of adolescence to continue longer. Young adults today are generally not expected to seek full-time employment until well into their 20s. In fact, recent laws have endorsed this extended adolescence in one specific way by allowing young adults up to age 26 to remain beneficiaries on their parents' health insurance.[80]

Developmental psychology research has extensively addressed developmental issues of maturity and decision making for children and adolescents. Developmental psychologist Erik Erikson was an early contributor who focused on the psychosocial theory of development that included a stage generally occurring in young adulthood where the central feature is the battle between intimacy and isolation.[81] According to Erikson, this stage generally spans the 20s and 30s.[82] According to some theorists, the ability to achieve intimacy in a romantic relationship is considered a crucial step in laying the foundation for a healthy adulthood.[83] Of course, with modern marriage delay many people are not getting married in their 20s or even their 30s. Indeed, in 2000 psychologist Jeffrey Arnett proposed a new period of development from the late teens through the 20s that he called emerging adulthood.[84] This new phase between adolescence and adulthood provides a demarcation during a time when people in our modern industrialized society do not see themselves as either an adolescent or an adult.[85] According to Arnett, emerging adulthood represents a time when romantic relationships transition from recreational to more intimate and serious. Relationships tend to last longer and are more likely to include sexual intercourse. In addition, emerging adulthood is a time of residential instability and transitions in work life and worldviews.[86] During this time, the ability to achieve intimacy in a romantic relationship is considered a crucial step in laying the foundation for a healthy adulthood.[87] Of course, with modern marriage delay many people are not getting married in their 20s or even their 30s. Some scholars see this as deferring developmental tasks that can have harmful impacts.[88] And those who do marry young often find themselves remarrying later in the life after their first marriage has ended.[89]

What standard should we apply for age restrictions and marriage? It turns out that if we want to base the standards on developmental psychological research concerning adolescent decision making, then we need to first determine whether the decision to marry is one that is more deliberate and cognitive or is more impulsive and emotional. Although the research has not directly addressed the issue of marriage,[90] some complementary work in the areas of abortion rights and medical decision making suggest that depending on the situation, adolescent decision making can be quite similar to or very different from adults.[91]

The APA can attest that the decision-making context is an important distinction when it comes to age-defined rules for adolescents. The APA submitted *amicus curiae* briefs in two cases involving adolescent decision making. The first case, *Hodgson v. Minnesota*,[92] involved a newly passed Minnesota statute that required that both parents of a minor under 18 years of age be notified at least 48 hours prior to the minor obtaining an abortion.[93] The APA argued *inter alia* that adolescents are competent to make informed decisions about life and have the capacity to make sound health care decisions and therefore should not be required to obtain parental consent for an abortion.[94] In *Roper v. Simmons*[95] the APA once again submitted an *amicus* brief in support of adolescent decision making, but this time the focus was on adolescents' inadequacies and developmental immaturity.[96] The brief argued that 16- and 17-year-olds should be excluded from the death penalty because research demonstrates that their brain development is still occurring throughout adolescence and that adolescents display less mature decision making, greater impulsivity, and greater risk-taking. In addition, the APA cited research that demonstrated that adolescents are more peer-oriented than adults and have less ability to consider long- and short-term consequences of their decisions.

Because of these two seemingly conflicting briefs, the APA has been accused of "flip-flopping"[97] when it comes to claims concerning adolescent decision-making abilities. That is, according the APA, a juvenile has the decision capacity for an abortion decision but not for committing a crime. Temple University psychology professor and expert on adolescence Laurence Steinberg and colleagues address this alleged incongruence by dividing the adolescent behaviors in question into two categories: (1) cognitive capacity and (2) psychosocial maturity. That is, the decision to seek an abortion, although likely emotional, is generally an issue of cognitive capacity. The decision is generally entered into only after consulting with adults and after a certain period of time either by desire or legal requirement.[98] A decision to commit a crime, on the other hand, is more likely to occur impulsively, unplanned, and under the influence of peer pressure. Using almost 1,000 individuals ranging in age from 10 to 30 years, Steinberg and colleagues demonstrated that adolescents are very similar to adults after the age of 16 when it comes to cognitive capacity, but their psychosocial maturity continues to develop throughout their 20s. Steinberg and colleagues conclude that in situations where adolescents have a chance to consult with adults and have time to weigh costs and benefits, an adolescent 16 years and older is likely to make a decision very similar to an adult. In contrast, in situations involving peer groups and impulsive decisions, adolescents are less likely to make adultlike decisions. Therefore, the law allowing marriage at 16 (with parental consent) but restricting alcohol purchasing to 21 fits the cognitive capacity–versus–psychosocial maturity dilemma outlined by Steinberg and colleagues and explains the seemingly conflicting APA briefs.

Incest as a Barrier

A close relationship between potential spouses is not permitted for a valid marriage, and in many instances states criminalize the resulting sexual conduct.[99] Beyond the restrictions of the immediate family (i.e., parents, grandparents, and siblings), the definition of what a "close" relationship is varies between states.[100] Although across the world marriage between cousins is common,[101] only about half of U.S. states allow marriage between first cousins.[102] For example, Arizona and a few other states do not allow marriages between first cousins unless the cousins are of a certain age (65 years or older in Arizona) or a judge approves of the union based on presented facts that the cousins will not be able to reproduce.[103] Although Florida does not restrict first-cousin marriages, it does define incest as sexual intercourse between lineally related individuals and blatantly provides that sexual intercourse need not involve emission of semen.[104] North Carolina extends the restriction to "double first cousins," which occur when siblings marry siblings.[105]

Some states have written their statutes restricting incest because of genetic concerns. For example, Maine allows aunts/nephews and uncles/nieces to marry so long as there is evidence that they have received genetic counseling.[106] The Colorado Supreme Court struck down its statute prohibiting marriage between adopted siblings because the prohibition was illogical and did not meet minimum rationality requirements.[107] Other states seem concerned with something aside from genetic issues because they extend their marital restrictions to nonblood relations. In Alabama, it a Class C felony for a person to marry a family member such as a parent, child, sibling, aunt/uncle, or niece/nephew even if the relationship exists through adoption or half-blood.[108] Kentucky specifically notes that persons will be guilty of incest if they have sexual relations with the normal prohibitive relatives but also denotes the relationship of stepparent and step-grandparent as within the purview of incest.[109] In Louisiana, "collaterals within the fourth degree" may not marry, and the restriction applies whether it is by whole or half-blood.[110] If two people are related in the fourth degree by adoption, then the couple may request a judicial authorization to allow their marriage. Several states such as Michigan, New Jersey, Rhode Island, and South Carolina provide complementary lists for both men and women concerning whom they may not marry.[111] For a man in Michigan, these people include some who are related by blood and others who are not. The statute states that he may not marry his wife's mother or grandmother and the wife of his grandfather, father, or son.[112] Similarly, for a woman in Michigan, the restrictions include her husband's father or grandfather and the husband of her grandmother, mother, or daughter.[113] Montana and South

Dakota specifically note that adopted relations are included in the marriage prohibition.[114] Utah prohibits marriage between stepparents and stepchildren while the marriage creating their relationship still exists,[115] but a number of states such as Tennessee do not clearly require the marriage creating the relationship to still be intact.[116]

Some states include an age component with their incest statutes. For example, North Carolina includes the general definition of incest and includes disparate crime classifications based on the ages of the parties to the incest.[117] In Illinois, sexual relations within families are punished as a Class 3 felony, and the relationships extend to great-aunts and great-uncles when the great-niece or great-nephew is younger than 18 years of age.[118]

Notably, virtually all the statutes assume or focus on heterosexual relationships[119] with several clearly focusing on reproduction issues.[120] Other states, such as Massachusetts and Texas, provide a wide list of sexual activities, offering a broader definition beyond heterosexual relationships and sexual activity for the purpose of procreation.[121] This raises an important consideration concerning the rationale for these statutes. Certainly, there are genetic considerations even though many of those are not as certain to cause problems as once believed.[122] But if genetic considerations are the sole ground for the prohibition against incest, homosexual relationships between relatives, even very close relatives, should be permissible. If a homosexual relationship between brothers or a father and son makes you uncomfortable in the same way a relationship between a brother and sister or a father and daughter, then you have to ask yourself, "Why?" Genetic concerns for offspring cannot be part of the equation, which means it must be something else.

Most likely that something else is something psychological. Generally referred to as incest aversion or the incest taboo,[123] there is a relatively universal incest prohibition for close-family incest[124] despite it being a relatively common occurrence historically.[125] Although physical attraction to similar kin is not uncommon,[126] research repeatedly demonstrates a disgust response toward incestuous relationships even when those relationships are unlikely to produce offspring.[127]

The Supreme Court set out some important language in the 2003 landmark case, *Lawrence v. Texas*.[128] The majority opinion held that the state cannot make private sexual conduct between consenting adults a crime. This broad-sweeping language suggests that the right to incest (and polygamy/bigamy, discussed in the next section) should be protected, but courts have been reluctant to adopt that stance. For instance, the Sixth Circuit U.S. Court of Appeals rejected a stepfather's argument that the *Lawrence* opinion should invalidate Ohio's incest statute when applied to consenting adults. The court rested its disagreement on the state's lesser interest in prosecuting homosexual sodomy, at issue in *Lawrence*, as compared to the "destructive influence of intra-family, extra-marital sexual contact."[129] Such assumptions of destructive influence have been called into question with modern birth control and by focusing on incest between consenting adults,[130] as have the genetic and biological arguments against allowing consanguineous marriages.[131]

On the other hand, if we focus on psychological reasons for prohibiting incestuous relationships, then the statutes should be updated, especially now that same-sex marriages are permitted. Rather than focus on issues of reproduction, the concern is one of unfair power dynamics and psychological impacts,[132] and the statutes should be adjusted to reflect this. For example, research in this area has demonstrated that this use of power for an older sibling over a younger sibling can have long-term effects on future relationships and trust.[133] Other psychological research demonstrates the long-term deleterious impacts such as mental disorders later in life.[134] Such empirical research could form the foundation for updating legislation.

Polygamy and Bigamy as a Barrier

"Monogamy is inextricably woven into the fabric of our society. It is the bedrock upon which our culture is built,"[135] the court noted in Royston Potter's case challenging Utah's law banning plural marriages. The court disagreed that Potter's First and Fourteenth Amendment rights had been violated when he was terminated from the police force because he was married to two women. The *Potter* holding follows the same line of reasoning dating back to the 1878 Supreme Court case of *Reynolds v. U.S.*[136] in which a leader of the Mormon Church challenged the federal antibigamy statute as applied to him in the then Utah territory. Reynolds unsuccessfully argued that the prohibition violated his First Amendment right to religious exercise. The Supreme Court was unsympathetic and equated bigamy with human sacrifice as two religious practices that would not be exempt from criminal prosecution.[137] Generally, polygamy and bigamy do not comprise many pages in family law textbooks and are mostly explained by a case or two usually stemming from the Mormon Church.[138] However, this could be a new area of legal activity with a new movement afoot both from formal polygamist advocates and from the polyamory community.

It seems reality television has permeated every topic, with not even polygamy being spared. The popular TLC show *Sister Wives* features a polygamist family—one husband, four wives, and 17 children. The husband, Kody Brown, argues that he is only legally married to one of the wives and has "spiritual unions" with the other three women.[139] Nonetheless, criminal charges were brought against Brown because the Utah state code banning bigamy includes not only marital contracts but also cohabitation with another person while married.[140] The criminal charges were dropped against the Browns because the state said it did not have the resources to pursue polygamist relationships in the absence of child maltreatment.[141] Nonetheless, the Browns filed a complaint challenging the antipolygamy law.[142] The Tenth Circuit Court of Appeals eventually dismissed their complaint for a lack of standing because the only polygamist relationships prosecuted are those involving child bigamy, violence, or fraud.[143] In the end, the antipolygamy law remains, but so do the polygamists.

Relationships involving bigamy and polygamy[144] have received very little scholarly psychological attention, other than public opinion surveys. Some research speaks to the life satisfaction and marital satisfaction of those involved in these relationships.[145] As noted earlier, the institution of marriage has changed over the past several decades. Not only are couples delaying marriage, but some are also not getting married at all, and others are marrying and divorcing at rapid rates. We have also seen the legal recognition of same-sex marriages. This shift in marital views and practices combined with more accepted notions of sexual fluidity[146] unite to create committed relationships that look very different from one man and one woman. For example, a polyamorous relationship is one that involves romantic relationships with more than one person at the same time.[147] Consent and support separate polyamory from infidelity. Polyamory is distinguished from the swinging lifestyle by a focus on the relationship and commitment rather than sex.[148] Recent research suggests that polyamorous relationships are more common than once thought, with as many as 33% of bisexual men and women indicating that they were involved in a nonmonogamous relationship and 54% saying they preferred nonmonogamous relationships.[149] Other research suggests that people involved in polyamorous relationships are not significantly different from general population norms on psychological well-being.[150] This research, albeit scant, lends some support to what the family from *Sister Wives* has argued—that the *Obergefell* case holding that marriage between same-sex couples is a fundamental right should open the door not only to same-sex marriage but also to plural marriages or relationships.

Fraud and Duress as a Barrier

The fourth and last barrier to marriage develops when the marriage is not what it seems because it was entered into under either duress or fraud. Duress occurs when a person enters into a marriage because of threats or fear. Fraud occurs when there is deceit in entering the marriage. In what seems like a recognition that all marriages have some thread of untruth woven within,[151] courts have held that for the fraud to lead to a voidable marriage, such deceit must go to the essential elements of the marriage and that the lied-to spouse must have relied on the lie in the decision to enter the marriage.[152] A California court held that lies about finances did not go to the essence of a marriage[153] and really only matters related to sex and procreation are essential issues.[154] In contrast, an Illinois court provided a more subjective approach to defining "essential" such that the focus was on what matters were essential to the parties getting married. In other words, would the wedding have happened if not for the fraud?[155]

Fraud can also occur because the entire marriage is a sham—where the victim is the public and not the defrauded spouse.[156] This situation most commonly occurs today for immigration purposes. U.S. citizen spouses can circumvent the normal immigration process by petitioning for permanent residence status for their immigrant spouse. The 1986 Immigration Marriage Fraud Amendments sought to restrict the pipeline by imposing a two-year waiting period to obtain permanent residency status and additional demonstrable requirements such as joint property ownership, commingling of financial resources, and affidavits of others acknowledging the marriage to be real.[157] The immigration official's investigations into such marriages reach deep into the privacy of marriage and, arguably, expect more conformity to the marital ideal than is expected of citizen couples.[158]

Very little empirical research has examined marriage among immigrants and U.S. citizens.[159] No doubt the looming legal consequences of deportation have a chilling effect on any research specifically targeted at those who marry for the purpose of obtaining citizenship. As a result, interesting psychological questions remain unanswered in this area. For example, when the citizen spouse knows the marriage is a sham, what is his or her motivation? News stories focus on the criminal charges brought against businesses (i.e., marriage brokers) paying someone who will purport to be a loving spouse,[160] but there are certain to be other reasons beyond money that dance on the line of altruism. When the citizen spouse is unaware of the fraud at the time of the wedding, a whole different set of questions arise about the citizen spouse and the immigrant spouse. For example, are there prototype citizen spouse victims who are easy targets for the immigrants? Are there any long-term ramifications on well-being for either or both spouses if the marriage is ultimately deemed legally illegitimate? And what about the children of these relationships?

Effects of a Barrier to Marriage

Marriages that are not valid are either void or voidable. A void marriage is one that cannot legally occur. A void marriage never was, nor can be, valid and therefore does not need to be formally dissolved. For example, marriages involving incest or a person not of the minimum age are considered void. These marriages are not legally binding and can be ignored for legal purposes.[161]

In contrast, voidable marriages are those that require at least one party to seek judicial declaration of the marriage's invalidity. These may be based on issues such as fraud by one of the parties. A voidable marriage has the potential to be valid and will be presumed valid until declared otherwise. Marriages involving fraud or mistakes are generally considered voidable marriages.

Often the issue of a void or voidable marriage arises when the marriage is being dissolved and there is a reason to want the dissolution to occur via annulment rather than divorce. An annulment renders the marriage invalid from the beginning and retroactively applies so that it is as if the marriage never existed and is void.[162] Because annulments are so extreme, courts only permit them when there was something fatally wrong with the marriage—when the marriage is void or voidable. Generally, the desire to have an annulment rather than a divorce occurs for religious reasons. For example, religions such as Catholicism do not permit or recognize divorce, and if there has been no divorce there can be no valid remarriage.[163] Therefore, an annulment is desired because it makes it as if the marriage did not occur and thus a new marriage can.

Conclusion

No other area of law is as relevant to daily life as family law, and no other area seems to be fluctuating as much, especially as we consider who can and cannot get married. Marriage has moved from little legal involvement to highly regulated state involvement and back to few regulations.[164] Has the changing legal landscape altered what happens inside the home? Or was it the inner workings of the relationships that led to the legal changes? Perhaps it is *because* intimate relationships are so relevant to daily life that marital law has seen such sweeping changes. As Justice Field wrote about marriage in the Supreme Court opinion of *Maynard v. Hill*, "[i]t is an institution, in the maintenance of which in its purity the public is deeply interested, for it is the foundation of the family and of society, without which there would be neither civilization nor progress."[165] As this chapter has demonstrated, personal attitudes and decisions have led to new marital barriers forming and some of those barriers later falling. The next chapter steps into the world of getting and being married, for those who have such a right.

2

Leading Up to Marriage and Family

Reaching back into history far before modern family law and well before the birth of the United States, the Code of Hammurabi provides some early insights into marriage and family governance. Hammurabi's code from around 1750 BCE is often referred to as the longest and best organized of the Mesopotamian laws.[1] In this code, marriage and parenting come with certain legal obligations, and it is clear that the act of having children changes the marriage relationship. For example, the code provides that if there were no children born from a marriage and the man divorced his wife, he was only responsible for restoring her wealth and dowry to its premarital state.[2] In contrast, if a man divorced his wife *who bore him children*, then the wife was entitled to get back her dowry and one-half of her husband's property.[3] The relationship between a father and his children was also distinct compared to the harsh penalties and swift judgments common in the code. This is exemplified best in the following passage concerning the disinheriting of a son:

> If a man should decide to disinherit his son and declares to the judges, "I will disinherit my son," the judges shall investigate the case and if the son is not guilty of a grave offense deserving the penalty of disinheritance, the father may not disinherit his son. If he should be guilty of a grave offense deserving the penalty of disinheritance by his father, they shall pardon him for his first one; if he should commit a grave offense a second time, the father may disinherit his son.[4]

Such forgiveness and second chances are in stark contrast to the code's treatment of nonfamily members, such as casting a woman innkeeper into the water if she reduces the value of beer in relation to the value of grain.[5]

Similar legal examples of special family relationships abound throughout history. The Egyptian sage Ptahhotep extolled the parent-child relationship, writing how fathers should teach their children because wisdom is passed down through the generations.[6] A similar Hebrew biblical proverb provides "Train up a child in the way he should go and when he is old he will not depart from it."[7] Indeed, these laws of old seem to have influenced the early modern systems of law; the Elizabethan Poor Laws made poor parents and children responsible for each other.[8] All these examples demonstrate the foundational constant of families and the law. In contrast, the Greek philosopher Plato provides a systematic rejection of the notions of family as we know them. According to Plato's theory, the responsibility of being in what he called the Guardian class would be hindered by raising children; however, procreation was important for the purpose of continuing the best and brightest genetic lines. Therefore, Plato proposed that the wives and children of the Guardians were to be common; no parent was to know his own child or any child his parent.[9] Perhaps because of the importance of marriages throughout history, no respected society has ever taken Plato's eugenics proposal seriously; it does shake everything we take for granted about family law.

Even today in the United States, when marriage rates are at an all-time low, our society still holds marriage in high esteem.[10] Unmarried couples do not receive tax benefits and often do not receive insurance benefits until they get married.[11] When couples only move in together without marrying, they do not generally have big parties where people bring presents. That type of celebration is reserved for a wedding. Amid these wedding celebration parties, there are some serious legal and psychological issues at play prior to the exchanging of vows and entering into the legal union of marriage. The next four sections address these premarital issues such as dating, breach of promise to marry, prenuptial agreements, and changing of surnames. The fifth and final section addresses nonmarriage both in terms of people remaining single and not in a committed relationship and people remaining unmarried but in a committed relationship.

Courting, Dating, and Hooking Up

A popular reality television show in recent years has been the *Bachelor* (and complementary *Bachelorette*), where, since 2002, once or twice a year young men and women attempt to find a spouse on national television. On the show, one Bachelor (or Bachelorette) has the chance to meet 25 individuals and one by one deselect until there is only one person who will ideally be his or her spouse. Although the show purports to be about finding the "one true love"[12] that will lead to marriage, very few of the relationships lead to a wedding, and even fewer have successful marriages.[13] Perhaps it is the not-so-real nature of the reality show that leads to so many defunct relationships.[14] Or, perhaps, it is simply a reflection of the larger culture of marriage.

Although there is the obvious issue of the additional women (or men) who are also vying for the Bachelor (or Bachelorette), the whole premise seems to be one of glorified romance and of finding a soul mate. The dates are like modern-day fairy tales complete with private jets and secluded island resorts. In contrast, the modern mate selection process seems to be much more about instant gratification than long-term commitment and romance. Why the romancing of romance on the *Bachelor*? Is there a desire for something more than our modern dating system tends to provide? More important, how did dating become what it is today? It turns out that, like the other topics addressed in this book, it is a combination of both legal and psychological developments.

There is clear supporting evidence for romantic relationships across societies.[15] But how those relationships emerge seems to depend on the culture. The history of mate selection in the United States is relatively void of arranged marriages and, instead, rests on individual selection.[16] With that choice comes the need for some way to make that choice. In the United States, couples usually choose each other rather than their parents arranging their marriage.[17] Even in colonial America, parents only provided approval for a marriage.[18] For approximately two centuries, this spouse selection was based on courting,[19] also known as calling.[20] Calling relied heavily on parental supervision and structured visits to the woman's home.[21] Around the end of the 19th century and beginning of the 20th century, calling transitioned into dating.[22] No longer did young men and women need to restrict their interactions to the family parlor (with parents usually within earshot); they could venture out to dance halls, movie theaters, and anywhere the new American automobile could take them—with the automobile sometimes being the destination itself.[23]

Dating was not only about ventures outside the home but also about increasing the number of partners someone might have. Dating became more about fun, popularity, and filling dance cards[24] rather than spousal selection. Whereas in courting women had much of the power to extend the invitations to men, dating was largely controlled by men because dating relied heavily on money, and men at the time controlled the money.[25] Indeed, sociologist Willard Waller published a study in 1937 noting the new phenomenon of dating that was occurring on college campuses that were more coeducational than ever before. Waller's "rating and dating complex" was largely tied to a man's popularity, which was directly related to his material possessions and group memberships, such as his car, his clothing, and his fraternity. In contrast, a woman's popularity was tied to being seen with popular men and cultivating an impression that she was in great demand.[26] Women had to date to rate and had to rate to get a date.[27]

World War II ironically brought a stabilizing force to dating. In fact, the idea of "going steady" and getting married earlier in life was more the norm during and after the war.[28] One possible explanation for this is something known as excitation transfer.[29] Excitation transfer occurs when arousal, or excitement, from one source intensifies emotions toward another source. In the classic experiment on excitation transfer and sexual attraction, male participants in the fearful manipulation had a misattribution of arousal and experienced more sexual or romantic attraction than did those in the nonfearful manipulation.[30] In other words, the original fear arousal from the events of war may have transferred into romantic attraction, which led to an increase in marriages. Not only did the war limit the number of male suitors, but it may have refocused and intensified the desire for romantic partnerships and marriage.

The sexual revolution of the 1960s once again changed the dating scene and further empowered women's selectivity and seriousness. The legalization of the birth control pill opened many doors for women and their sexual freedoms.[31] These freedoms expanded with the legalization of abortion,[32] leading to even more casual dating over the next several decades.

Similar to the early days of dating, modern courtship seems focused on popularity rather than marriage. In contrast, however, the current trend is more explicitly sexual rather than filling dance cards and, as such, has been termed "hooking up" rather than dating.[33] The hookup culture is characterized by casual sex with no further attachments or requirements, but there are many different definitions of hooking up. These definitions range from kissing to intercourse and everything in between and can be a onetime interaction, occasional, or much longer in duration.[34] And these definitions are important in determining outcomes of hooking up.[35] Some argue that this hookup culture is a direct result of and to the benefit of the feminist revolution because too-serious relationships can stand in the way of the upward mobility of young women.[36] In fact, even a female student involved in a Title IX complaint at Yale[37] said, "I would never come down on the hookup culture."[38] She defended this view because, she said, many women enjoy casual sex.

The hookup culture is most prevalent during and around the college years, such that most people are not meeting their spouses in college as was once the case. This delay in marriage, combined with demanding work schedules and the potential for sexual harassment issues at work, provides a gateway for online dating that "isn't just for geeks anymore,"[39] and the proliferation of mobile apps on smartphones has further transformed dating into hooking up.[40]

Mobile or online dating also provides quantifiable options and opportunities to falsify profiles to virtually improve oneself.[41] But, as social psychologists know, people often do not know themselves as well as they think they do and often do not know what they want or how they will behave.[42] This lack of accurate introspection can be referred to as mental blind spots.[43] People are able to report their thoughts but not the underlying processes that lead to their behaviors.[44] In fact, early online dating algorithms were based entirely on what the customers said they wanted, which caused them to veer from what they truly wanted.[45] It turns out that how someone looks in his or her profile picture may often be the only thing that matters for choosing a person to date.[46] Tinder,[47] a dating site that relies on photos and quick swiping decisions, has created a secret desirability rating and provides its users with people who have similar desirability ratings.[48] Some of the emphasis on physical attractiveness could be related to the halo effect, which is the belief that physically attractive people also possess other positive qualities such as having higher incomes, more positive attitudes, and more intelligence.[49] Alternatively, it could be related to the purpose of using the dating site.

Evolutionary psychological research on attraction suggests that while physical attraction may be important for short-term relationships, physical attractiveness becomes less important for long-term and committed relationships.[50]

Many young males and females feel an enormous pressure to engage in casual sex as part of the modern dating scene.[51] Women especially report feelings of regret after these casual sex encounters[52] that seem to have neurobiological bases.[53] But, even with the more insidious effects from hooking up, such as increased risk of sexual assault[54] and exposure to sexually transmitted infections,[55] short-term well-being is not always negatively influenced by hooking-up behaviors.[56] The complex connections between hooking up and long-term well-being are difficult to determine. Definitional differences for hooking up[57] and the lack of longitudinal research on the topic make it difficult to fully understand the implications of hooking up both at the individual and societal levels. Recent research has confirmed that a hookup can lead to marriage—almost one-third of a nationally representative sample of married people reported their relationship started with a hookup.[58] Thus, whether it be courting, dating, or hooking up, on average the compass seems to be generally pointing toward marriage.

For the most part, laws have kept up with the dating fads. Very few "fornication laws" forbidding premarital sex remain as state statutes, and it is unlikely any would withstand judicial scrutiny.[59] But, as technology continues to play a larger role in dating with the increase in dating apps, the law will likely struggle to keep up as evidenced in other areas involving technology.[60] For example, should it be sexual assault to send an unsolicited "sext," that is, to send illicit photos to someone? And should dating sites screen potential sex offenders from using their services[61] even though the U.S. Supreme Court unanimously struck down a North Carolina law that banned sex offenders on social media as violating the First Amendment?[62]

Breach of Promise to Marry

The Ring Cam was launched in October 2013 as a way to capture—from the vantage of the engagement ring—the engagement proposal recipient's reaction.[63] A tiny camera and a microphone record and store the moment when the ring box is opened and the proposer pops the question. In the social media age, big proposals and even bigger diamonds[64] garner big attention.[65] A less visible but legally important scenario sometimes arises after the big proposal: Who owns the ring if the couple splits? Does it matter if the engagement fails to transition into a marriage?

Social psychologist Jonathan Haidt outlines two points of vulnerability for relationships.[66] The first is the initial passionate phase when couples may decide, rather irrationally, to move in together or plan to get married. The second is the end of the passionate romance. If the fiery passionate love does not transition into companionate love, then the relationship is likely to end. According to Haidt, companionate love is the kind of life-sustaining love that makes for golden wedding anniversaries. Psychologist Robert Sternberg focuses on the following three components in his triangular theory of love: intimacy, passion, and commitment, with each component manifesting a different aspect of love rather than a phase.[67] According to Sternberg's theory, the three types of love interact with each other in different ways across time and individuals.[68] Sternberg's consummate or complete love results when all three components of the triangle are present. For both Haidt and Sternberg, relationships succumb to their demise because they are not complete and not focused on all components. If this happens during the engagement it may simply mean sending the "Never mind, no need to save the date" cards, but for others there are serious psychological and legal implications.

Psychologically, ending an engagement is likely to have negative effects for at least one of the partners. Indeed, research demonstrates that people experience reduced self-concept clarity after a breakup that can also lead to emotional distress.[69] Although there is some evidence to suggest that positive emotions can be fostered, especially when the relationship contributed to expanding one's sense of self or self-improvement, breakups can lead to depression, loneliness, and distress.[70] Clearly, the more serious the engagement, the more emotionally difficult its dissolution will be, at least in the short term.

In some jurisdictions a jilted partner may bring a lawsuit based on the breach of promise to marry. Such a "heart balm" remedy was meant to sooth the brokenhearted by leveraging a combination of both contract and tort law at common law.[71] Early in the 20th century, abuse of such remedies led to statutory restrictions.[72] For states that still allow this cause of action, contract reliance damages may be for expenses incurred in preparation for a marriage or in planning a wedding and honeymoon. In addition, damages for mental anguish and psychological harm not generally recoverable in a contract case can be sought in a breach of promise to marry case.[73] Even punitive damages are sometimes granted in these cases.

What about the engagement ring for which that the Ring Cam so beautifully recorded transfer of ownership? It depends. Courts have generally held that recovery of an engagement ring rests on whether the ring was obtained conditioned on the performance of the marriage or was simply a gift not conditioned on the marriage. In making this determination, courts generally focus on the giver's intent with the gift being conditional on a wedding and marriage in the future.[74] Perhaps footage from the Ring Cam could come in handy as one piece of information in making this determination.

Prenuptial Agreements

A popular music artist sings, "If you ain't no punk, holla, 'We want prenup!'"[75] Such blatant affection for such agreements is also reflected in the public's increased use of prenuptial agreements. By some accounts, there has been a fivefold increase over the past two decades, and it is not only the wealthy and celebrities who employ these contractual arrangements anymore.[76] In fact, one reason many couples are creating these agreements is to limit liability for prior-marriage debt, or in some instances student loan debt.[77] Prenuptial agreements are also popular for second and subsequent marriages, especially when children from the prior marriages are involved and there is a desire to protect assets for those children.

Historically, prenuptial contracts sought to alter the legal consequences that ordinarily follow the end of marriage by death or divorce. These were allowed in the case of death, but their allowance in divorce proceedings is a more recent phenomenon. The former belief was that allowing prenuptial agreements for divorce would be contrary to public policy and would encourage and facilitate divorce. Within the past 40 or so years, legislatures and courts have been persuaded by economic theory that the opposite can be true. If the parties know in advance the financial implications of a divorce, then they will be less likely to get a divorce.[78] This is an impossible empirical question to answer ethically with true experimental methodology because it would require randomly assigning engaged couples to either be forced to enter into a prenuptial agreement or be prohibited from doing so.

To be enforceable, prenuptial agreements must (1) be truly voluntary, (2) involve informed agreement, and (3) not be unconscionable or otherwise offensive to public policy.[79] Voluntariness is generally required for any contract. For prenuptial agreements, the courts tend to be somewhat more sensitive than usual to claims that the agreement involved fraud, duress, or coercion, for instance, when prenuptials are introduced very close to the wedding date such that the timing does not allow adequate review to obtain full knowledge and voluntariness.[80] To be informed, generally the courts hold that the spouses must have truthfully disclosed their financial circumstances. In addition, some courts have considered whether both parties were represented by legal counsel in determining whether the parties were truly informed. Unconscionable agreements are harder to define, but it is clear that even if one partner was a better negotiator, it is not automatically unconscionable. In Missouri, the court held a prenuptial agreement entered the day before a wedding was both procedurally and substantively unconscionable because of the timing of the agreement and because the agreement was clearly unequal and weighted too much in favor of the husband.[81]

Indeed, there are core psychological principles at play that will likely lead people to be less likely to enter into a prenuptial agreement. Additionally, if they do enter into one, some people may be more willing to accept terms that are one-sided and less favorable than they should be. The main psychological principle is the "superiority bias." Sometimes referred to as the "illusory superiority effect,"[82] the superiority bias leads to a majority of people having a more positive perception of themselves than they have of others, so much so that it is mathematically impossible for the beliefs to be true. Statistically, no more than half of people can be above average. This finding has been demonstrated with high school students, university faculty, college students, and the public.[83] People tend to believe that they are more likely to succeed and have positive experiences in their own lives than others will and will be less likely to fail or otherwise have negative experiences.

Relevant for prenuptial agreements is research that demonstrates that people feel their own relationship is better than the relationships of most others.[84] In a survey of marriage license applicants, respondents reported that they knew 50% of marriages end in divorce, but, ironically, also reported a 0% chance that their marriage would be one of those.[85] Of course, the decision to have a prenuptial agreement is a complex one, but according to the superiority bias, one possible factor may be that many people believe prenuptials are for other people—people who will get divorced and are not as superior.

There are also psychological ramifications when a couple has a prenuptial agreement. Divorce legal expert Samuel Margulies argues prenuptial agreements highlight the juxtaposition of the adversarial system in which they arise and the fragility of human relationships they are meant to address.[86] As Margulies notes, prenuptial agreements are complex because the relationships they address are complex. They highlight underlying emotional concerns such as potential family interference and distrust. He also notes that attorneys working on them should refrain from zealously advocating the same way they might if they were negotiating a simple business agreement. There are real, and potentially permanent, relationship costs if the negotiations in a prenuptial agreement are done incorrectly because each request will likely have emotional underpinnings. Indeed, clinical psychologist Florence Kaslow argues that a therapist could be a useful mediator for a couple discussing a prenuptial agreement so that they can explore the motivations and intentions underlying the agreement.[87] Kaslow also suggests that couples should formulate their psychosocial prenuptial agreement before embarking on their legal prenuptial agreement. Such psychosocial agreements would address issues such as the couple's views on fidelity, psychological needs, and in-laws.

Surnames

Another decision that is generally made prior to getting married is one related to surnames,[88] also known as last names. Surnames are an interesting example of human behavior that became legalized.

Surnames developed organically with the aristocracy first[89] and then moved down the social ladder, so they were generally descriptive of where the person lived or what he did as a profession.[90] So John the metalsmith would become John Smith, and his wife would generally take on that same last name as she was unlikely to have an occupation outside the home. Surnames in England were not even consistent for an individual or within families until the 1300s, when some laws began to require registering one's name, but most names continued to be adopted through informal processes or personal choice.[91] The informal common law custom became legalized in the United States mostly through court dicta adopting a requirement for a wife to adopt her husband's surname.[92] There was a presumed psychological connection for men with their names, and courts have relied on this connection to support decisions in favor of male naming.[93] This connection is an artifact of cultural conventions in Western Europe and not seen universally in other cultures.[94]

Even as late as 1972, the U.S. Supreme Court seemed to support the requirement that women adopt their husband's last names.[95] Today, the legal default is for both spouses to keep their last names,[96] although in all 50 states, a woman can easily change her last name to her husband's upon marriage.[97] And most do so.[98] For men, it is not so easy.[99] Absent statutory provisions allowing a surname change of either spouse upon marriage,[100] a husband is forced to obtain a formal court order to change his surname.[101] Not only do such gender differences arguably violate the Fourteenth Amendment equal protection clause, because there seems to be no compelling government interest in not equalizing the name-changing abilities between men and women,[102] but they also suggest what society expects from marrying couples.[103] Indeed, the etiquette standards of the Emily Post Institute still indicate that when addressing your wedding invitations to a married couple they should follow the form "Mr. and Mrs. John Smith."[104]

Many psychological principles are likely at play in a couple's surname decision, but the endowment effect combined with cultural shifts could swing the pendulum back toward more fluidity and choice regarding surnames. The "endowment effect," also known as the "mere ownership effect," is the principle that people attach more value to something because they own it. In the classic experiment, half of the participants were given coffee mugs.[105] Those who "owned" the mugs valued them approximately twice as much as did those who did not "own" the mugs. These results have been explained as either an effect of loss aversion—people do not like to lose something once they have it—or the way we attribute items to ourselves once we own something.[106] Either way, for a man who has grown up in a society where the expectation is that he will keep his last name and for a woman who has grown up in a society without that as her expectation, there very likely could be different notions of surname ownership in the decisions to change one's name. As the customs change and more women keep their birth surnames and men change their names, little boys and girls may grow up with very similar expectations and feelings of surname ownership.

In addition to deciding surnames for the marrying couple, if the couple chooses to have children, the children's surnames must also be determined. Interestingly, for most children of women who choose to hyphenate or keep their surname, they bear their father's name.[107] For those who do hyphenate their children's names, what will happen to that hyphenated name when that child gets married? What if both future spouses have hyphenated names? Absent a legal reason why surnames should be differently chosen than first names, the law should be able to accommodate the changing social customs related to surnames. Of course, if the law responded to surname customs once, it surely can again and overcome the psychological heritage that seems to be influencing their use.

Nonmarriage

The popular music artist Beyoncé sings to "all the single ladies," telling them their ex-boyfriends cannot get mad when someone else shows interest because those ex-boyfriends "should have put a ring on it."[108] Despite Beyoncé's call for marriage proposals and our very marriage-focused society, remaining unmarried today has become a culturally accepted lifestyle. For some, being unmarried is about being truly single and unattached, whereas others are in committed, and even cohabitating, relationships without the marriage.

Still, most people do want to be married, and most do eventually get married.[109] Of course, the age at which that is happening continues to increase. Women, on average, are getting married at 27 and men at 29 years of age.[110] Part of this delay is related to a longer period of adolescence, with more people attending college and obtaining postbaccalaureate degrees.[111] Another factor has been the increase in prevalence and social acceptability of cohabitation. What was once shameful[112] and illegal[113] is now the most common first union experience of young adults.[114] As we will see, some of the shift is attributable to the availability of birth control that better equalized between men and women the potential outcomes from premarital sex. More generally, the sexual revolution of the 1960s better equalized the potential reputational effects between men and women who have premarital sex.[115]

For those couples who choose to cohabitate, there is not always a direct pathway to marriage. It turns out that couples who cohabitate and then get married are very different from couples who have been involved in serial cohabitation—that is, cycling through a series of cohabitation relationships.[116] Although some empirical research suggests that cohabitation puts those who marry at a higher risk for lower marital quality and divorce than married couples who do not cohabitate,[117] this seems to be related more to the number of cohabitation relationships than to the act of cohabitating. It could be that those who are serially cohabitating, and not planning to marry, are more likely to delay discussing the truly difficult issues, such as pooling their monetary resources, purchasing a home, or planning to have children.[118] Indeed, empirical research from the late 1990s demonstrated that most cohabitating couples do not enter into written agreements regarding their property.[119] In other words, they delay having those difficult conversations until marriage, thus allowing the cohabitation period to be something they slide into rather than decide to enter while leaving potentially relationship-ending discussions for marriage.[120] Additionally, one study found that serially cohabitating women who married had a more than double risk of divorce than did women who only cohabitated with their future husbands. This may be because those who are more likely to serially cohabitate generally have other risk factors that interfere with marital longevity. Other research demonstrates that the reasons for cohabitating impact relationship quality. For example, couples who cohabitate to test their relationship have poorer relationship quality than do those who cohabitate to spend more time together.[121]

Conclusion

Although the centrality of marriage and family remain similar to the antiquated notions of our ancient ancestors, modern life has brought more options for virtually everything, including finding a spouse. Historically, marriage was much more of a private issue compared to the legal and religious involvement we see today. The families, or rather the parents, controlled the decision to marry, and there was very little to discuss about family law prior to the actual marriage. As we have seen, there are important legal and psychological issues at play prior to the solemnization of the marriage in today's society. These premarital changes are important to contextualize the current status of marriage. In particular, the greater opportunity for finding a mate and the increased fluidity with which people seem to enter into marriage and marriage-like relationships are particularly important when thinking about the quality and longevity of a marriage. If our notions of dating are more relaxed, then it seems this could translate how we view marriage more generally. The next chapter addresses being and staying married and shows how public opinion can have a real influence on legal regulations of the family.

3

Getting, Being, and Staying Married

As singer Frank Sinatra famously crooned, "[l]ove and marriage, go together like a horse and carriage . . . You can't have one without the other . . . It's an institution you can't disparage."[1] Marriage is a relationship changer not only socially but also legally. Consider two friends who are roommates. Even if those two people have lived together for many years and are emotional confidants, their legal status as individuals remains unchanged. There are no legal rules for friendships, and their status as friends will have no legal consequences. Even if those two friends are romantically involved exclusively with each other, their relationship will not have automatic legal consequences. In contrast, the moment a marriage occurs, that status changes the way the law sees the couple both individually and together. This chapter addresses how psychologists may be involved in premarital counseling, how a marriage legally occurs, and the legal effects of that marriage. In addition, the chapter ends with a section on empirical research related to staying married.

Premarital Counseling

Premarital counseling, or premarital education as it is sometimes called, brings together the two worlds of psychology and law because the person providing the counseling often will be a psychologist. In fact, research suggests that couples prefer a licensed therapist over other professions to serve in that role.[2] At this point, premarital counseling is usually voluntary, although there has been some movement to try to require courses or counseling.[3] Many states incentivize counseling participation by lowering or canceling the marriage licensing fee for couples who attend state-approved counseling or premarital classes.[4] Some officiants require the couples to participate in premarital counseling before they will agree to officiate over the wedding, but that is generally when the officiant is from a religious sect.

The reasoning behind incentivizing or requiring premarital education or counseling is straightforward: Couples who are educated about marriage and spend time thinking and planning for their marriage should be better equipped to have a healthy and stable marriage. Additionally, some argue that it is necessary to require the counseling or education because couples do a poor job predicting their future marital satisfaction. Indeed, premarital counseling providers are generally supportive of state policies encouraging and incentivizing counseling.[5] But most newly married couples believe that their high levels of relationship satisfaction will continue and therefore that there is no recognized need for premarital counseling.[6]

For those who do participate in premarital programs, evidence suggests they are successful in increasing positive short-term outcomes, such as communication processes, conflict management, and general relationship quality.[7] In addition, couples participating in premarital counseling report higher marital satisfaction than those not participating in counseling.[8] But individual couple characteristics are likely to influence how beneficial the counseling will be.[9] Additionally, there is some evidence to suggest that couples who are more religious and less likely to cohabitate before marriage are the ones most likely to participate in premarital counseling.[10] Similarly, even though second marriages are more likely to end in divorce than first marriages, research suggests those entering second marriages are less likely to participate in premarital counseling.[11] In other words, some factors known to correlate with increases in divorce rates are the same factors correlated with less likelihood to participate in premarital counseling. This leads some scholars to suggest that those who need the counseling the most are the least likely to get it.[12]

Longitudinal research in this area is lacking, so less is known about the long-term effects of premarital counseling. However, large sample studies demonstrate positive outcomes across demographic factors such as race, income, and education level.[13] Some research suggests that using premarital counseling serves as a gateway for couples to seek counseling support later in their marriage,[14] which could help stabilize a marriage and decrease the divorce likelihood. Researchers in one study interviewed divorced couples who had received marital education when they were engaged to find out what they would suggest to improve premarital programs.[15] Interestingly, one common recommendation was that the education should have occurred much earlier and before the couple was engaged. The study respondents explained that by the time they were engaged, it felt like it was too late to change their minds about marriage even though the premarital counseling or education was raising concerns for them.[16] Still, because no states require premarital counseling there is also no research demonstrating that such a requirement will significantly reduce divorce or increase marital well-being. Even if such research existed, what proof would be enough to justify that kind of government intrusion?

Getting Married

Becoming married can occur through traditional solemnization or through common law means. In both instances, the parties must intend to be married, and there must not be any legal barriers present.[17] The two sections that follow address the differences between these ways of becoming married.

Solemnized Marriage

Most states require certain formalities when recognizing a couple as married. First, the couple must obtain a marriage license. Such licenses are generally issued by the county clerk and include small fees paid to the county. Some states require a waiting period between issuing the license and when the couple can get married. These waiting periods are usually only a few days and can often be waived for good cause. Despite many "must-have . . ." wedding lists available online,[18] the legal requirements for the ceremony are quite open. In fact, the Uniform Marriage and Divorce Act §206 provides that the solemnization of a marriage can be done by a judge, any public official who has the powers of solemnization of marriages, or any way that is recognized by any religion or Indian Tribe.[19] Therefore, all the "must-haves" of wedding photographs, bride emergency kits, and fresh flowers are clearly culturally defined rather than legally required.

Still, there are psychological benefits to all kinds of ceremonies and rites of passage; therefore, solemnization does appear to serve a psychological purpose. Scholars argue that a wedding ceremony is a rite of passage that symbolically ushers in a new life with new expectations.[20] Interviews with brides and grooms confirm not only this symbolism but also that the ceremonies represent something deeper for them.[21] For many of those interviewed, the ceremony was a way for the couple to meet each other's families and to publicly link the two families together.[22] Wedding celebrations also serve as a way to involve the couple's social circles and cultural institutions—such as churches—that are important to the couple.[23] For a remarriage, the ceremony provides the ability to include the children from a previous marriage or relationship.[24] This involvement and contextualization are magnified when the couple is intercultural and bringing together two different cultural backgrounds.[25] In fact, a study by the National Marriage Project (NMP) found that American couples who had large weddings with lots of guests reported higher-quality marriages than did couples with smaller weddings.[26] Even when adjusted for race/ethnicity, education, personal income, and religiosity, couples with 50 or fewer attendees had a mere 31% likelihood of a high-quality marriage. In contrast, couples with 150 or more attendees had a 47% likelihood of having a high-quality marriage.[27] Results from a study by the two economists, Andrew M. Francis-Tan and Hugo M. Mialon, confirm the NMP's results and separate the size of the wedding from the cost of the wedding. Using approximately 3,000 online participants, the researchers asked, among other questions, how much respondents had spent on their weddings and engagement rings and whether the marriage was still intact.[28] Their results demonstrated that the higher the wedding costs, the greater the risk of divorce. For example, for male respondents, spending between $2,000 and $4,000 on an engagement ring was associated with a 1.3 times greater likelihood of divorce compared to those who reported spending only between $500 and $2,000. But higher wedding attendance and going on a honeymoon were both associated with lowering the chance of divorce. This link between a larger wedding and marriage quality potentially exists because the larger celebrations are more purposeful in including the couple's community and demonstrate a stronger psychological network for the couple.

Aside from the license and some sort of solemnization, there really is not much else that is required. In fact, even the couple does not always have to be present. Some states allow a wedding by proxy.[29] A proxy wedding is one in which someone stands in for one of the parties getting married. Generally, these weddings by proxy occur because one party is unavoidably unavailable and most often because that one party is in the Armed Forces. In the state of Montana, neither party needs to be present in this situation, as they allow double proxy weddings when one member is actively serving in the military. Several Internet-based businesses have capitalized on Montana's law with catchy slogans such as "Why be apart from your partner? Don't wait any longer!"[30]

If larger celebrations lead to more marriage stability, then presumably these proxy weddings would not have glowing success rates, but no empirical research has examined marriages formed by proxy weddings. Indeed, correlational research questions emerge in considering whether the kind of wedding is predictive of the marriage longevity. For example, does it matter whether the guest list was large because it was filled with more family members or friends? Is the length of the guest list or the actual amount of money spent that is important? After all, a destination wedding may have fewer guests but still cost more than having a large wedding. Related, what role do the wedding photographs play? For instance, will having more Pinterest-worthy poses lead to a happier and longer marriage? Unrelated research on the role of photographs suggests that the opposite effect could occur because pictures can distort memories[31] and the act of taking pictures may interfere with forming the memories.[32]

Common Law Marriage

In the 2012 Hallmark Channel movie *The Seven Year Hitch*, two friends who live together for seven years find they have "accidentally" gotten married.[33] Despite this movie plotline and the commonly held belief, there is not a seven-year or any number of years requirement for common law marriages.[34] A common law marriage is simply a marriage that occurs without solemnization. The couple is legally recognized as married even though they have not taken the normal necessary steps of acquiring a marriage license and having a marriage ceremony. Generally, the couple must live together and hold themselves out as married.[35] At one time, U.S. common law marriages were quite numerous. Some theorize their ubiquity was born out of necessity during the westward expansion when there was less availability of clergy to solemnize marriages.[36] Common law marriages in the United States became less acceptable legally by the beginning of the 20th century. Today, only a few states recognize common law marriages. States began not recognizing common law marriages for eugenics purposes. If the state did not recognize the marriage, then it allowed the state to control legitimate births.[37]

For couples who validly enter into a common law marriage in a state that allows such unions, those marriages are recognized even in states that do not allow common law marriages.[38] Additionally, common law marriages can only be dissolved through traditional divorce proceedings—there is no common law divorce.

Case law regarding common law marriages generally arises because there is a need to divide property upon the death of at least one spouse or there is a desire to dissolve the relationship. In such instances, the courts generally focus on whether the couple was holding themselves out as married. This piece is important because there is no such thing as a secret common law marriage.[39] Courts rely on evidence such as tax returns, hotel registers, and hospital records in determining whether the couple held themselves out as married.[40] Inevitably, these court determinations of whether the couple held themselves out as a married couple are founded on traditional notions of marriage. For example, in one case the court used the fact that the woman did not change her surname as one of the reasons there was no common law marriage.[41] Yet, as detailed in Chapter 1, more and more women are deciding not to change their surnames when they get married. Indeed, in the rapidly changing marital norms, what does it mean to hold oneself as if married? Are there unintended stereotypical biases that occur because the judges making these decisions have a particular schema for what a marriage should look like? In addition, most legal actions brought that rest on a common law marriage determination are for the benefit of women, especially those from a lower socioeconomic status because they are seeking some sort of spousal benefits.[42] This disproportionate effect has led some scholars to argue that common law marriages should be more widely recognized as a protection for women and minorities.[43]

Being Married

A marital union, whether solemnized or through common law, brings with it a number of legal privileges and protections, as well as responsibilities and liabilities. Highlighting how much family law seeps into virtually every other area of law, the following sections outline those privileges related to property, taxes, medical decisions, torts, and evidence. In one instance, spousal rape, the marital privilege is only for the perpetrator and not the victim.

Marital Property

Although the family law notion of property ownership in the context of dividing property during a divorce is addressed later in this book, there are also important property issues within an intact marriage.[44] States are considered either common law or community property states for the purposes of marital property. Most states are considered common law states, and in these states the property acquired during marriage is owned by the person who acquired the property.[45] In community property states, property acquired during the marriage belongs to both partners—the "community."[46] Therefore, both spouses own an equal 50/50 division of their property.

Prior to the 19th century, women in the United States were subsumed within their husband's property rights. A married woman was not permitted to contract or own property because she had little legal existence separate from her husband. Similarly, married women (and sometimes all women) were barred from certain professions based on their inability to contract.[47] By the mid-1800s, a legislative movement was afoot providing women with basic property rights. Referred to as the Married Women's Property Acts, these state laws allowed women the basic property rights of entering into contracts in their own name and owning property.[48] These laws had psychological as well as legal implications. In Western cultures, the ability to own and have control over property is considered of utmost importance in defining self and one's power.[49] But, as law-psychology scholar Jeremy Blumenthal highlighted in his work on property law and psychology, much of what scholars believe about the psychological perspectives of property law are empirical questions left to be answered.[50] The family law context certainly provides fertile ground on which to do the interdisciplinary work Blumenthal outlined.[51]

Any vestiges of property ownership inequality are now tradition rather than the law. No longer are men required to provide for their wives, but rather, both partners share equally in the legal obligations of spousal support. Of course, in practice, there is still a great deal of inequality between men's and women's financial security because of gender inequality in earning, more women staying out of the workforce, and women working fewer hours and at lower-paying jobs.[52] As such, there is still often a power differential in marriages because men, on average, still bring in more resources, making women dependent on men for those resources.[53] With women continuing to increase their resources and shrink the wage gap, research suggests that there will be a greater likelihood of egalitarian decision making within marriages.[54] Such a shift could certainly exert great change within marriage that could even be greater than when women earned the right to own property.

Spousal Rape

Based on the historical idea that a wife was the property of her husband, rape of a wife by a husband was a legal fiction and inconceivable until the mid-1970s in the United States.[55] The status of being married was viewed as providing consent. From the late 1970s to early 1990s, state courts began striking down rape laws that included a marital exception. By 1993, all states recognized marital rape as a crime.[56] Nonetheless, a number of state statutes still treat marital rape differently from nonmarital rape. For example, marital rape is held to a higher standard than nonmarital rape in South Carolina such that the force must be elevated with a weapon or a threat of a weapon or some other aggravated nature.[57] Additionally, in a number of states, it is not a crime for a husband to have sex with his wife when she is drugged or unconscious to the point of not being able to provide valid consent.[58] Such an act would be a crime if he was not married to the victim.[59] There are also additional reporting requirements for spousal rape, such that victims must report the incident sooner compared to victims of nonmarital rape.[60] In contrast to these legal positions that suggest marital rape is less serious than nonmarital rape, psychologically, marital rape is devastating. Arguably marital rape is worse than nonmarital rape because of the broken trust and intimacy with someone they chose to be married to.[61] As such, legal scholar Michelle Anderson argues for the need for revisions of sexual offense statutes that would remove any reference to marital status, thus removing this area of the law that treats an issue differently when it involves married versus nonmarried individuals.[62]

Government Benefits and Taxes

If money tells us how much something is valued, then the U.S. government clearly values marriage. The list of government benefits for married couples is extensive. Some examples include the benefits married persons get with taxes, Social Security, retirement, and the military. In each instance, there is some discount or additional monetary benefit because of the marriage. The quality of the marriage is completely irrelevant, and as noted in the opening of this chapter, no similar benefits naturally flow for other personal relationships.

Using taxes as an example, when two people get married, they enjoy an unlimited marital tax deduction. This means that a married couple can transfer tax-free money between themselves as much and as often as they want, even after death in an estate.[63] Additionally, married couples have the option of filing their taxes jointly. Filing jointly generally results in fewer taxes due and therefore often a larger refund.[64]

An interesting question to consider is whether single penalties would garner less public support than the marriage benefits. From an economic perspective, these are the same, but we know people are loss averse.[65] Indeed, law professor Edward McCaffery and psychology professor Jonathan Baron examined public perceptions of tax laws and found this penalty aversion, such that their participants were more supportive of a marriage bonus rather than of a single tax. They saw the marriage bonuses as fairer than the single surcharges.[66]

Additionally, spouses are liable for each other's owed taxes unless one was an "innocent spouse" in errors made by the other spouse. To qualify as an innocent spouse, the taxpayer must prove to the Internal Revenue Service (IRS) that they did not know or have reason to know that their spouse underpaid their taxes. How does the IRS determine when a spouse knew or should have known? Is it possible that biases underlie this decision? One former spouse, Carol Joynt, thinks so. Joynt was married to a successful Washington, D.C., business owner who also happened to have underpaid his taxes by approximately $3 million. Joynt, herself a successful journalist and news producer, claimed to be unaware of the tax evasion. When she first met with her attorneys to claim innocent spouse relief, they told her that she "didn't look like a woman who was unaware of her husband's financial affairs."[67] Joynt says she never wore a suit to meet with her attorneys again. It is impossible to know whether it was her clothing choices or not, but she was awarded innocent spouse relief.[68] Is it possible that what Joynt wore influenced how supportive her attorneys were of her case and the ultimate outcome of her case? The IRS indicates that it will consider, among other factors, the couple's financial situation, the health of the requesting spouse, and whether domestic violence was present in the marriage.[69] Might stereotype notions also play a role? For example, what role does the requester's gender play? That women are the vast majority who seek this relief is clear,[70] and it is a highly litigated area of tax law with wildly disparate outcomes based on jurisdictional differences.[71] Would the race of the requester also interact such that White males would be least likely to obtain the relief because they are presumed to be knowledgeable about financial matters? Additionally, IRS employees and tax court judges are likely largely uninformed about domestic violence and the role it can play in a person's decision-making abilities.[72]

Medical Decisions

State statutes dictate who has surrogate medical decision-making power if someone is incapacitated and without a power of attorney in place. The Uniform Law Commission sets out a priority list starting with the spouse.[73] This means that the law designates the spouse to be the person best suited to make medical and life-sustaining decisions. Some empirical research has examined how well spouses do at making these decisions. Unfortunately, surrogates projected their own desires and preferences on their spouses, resulting in decisions that were inconsistent with the ailing spouse's desires because of this projection bias.[74] Both husbands and wives in the study were similarly bad at making accurate predictions. Even discussions about end-of-life issues prior to the decision making did not change these inconsistencies. It seems surrogate decision makers are highly influenced by their own desires.[75] This may be because of the surrogate's overestimation that others share their same preferences, otherwise known as the "false consensus bias."[76]

Other psychological factors are also likely at play that interfere with a spouse making true substituted judgments in a medical surrogate decision-making situation. For example, because it is your spouse who is in need of medical care, emotions will be heightened in a way that is certain to influence and cloud decision making. It is also more difficult to separate the needs of your spouse from your own because his or her medical outcome is inextricably linked to your own future. Even when spouses were provided with an advanced directive and given the opportunity to discuss the directive immediately prior to making a prediction about what the patients would want, their predictions were no better than spouses who had neither the benefit of the directive or discussion.[77] Indeed, some research suggests that unacquainted physicians are better than family members or the patient's primary-care physician at interpreting the desires of the patient.[78] Nonetheless, the law has chosen to provide spouses with this special role even though it is clearly not a perfect system, and that is partly because it is hard to imagine a more appropriate person to make these decisions.

Tort Actions

Spouses (and some family members) can recover damages for loss of consortium in a negligent or intentional tort case. Loss of consortium refers to the resulting interference with companionship, services, and sexual relationship because of an injury or death of the spouse. In other words, the unharmed spouse brings a suit against a responsible party to recover what they have lost because of the injury or death to their spouse. Although the law may be evolving on the matter, loss of consortium between couples is reserved for those who are married. A California case concerning an automobile accident that resulted in one partner's death highlighted the concerns with opening this tort action to unmarried couples. The court noted that the state had an interest in promoting marriage and that it would be too difficult to assess the "emotional, sexual, and financial relationship of cohabiting parties to determine whether their arrangement was the equivalent of a marriage."[79] In addition to excluding nonmarried partners, the loss-of-consortium standards are often vague at best.[80] Such vagueness likely allows bias to creep in. For example, we know from other areas of research that jurors place a higher value on plaintiffs who are physically attractive.[81] And this effect is not reserved only to juries; more attractive people on average make higher wages in their jobs,[82] and because of the "halo effect," we have more positive feelings toward the more attractive and imbue them with superior characteristics objectively unrelated to physical attractiveness.[83] Applying this research to the loss of consortium cases, will the more physically attractive couples and those who fit the stereotypes for a traditional marriage garner more and higher loss of consortium awards?

Evidentiary Privileges

In evidence law, there are certain testimonial privileges that permit someone to refuse to disclose, and prohibit others from disclosing, certain confidential information during judicial proceedings.[84] The law provides these privileges for practical purposes and to encourage certain relationship confidences.[85] Indeed, protecting the confidentiality of these relationships is said to be more important than the potential for lost information. For example, if the law did not protect physician–patient confidentiality, then the knowledge that a person's condition would not remain confidential could have a chilling effect on his or her obtaining medical care. Spouses are granted these special evidentiary privileges. Although other relationships are granted similar protections, those relationships are always professionally rather than personally based and are only for private communications.[86] For example, the profession is foundational for the privilege between a clergy and a parishioner, a physician and a patient, or an attorney and a client. Two best friends are not granted any such privilege even if they tell each other they are in the cone of silence. The foundations for the spousal privilege date back many centuries to English law when a husband and a wife were considered legally one person and both were considered incompetent to testify for or against each other in legal proceedings during marriage. Today, the laws are more complex but still based on the notion that the spousal relationship should be given special status. There are two spousal privileges. The first is spousal immunity, which is the privilege not to have one spouse testify against the other spouse while married.[87] A spouse can use this privilege to refuse to testify or to prevent the other spouse from testifying.[88] The second is the privilege for confidential marital communications that occurred during the marriage.[89] Neither privilege applies in actions between the spouses or when the case is concerning a crime against the testifying spouse or either spouse's children (e.g., child abuse).

Early in the 20th century, the Supreme Court addressed the first privilege, spousal immunity. In *Funk v. United States*,[90] the Court examined whether a wife could be a competent witness on behalf of her husband's defense. Abandoning the antiquated notions, the Court held that she could do so. The *Funk* Court did not address whether a spouse could prevent the other from testifying against the first spouse. Not until *Trammel v. United States*[91] did the Court tackle this issue. In *Trammel*, a wife testified against her husband concerning their combined drug smuggling. The wife did so in exchange for leniency for herself. Not surprisingly, the husband did not want his wife to be able to testify and claimed that she was precluded from doing so because of marital privilege. Holding that in federal cases the witness-spouse has the decision-making power, the *Trammel* Court noted,

> The long history of the privilege suggests that it ought not to be casually cast aside. That the privilege is one affecting marriage, home, and family relationships—already subject to much erosion in our day—also counsels caution. At the same time, we cannot escape the reality that the law on occasion adheres to doctrinal concepts long after the reasons which gave them birth have disappeared and after experience suggests the need for change.[92]

Although a witness-spouse cannot be compelled to testify, that spouse also cannot be prevented from doing so if she or he so desires. State courts vary on their handling of this issue, with some giving the party-spouse the decision-making authority.[93]

The second marital privilege is that of the confidential marital communication.[94] This privilege allows for either spouse in a civil or criminal case to choose not to disclose, or prevent the other from disclosing, that information that was confidentially communicated between a married couple while they were married. The communication must have had a confidential intent and not constitute day-to-day conversations.[95]

The rationale for this privilege is to encourage confidence and trust between marital couples. Again, no such similar privilege exists for other personal relationships. In fact, most states do not permit even a parent–child privilege.[96]

With these evidentiary privileges, we can once again see how tenderly the law views the marital relationship. Even though research demonstrates that married couples often are not fully honest and open with each other,[97] the law still places a premium on encouraging such openness. Of course, as has been detailed in this book already, marital rates are decreasing. Is it possible that these privileges are outdated and inappropriate to handle modern family life? If a mother is raising her son from a sperm-donor father while living with her widowed mother, no privilege exists between mother and grandmother, yet these people are a family for the purposes and best interest of that son. As the *Trammel* Court noted in the quote earlier, sometimes the law needs to look to the changes in society and adjust to those changes.

As law-psychology scholars Michael Saks and Barbara Spellman have noted, the area of evidentiary privilege is not well-researched empirically, but there are a number of behavioral assumptions the law makes in this area.[98] For example, do people know about the privileges, and would marriages suffer if the privileges were not in place?[99] If the intent is to encourage marital openness, it seems these questions are important for determining the continued validity of the privilege. If people do not even know about the privilege and it has no bearing on marital behaviors, should we maintain it as an evidentiary privilege? More broadly and theoretically, should our country provide such benefits of marriage?

How to Stay Married

As we will see, getting married is no guarantee for staying married and a large area of family law is primarily focused on the dissolution of a marriage. Yet, it seems prudent not to ignore the couples who do not divorce and celebrate their 50th and 75th wedding anniversaries. What are their secrets to a long marriage? What differentiates the 50% who do stay married from the 50% who do not?

Across the past century, research on marriage and marital longevity has become increasingly more sophisticated.[100] Psychologists have isolated a number of factors as being important in marital longevity. Some of the factors are demographic and not easy or impossible to change. According to the National Center for Health Statistics (NCHS) data, Asian women and foreign-born Hispanic men have the highest chance (70%) of staying married to the 20-year mark, whereas Black women have the lowest rate (37%).[101] More education, marrying later, and financial resources when married also all play into increasing marital longevity.[102]

Unfortunately, culturally, we have unrealistically hopeful expectations about marriage.[103] Historically, we are in what scholars refer to as the Romanticism period—having started around the mid-18th century. This period is characterized by the interweaving of sex and love. But marriage is about more than just love. In addition to the demographic factors that increase marital longevity, there are other factors more within the control of the couple. For example, research demonstrates that married couples who stay together are more likely to deal with unresolved conflicts in kinder ways[104] and have less pessimism and anger in the way they communicate with each other early in the marriages.[105] Additionally, simply the shared desire to stay married plays a role.[106]

Leslie Bachand and Sandra Caron conducted a qualitative interview study in which they asked couples who had been happily married at least 35 years about their marital longevity. Most common responses from the couples about why they remained married related to their mutual friendship, love, and similar interests.[107] In a similar interview study focused only on African American couples, the most common responses focused on the couples' faith in God, their love, and good communication.[108]

Samantha Joel writes for the blog called the Science of Relationships and outlined ten vows she and her fiancé planned to use in their wedding.[109] The vows are based on empirical research. For example, one was promising to the see the best in each other because research demonstrates that engaging in positive illusions about your partner—that is, seeing positive rather than negative qualities—leads to greater relationship satisfaction.[110] Another vow focused on showing gratitude because research has shown that people who feel more appreciated by their partners report more commitment to their relationship.[111] To note, none of Joel's empirically based promises were related to the law valuing marriage or had anything to do with the law. As is often the case, people may not be aware of the role of law in their lives, or it may be that the law, despite its valuing and emphasis on marriage, has very little to do with keeping marriages intact.

Conclusion

A founder of sociology, Émile Durkheim, studied suicide rates and found that constraints or ties to others, in particular, a spouse and children, were the greatest predictors for reduced suicide rates.[112] Strong social relationships make us happier, and the main social relationship that has been legally endorsed is a marriage and family. No other chosen personal relationship has the same gravity of legal effects. When people decide to be running buddies, book club co-members, or even best friends, legal consequences do not follow. There will be no tax benefits or special evidentiary rules applied.

Yet, we live in a time when marriage is not the automatic choice it once was. Our current society is fighting against a shadow of the "ideal" family. That ideal image includes a working father, a stay-at-home mother, and at least two children. Oddly, such a dominant nuclear family was more of a blip in history that occurred because of the exceptional circumstances in the 1950s both economically and politically because of the end of World War II.[113] It did not take long for this unique confluence of factors to break under the weight of a social rebellion, and the picture-perfect *Leave it to Beaver* family life dissolved. That shift brought dramatically new attitudes toward marriage and parenting. The next chapter addresses current notions of what makes a family.

4

Becoming a Parent and "Making" a Family

Jennifer Hopkins is a wedding and family photographer in Jacksonville, Florida, who is known for capturing perfect pictures of families and especially infants.[1] She longed to be a mom herself, but at 31 years old she was not in a romantic relationship and had fertility concerns because of complications with endometriosis. She decided she would use a sperm donor and chose one based on an extensive donor's profile that included his favorite subjects in school, baby pictures, and SAT score. After three failed attempts, Hopkins had a baby boy, Sawyer. Although she does not know the identity of Sawyer's biological father, she used the donor number and social media to find nine other mothers who used the same donor father as she had. All had sons—half brothers for Sawyer. They have a private Facebook page where they exchange pictures and stories. Some of the half brothers and their parents even got together for a trip to Disney World.

How we define who are the members of our family is ever evolving. If family is biologically defined, then donor offspring are related as half siblings. But, are there legal and psychological relationships? What effect should biological relationships have in the law? This chapter addresses reproduction options in the context of family law. First, the chapter addresses the use of assisted reproductive technology in becoming a parent. Although assisted reproduction is a booming business, it is still relatively new. In contrast, adoption has been part of the cultural fiber for much longer and raises similar, yet distinct, issues of legal and psychological relationships. The chapter therefore highlights those family law issues related to adoption. Finally, the chapter addresses the issue of controlling reproduction and the decision not to become a parent.

Assisted Reproductive Technology

Who hasn't watched a loving and upstanding couple struggle to conceive while also hearing about abandoned or abused infants born into unlivable conditions? The physical ability to become a parent seems unrelated to the social ability to be a parent. Indeed, becoming a parent through assisted reproductive technology or adoption requires a great deal more financial investment, demonstrable abilities, and patience than becoming a biological parent. Although it can be expensive and a great deal of work, assisted reproductive technologies have made biological parenthood a reality for many for whom it would have been an impossibility. Modern reproductive assistance often involves advanced medical technology that can easily outpace the legal doctrines meant to regulate it. Indeed, the bundle of joy comes with a bundle of legal and psychological issues. The current section addresses the most popular reproductive alternatives and their related legal and psychological issues.

According to the Centers for Disease Control and Prevention (CDC), assisted reproductive technology (ART) is any procedure where both the eggs and sperm are handled.[2] The egg and sperm are combined in a laboratory and then inserted. Often one or both are donations from another person outside the couple desiring to have a child. According to the CDC, ART does not include artificial insemination or any fertility treatments that do not result in eggs being removed, so ART represents a medically extreme form of reproductive assistance. Outside the CDC[3] and colloquially, ART refers more generally to any reproductive assistance including artificial insemination, *in vitro* fertilization, and surrogacy. The next sections address first those instances without a surrogate and then issues surrounding surrogacy.

Artificial insemination (AI) is the oldest, most common, and most basic of the reproductive technologies.[4] The first recorded procedure occurred in the late 1700s and involved inserting into the wife her husband's sperm without intercourse.[5] Later, sperm donors were used rather than sperm only from the husband. Shrouded in secrecy, the first instance used a medical student as the donor—chosen because he was the best-looking of the lot—and did not tell the wife that the sperm came from someone other than her husband.[6] From this clandestine procedure in 1855 to today, the process became much more standardized and somewhat less concealed. In the ensuing years from that first procedure, many legal and ethical issues arose. In some instances, the law considered artificial insemination a form of adultery and considered the resulting child illegitimate.[7] To avoid a long list of feared, unpleasant outcomes, doctors worked to keep the process a secret and encouraged the couples to do so also.[8]

The 1973 and 2002 Uniform Parentage Acts attempted to bring some legal clarification to issues surrounding artificial insemination. Most important, the act indicated that a donor is not a parent and that a husband of a wife who gives birth to a child through artificial insemination is the presumed father unless specific exceptions are met.[9] Today, the AI procedure does not require medical intervention, and self-insemination can be easily accomplished. In fact, the procedure has become so common and accepted that some prefer to call this technique "alternative insemination" rather than artificial insemination.[10] But legal cases are far from completely consistent. One sperm donor in Kansas, for example, was ordered to pay child support because he provided his donation privately through a Craigslist ad rather than with the help of a physician.[11] William Marotta donated his sperm to a lesbian couple who performed the insemination at home without the aid of a physician. Marotta signed documents waiving his parental rights, but the court said he did not have the legal ability to do so because Kansas law only allows physician-assisted insemination.

Aside from potential legal ramifications, are there other repercussions? In Naomi Cahn's book *New Kinship*, she notes that the way in which the law chooses to regulate donor families can transform the cultural norms surrounding AI.[12] A survey conducted in Australia at the end of the last century signified that most parents of donor-conceived children do not believe the children have a right to know they were conceived with AI and do not tell their children.[13] But, as more donor families include gay and lesbian parents or single parents, it is difficult for the children not to figure out their origins. Keeping donation conception a secret is more difficult in these family settings than it is when there is a husband and wife. Perhaps for that reason, today there is less secrecy surrounding AI, and more people are seeking out information about the donor and potential donor siblings.[14] Even donor grandparents, that is, the parents of a donor, also desire to know more about their donor-conceived grandchildren,[15] which clearly reflects an expansive definition of family. Cahn notes that it is unclear whether there are psychological effects for donors. Donors could experience some psychological ramifications after donating, as they realize that their donation could make a child and will no longer be an inanimate object.[16] Because adoptions have been occurring far longer than AI, future research in this area could potentially borrow from the psychological literature focused on the grief of parents who relinquish their children by adoption.[17]

What about the psychological effects of parents who go through an assisted reproductive process? Contrary to the early fears of eugenics swirling around assisted reproduction, self-report research found that parents who are in the process of using some assistance are less likely to focus on genetic selection and genetic perfection of their unborn child than those not using assistance.[18] The respondents in this research were told, "Imagine that you have a magic wand and can control what your future child will be like. We want to know how you would use your magic wand to choose traits in your child."[19] The respondents were then shown 14 traits, such as increased IQ, having a certain hair color, and having a good memory, and were asked how likely they would be to choose to improve those traits. *In vitro* fertilization (IVF) couples and pregnant couples without IVF were not statistically different in their responses to improve their unborn children.[20] Additionally, for those people who go through successful assisted reproduction, there seems to be a positive psychological bump as compared to natural pregnancies. In one study done in Australia, several hundred women in their third trimester who conceived with assisted technologies reported a more positive pregnancy experience than did those who conceived spontaneously.[21] In contrast, for those who do not have a successful assisted reproductive experience, there is often a decline in life satisfaction that takes several years from which to rebound.[22]

Surrogates and Gestational Carriers

Although surrogacy can be thought of as another assisted reproductive technology, it raises separate legal and psychological issues because it involves active participation by a woman separate from the intended mother. This other woman, the surrogate, generally contracts, for a fee, with a couple to carry a child through pregnancy and then relinquish that child at birth. In contrast, gestational carriers are implanted with an embryo that is not biologically related to her. In a gestational carrier situation, the sperm and/or egg may be from the intended parents or donated from outside the intended parental couple.

The most highly publicized surrogacy case, *In re Baby M*,[23] called into question societal notions of who we consider parents. In 1986, the surrogate in this case, Mary Beth Whitehead, upon giving birth, refused to surrender the child to the couple who had hired her to be their surrogate. The couple, William and Elizabeth Stern, had feared that Elizabeth would suffer complications from her multiple sclerosis if she got pregnant, so they offered to pay Mary Beth $10,000 to be impregnated with William Stern's sperm and carry the baby to term. Mary Beth agreed but changed her mind upon giving birth and decided to forgo the money and instead keep the baby. The case was full of underlying social dynamics. Mary Beth was a former bar dancer, and the Sterns were a successful professional couple—William a biochemist and Elizabeth a pediatrician.[24] The Sterns took to the courts and at first won, but the New Jersey Supreme Court invalidated the surrogacy contract as being against public policy. The court said that the contract conflicted with bans against baby selling. Nonetheless, the court granted custody to the Sterns because they said it was in the best interest of Baby M. Mary Beth was awarded visitation rights.

More recently, a California married couple, Mark and Crispina Calvert, contracted with a surrogate, Anna Johnson, to have the couple's embryo implanted, and Anna agreed to relinquish all parental rights in exchange for $10,000 and a life insurance policy taken out on Anna's life.[25] During the pregnancy, Anna had a change of heart and said she was not going to give the Calverts the baby. Once the baby was born, blood tests confirmed that Anna was not genetically related to the infant and that Mark and Crispina were its parents. At the time of the case, the California statutes referenced a mother as being the one who gave birth to a child and indicated that blood testing could be used as evidence of maternity. Clearly, the California code was written at a time when giving birth and blood tests would have pointed to the same person as the mother. The California Supreme Court concluded that either Anna or Crispina could be considered the mother under the code, but they held that legal parenthood should be assigned to the one who was intended to be the mother. For the court, the couple's intention prevailed, and they were granted custody.

The court noted concerns that surrogacy contracts can exploit and dehumanize women from lower socioeconomic status and can cause psychological harm to the surrogate. It also noted with concern that surrogacy can lead to children being viewed as commodities. The court went on to say that the proper forum for resolving surrogacy issues is the legislature, where "empirical data, largely lacking from this record, can be studied and rules of general applicability developed."[26] The court was right about the lack of empirical data on the topic.[27] But what empirical data would enable a legislature to answer these questions? Is a public opinion poll about surrogacy reducing children to commodities the answer? How many people would need to have this notion before it was too many and how informed must they be on the issue? What data would a legislature use to determine if surrogacy dehumanizes women and exploits those from lower-income brackets? What about the argument that allowing surrogacy recognizes a woman's moral agency and viewing the situation otherwise reduces women only to their wombs without sound judgment?[28]

Albeit limited, some empirical research has addressed surrogacy. Most of that research has focused on attitudes about surrogacy, characteristics and motivations of the surrogate mother (including experienced satisfaction with the surrogacy and effects of the surrogacy on her relationships with the intended parents), and personal characteristics of the intended parents.[29] Professor of psychology Susan Golombok and her colleagues have studied surrogacy families, comparing them to other assisted reproduction families (e.g., egg or sperm donation) and natural conception families across time points spanning from age 1 to age 10 of the children.[30] In examining the children at age 3, 7, and 10, there were no differences between those children who were born either with an egg or sperm donation. In contrast, children born through surrogacy, although normally adjusted, showed more adjustment problems at age 7 than did those conceived through donation.[31] The researchers conclude that one of the issues for the surrogacy children was that the surrogate could more easily remain in the family's life and was involved with the child, whereas the donors do not normally do so.

Likely because surrogacy arrangements differ drastically and often raise questions not easily answered with empirical data, the United States has no national policy about surrogacy, which leaves the decision of how to handle it to the states. That means that in some states, surrogacy is completely banned; in other states, only paid surrogacy is not allowed; and still other states, surrogacy for monetary gain is permitted.[32] Attitudes about surrogacy are also disparate, with one scholar arguing the best way to address the surrogacy issue is to simply avoid it with better infertility prevention.[33]

Adoption

Adoption legally severs the ties between blood relatives and creates new ties with the adopting family. Legally, the adoptee is treated as a blood relative of the adopting family. The law removes one relationship and creates another. Adoption, like many other topics in this chapter and book, is wide-reaching, but for current purposes the next section focuses on the process of adoption and postadoption issues with a particular emphasis on the surrounding psychological issues.[34] Despite its relatively common occurrence, there is still a level of unease in our common vernacular and social understanding of adoption[35] that will be apparent in the sections that follow.

Process of Adoption

The reasons for adopting can be organized into two categories. First, there are the parent-centered reasons, such as an answer to infertility. Second, there are the humanitarian child-centered reasons, such as adopting a child with special needs or adopting sibling groups.[36] Historically, adoptions were almost entirely the first kind—meant to benefit the parents by providing heirs and preserving family lineage.[37] These are the "feel good" adoptions that classically occur because an unwed and young mother does not have, or does not think she has, the resources to care for a baby and gives the baby up for adoption to a more financially established couple who have been unable to conceive a child on their own.[38] This situation was historically described as a win all around for the birth parents, the adopting parents, and the baby.[39] Today, we know the process of adoption is much more complex, and deciding the best interest of the child may not be as simple as comparing parental financial resources and age.[40] Indeed, the legal question of best interest of a child has uniquely psychological undertones.[41]

CONSENT AND QUALIFICATIONS

One of the core principles of adoption is that both parents who have the right to do so must consent to the adoption of their child. In the current era of no-hassle returns[42] and 90-day trial periods for sneaker purchases,[43] it feels like any decision can be changed. But, for a mother deciding to give her child up for adoption, the time allowed for her to revoke her decision is often quite short. In fact, some state laws require irrevocable consents that can be signed almost immediately after giving birth.[44] Of course, there is the new family on the other side of the adoption wanting to establish permanence and be able to know that the child they have adopted will remain theirs.[45] Consent revocation cases are always heart-wrenching with no perfect answer; there is no way to divide the child.[46] Although adoption law takes efforts to prepare both parties for the decision of relinquishing parental rights or taking on new parental rights, psychologically it is quite difficult to predict how the change will affect them emotionally. As we will discuss further, we know that because of ineffective "affective forecasting," it is very hard to fully appreciate how each party involved will feel in the new situation.[47] State laws reflect this difficulty by requiring the consent to an adoption not occur until after the birth.[48]

In addition to requiring consent of the birth parents, state laws also require a certain level of competency for the adopting parents. In contrast to someone deciding to have a biological child, adoptive parents have more formalized steps they must follow and much more government involvement. For example, in Arizona, the state law provides that in an adoption, consideration should be given to the "prospective adoptive family's ability to meet the child's safety, social, emotional, and physical and mental health needs and the ability to financially provide for the child."[49] In Idaho, the state places an age restriction such that the person adopting must be at least 15 years older than the adopted child.[50] Other states require a domicile requirement. For example, in Minnesota, a person must have resided in the state for at least one year unless the adopting parent is related to the child or was an important friend with whom the child has had significant contact.[51] States also require home studies of the prospective adopting parents. For example, as part of a home study, a child-placing agency in Virginia will determine that "bedrooms shall have adequate square footage for each child to have personal space."[52] The home study is concerned with ensuring that the adopting parents are qualified to adopt and are prepared to take on the role of being parents. Adoption parenting classes are also frequently required.[53] Clearly, the requirements to adopt are vastly different from conceiving naturally.

"Private rehoming" is a process some families are using to circumvent legally regulated adoptions.[54] Private rehoming occurs generally through Internet sites where adoptive parents advertise their previously adopted children as being available for rehoming in a similar way someone might advertise a pet in need of a home.[55] Not surprisingly, the adopted children often suffer sexual exploitation or other forms of abuse after the rehoming.[56] These disrupted adoptions, as they are technically called, are more common when the original adoption occurred with an older child and when the adoptive parents are not provided with the necessary resources to have a successful adoption outcome.[57] Indeed, studies demonstrate that very few clinical psychology graduate students or medical students have had any training on specific issues related to adoptions.[58] There is a similar dearth of training for students gaining their teaching certificates.[59] Some argue there is a need for a dual legal and psychological response. Federal and state legislation might require closer attention to the postadoption situation and better psychological services so that adoptive parents are not drawn to such a drastic measure as rehoming their adopted child.[60]

The Stigma of Adoption

One issue for adoptive parents to decide is whether they will tell their same-race[61] adopted child about the adoption. Current adoption scholars almost universally advocate for disclosing the adoption to the adoptee.[62] But adoption was historically shrouded in secrecy. In fact, the U.S. Census only first started asking about adopted persons in the home on its 2000 census.[63] Adoptions generally involved an unwanted pregnancy that was viewed by society as illegitimate. As the negative stigma around unwed pregnancies has decreased, the level of secrecy surrounding adoptions has also declined. Still, the genetic family is often considered the ideal, with adoption stigmatized.[64] The reasons people give for why they chose artificial insemination over adoption are quite telling in terms of beliefs about adopted children. For the most part, these reasons focus on the fear of damaged children who have been put up for adoption and the perceived exorbitant costs associated with adopting.[65] Adoption stories most often start with a couple's fertility challenges.[66] The stories begin with couples describing their desire to have a child and failed attempts to do so.[67] Some of these couples consider artificial fertility treatments next, and if those do not work, they then move to the adoption option.[68] This means that the adoption is usually the second or third choice for the couple or individual adopting.[69]

Some scholars suggest that even the language we use to describe adoption may be creating an unnecessary and damaging stigma for those involved in the process.[70] For example, adoption scholar Amanda Baden describes the shift from the term *biological parents* to *birth parents* to *first parents*. The change from *biological* to *birth* was meant to emphasize a relationship beyond genetics and biology. The more recent shift to *first families* further emphasizes that tie and denotes the chronological primacy of the relationship. Yet, even with the scholarly language shift, adoptees are still likely to get asked about their "real parents."[71] Relatedly, Baden describes how popular movies and books like *Stuart Little* and *The Blind Side* create an adoption narrative that can vilify either the first families or adopted families.[72] In the 2016 Pixar film *Finding Dory*, audiences are rather bluntly confronted with adoption and first-family issues.[73] The basic plot of the cartoon movie is that Dory loses her parents when she is swept away from them in an undertow. Although she has found a family with two other fish, she still longs to find her parents, and she struggles with self-blame and parental loss. When she does find her parents, she forms a new family that includes the two other fish and her parents.[74] Of course, this movie is about a cartoon fish, but the underlying theme seems to be that a child adopted by a family should want to find his or her first family with the ideal goal being to form a new family that includes everyone. Not only is this not a realistic goal for most adoptees, but arguably, it further devalues the adoptive family relationship as well. Somewhat similarly, Kelly Jerome and Kathryn Sweeney[75] analyzed children's books about adoption. In their examination of more than 100 recently published books on the topic, these researchers found that many of the stories advanced both the altruism of the birth parents and their inability to care for the child.[76] Only two of the books they examined provided the birth mother's perspective, and only three included information about a termination of parental rights.[77]

In the news media, adoptees are more often portrayed in negative rather than positive ways. For example, in one content analysis of 639 news media stories on adoption, 41.4% mentioned the negative emotional issues of the adopted child.[78] More than one-third of the stories described antisocial behaviors and physical problems of the adopted child.[79] More than half of the stories focused on problematic family issues, such as adoption placement failures and aggressive interactions.[80]

Is the negative stigma of adopted children based on reality? To answer that question, research about post-adoption often focuses on the development, mental health, and stability of the adoptee. In a series of studies, Marinus van IJzendoorn and colleagues demonstrated that adoption is a positive intervention.[81] The researchers relied on studies that compared adopted children to the following four comparison groups: nonadopted birth siblings who remained with birth parents, institutionalized peers who remained institutionalized, postadopted classmates, and environmental siblings (biologically unrelated but living in the same adoptive home). Their results suggest that although adoptees show delays and issues related to IQ, school performance, and language abilities prior to adoption, postadoption comparisons show more similarities than differences between adoptees and the comparison groups.[82] The adopted children seem to catch up in most domains, especially when adopted before 12 months of age.[83]

Wrongful Adoption

Similar to wrongful birth, described later in the current chapter, wrongful adoption is a case brought by parents claiming that they would not have gone through with the adoption had they known some material fact about the child. The concept was first outlined in an Ohio case when adopting parents Russell and Betty Burr alleged they were given fraudulent information about their adopted son, Patrick.[84] In 1964, the Burrs had desired to adopt a boy and were working with their county's adoption division. The adoption division offered 17-month-old, Patrick, whom it described as coming from a single mother who was living with her parents while trying to take care of Patrick. The adoption division said the mother had decided to give Patrick up for adoption because she was relocating to Texas in search of better employment. In reality, Patrick's mother was a mental patient in a state hospital, and although the father's identity was unknown, he was presumed to be a fellow mental patient. In addition, Patrick had been placed in two separate foster homes, and the adoption division had conducted assessments of Patrick that indicated he had lower than average development and other concerns.[85] It seems the adoption division fabricated the entire story about the single mother moving to Texas. While raising Patrick, the Burrs only knew that he was not like other children.[86] He was classified as "educable, mentally retarded"[87] and was eventually diagnosed as having Huntington's disease as a young adult.[88] The diagnosis led the Burrs to obtain Patrick's prior sealed records from before his adoption, at which point they learned Patrick's true background and family history.

The jury awarded the Burrs $125,000 for the damages resulting from the adoption division's fraud and misrepresentations. The Ohio Supreme Court affirmed the lower court's decision, noting that it was not a matter of adoption agencies needing to provide guarantees of a good adoption fit but, rather, the blatant fraudulent claims that the adoption division provided in this instance.[89] The Burrs' case was an extreme example of an adoption agency fraudulently changing the adoptee's story. More recent cases have focused on adoption agencies' negligence and a legal duty not to mislead.[90] In one such case, the agency indicated to the adopting parents that the baby they were adopting had a "possibility of incest in the family."[91] As it turns out, the adoption agency knew the adoptee's biological parents were a 13- and 17-year-old sister and brother.[92] Fetal Alcohol Spectrum Disorder (FASD) is another hidden medical issue that appears to be more common in adoptees than nonadoptees.[93] Unfortunately, there is no clear diagnostic test for FASD. Nonetheless, an adoption agency may have indications of FASD based on the mother during her termination of parental rights[94] and could let the adopting parents know of the possibility.

Should adoption agencies have an affirmative duty to take reasonable steps to determine the physical and psychological health of their adoptees? If the best interest standard applies, is it in the best interest of the adoptee to have presymptomatic genetic testing? Some legal scholars think it is not and will only create unnecessary angst and potential discrimination.[95] If the goal is to equalize the knowledge between adopting and biological parents, is there a way to provide similar information that biological parents would naturally know? All these questions represent topics ripe for research inquiry.

Cultural and Racial Issues in Adoption

Only a few decades ago, a Florida trial court and a district court of appeals decided it would be in the best interest of a child to be removed from her mother to live with her father because her mother was in a relationship with an African American man. The court reasoned that it would not be in the best interest of the child to be raised in a racially mixed home.[96] The lower court found no other issues with the mother's care or ability to provide for the child. In *Palmore v. Sidoti*, the U.S. Supreme Court reversed with vehemence, noting that the Constitution cannot tolerate such prejudice.[97] Although *Palmore* took a hard stance against race-based child custody determinations, it did leave open the possibility of considering race in adoption instances. Indeed, there have been two major movements related to race and adoption. The first relates to Black families and the second stems from the Indian Child Welfare Act (ICWA).

In 1972, the National Association of Black Social Workers issued a position statement declaring that White homes were not appropriate for Black children and that efforts needed to be made to match the race of the adopting family with the adopted child.[98] This position paper remains on its website,[99] and leadership in the organization continue to stand behind this message, arguing that the unique needs of a Black child would not be met by a White family.[100] Their most recent position statement focuses on kinship care and advocates for a "family-focused" rather than "child-focused" approach.[101] One potential unintended negative consequence, however, is that more Black children could languish in foster care awaiting a racially matched family.[102] The Multiethnic Placement Act (MEPA)[103] and the Interethnic Adoption Provisions (IAP) Act[104] are two federal laws meant to address this issue and the complex array of other factors[105] by making federal funding dependent on adoption agencies not delaying or denying adoptions because of race, color, or national origin of the adopting parent or adopted child.[106]

The ICWA[107] was enacted to address the high rate of Native American children being taken out of their tribes and adopted by White families. Contrary to the MEPA and the IAP, ICWA placed more authority with the tribe by giving the tribe decision making authority.[108] One purpose of the law was to discourage placement of Native American children with nontribal families. The goal under the law is to place a child with the child's extended family. If the extended family is unavailable, then members of the child's tribe are the second choice. The final option is "other Indian families,"[109] which suggests a blending of all tribal cultures.[110] The law also permits a longer period for revoking consent to an adoption.[111]

The law has a sordid and tumultuous past regarding race and adoptions. Currently, approximately 40% of adoptions are transracial, with 85% of transracial adoptions being international adoptions.[112] For families in the process of adopting, race is often a consideration, with adoption agencies asking what races the adopting parents will accept.[113] Some agencies are less transparent about race and, instead, use terminology such as "healthy" as code for White children available for adoption.[114] In fact, there is even some evidence that adoption agencies have lower fees and costs associated with adoptions of minority children as compared to White children.[115]

In her narrative research about the experience of adoption, social work scholar Miriam Klevan asked her participants to describe their experiences with infertility and adoption. Klevan examined more deeply those participants who voluntarily mentioned race in their narratives. Parents who adopted children of the same race focused on the importance of being similar to their adopted child and tied skin color similarity to larger life themes.[116] These parents also expressed that they felt judged because of their desire to adopt a child of the same race.[117] Parents who adopted a child of a different race not only expressed their high awareness of the racial differences at the time of the adoption, but they also expressed their ability to make the transracial adoption work.[118]

Some parents in transracial adoptions felt isolated because of instances of prejudice from both the White and non-White communities.[119]

In a similar in-depth interview study, sociologist Kathryn Sweeney asked adoptive parents about their experiences adopting their children. Approximately one-quarter of the parents indicated that they were open to adopting a child of any race except Black. Some of those parents rationalized this because it would be more difficult for the child because the child would not have a support network of people of their same race.[120] One parent noted that she would not know how to care for a Black child's hair and that this was one of her reasons for not wanting to adopt a Black child.[121]

Despite the potential for difficulties, many transracially adopting parents see their legally created families as spiritually formed and part of God's plan and providing increased awareness and knowledge of racial issues for the parents involved.[122] Indeed, research, albeit limited, has found that transracially adopted children do not experience any more racial discrimination than nonadopted minorities.[123] Transracially adopted children seem to also fair about the same psychologically as same-race adoptees.[124] Additionally, a review of previous research suggests many positive outcomes for adoptees when their adopting parents provide ethnic identity information for their birth identity.[125] However, it seems the opposite is not necessarily true. Adoptees who are not provided with this information are not necessarily worse off.[126] One noticeable limitation in the area of transracial adoptions is the conflation of international and national adoption. More work is certainly needed to develop a clear theoretical understanding of the impact of transcultural and transracial adoptions.

Controlling Reproduction and the Decision Not to Become a Parent

Decisions to become or not become a parent are inextricably related to what is happening socially, economically, historically, and legally.[127] Between 1800 and 1900, U.S. families decreased in size from an average of 7 children to an average of 3.5 children.[128] The reasons for the decrease can be tied to the shift from an agricultural to industrial economy and more knowledge concerning reproductive processes.[129] That knowledge continued to grow in the next century; however, the law attempted to intervene. In 1873, the U.S. Congress enacted the Suppression of Trade in, and Circulation of, Obscene Literature and Articles of Immoral Use.[130] Colloquially referred to as the Comstock Law, the act restricted the use of the U.S. Postal Service to send, *inter alia*, contraceptives or any information regarding contraceptives. Many states also passed complementary statutes that restricted the possession and sale of such "obscene" materials. Even married couples in Connecticut could have been arrested and subjected to a year in prison for using birth control.[131]

In 1916, with the Comstock Law as the backdrop, a public health nurse named Margaret Sanger opened the first birth control clinic in the United States. Open for only 10 days, the clinic was raided, contraceptives confiscated, and Sanger arrested and convicted for distributing contraception.[132] The appellate court upheld Sanger's conviction but exempted physicians from providing contraception information for therapeutic purposes.[133] Not until the 1936 New York case of *U.S. v. One Package of Japanese Pessaries*[134] was contraceptive commerce among medical professionals permitted. Soon thereafter, the American Medical Association recognized birth control to fall within the purview of medical practice.[135] Approximately 20 years later, research programs were actively developing what Margaret Sanger referred to as a "magic pill" that would prevent pregnancies better than the current contraception available at the time.[136] In 1957, the Food and Drug Administration (FDA) approved a progesterone–estrogen combined pill, Enovid, not as a form of birth control but, rather, to treat severe menstrual disorders. The bottle even came with a warning label that the medication would prevent ovulation. Not surprisingly, "severe menstrual disorders" swept the country, with more than 500,000 women receiving Enovid prescriptions by 1959. In the following year, the FDA approved the Pill for use as contraception. Within three years, 2.3 million American women were using the Pill, yet Comstock Laws still cast shadows in some states by making contraception illegal. In 1965, the U.S. Supreme Court case of *Griswold v. Connecticut* invalidated Connecticut's Comstock Law that prohibited the use of a drug to prevent conception.[137] The case developed from the illegal establishment of Planned Parenthood clinics in Connecticut and the arrest of and guilty verdicts against the clinic's executive director (Estelle Griswold) and physician. The 7–2 Supreme Court decision focused on marital privacy in finding the laws unconstitutional. Writing for the majority, Justice Douglas noted that although the right to privacy was not explicitly detailed in the Bill of Rights, it was rather in the "penumbras" and "emanations" of other constitutional protections.[138] Although *Griswold* only focused on marital privacy, it did not take long before the Supreme Court extended similar privacy rights to the unmarried in *Eisenstadt v. Baird*.[139]

With the legalization of oral contraception in the 1970s came questions of actual use and education about use. Legalization allows contraception use, but many individual and societal factors influence whether contraception will actually be used. Indeed, approximately half of pregnancies in the United States are unintended, with women from a lower socioeconomic status experiencing more unintended pregnancies.[140] Other data suggest that contraception use is inconsistent even among people not desiring to get pregnant;[141] in fact, a lower desire for pregnancy is not statistically associated with an increased use of contraception.[142]

In addition, legalization did not change religious tenets against the use of birth control. In fact, the Catholic Church still forbids the use of birth control among its members,[143] although research demonstrates that many Catholics use contraception.[144] Why is there this seeming disconnect between what the law allows, biology requires, and people do? Psychological research suggests that we often maximize short-term gratification while neglecting to consider long-term consequences.[145] In addition, the research specifically on hot and cold decision making is also informative. George Loewenstein describes medical hot–cold decision making, noting how our current affective states cloud our predictions of how we will feel in the future.[146] For example, when people are in a hot emotional state, they are unable to completely appreciate how they will feel when they are not in the same state and will underestimate the influence of their effect on their decision making. A similar gap occurs when people are in a cold state and unable to predict how they will feel in a hot state. It is easy to see why contraception use can be affected by the hot-to-cold empathy gap Loewenstein describes, such that when a couple is in the hot state of embarking on sexual activity, they will believe they are behaving more dispassionately than they are and will overestimate the stability of their current preference. In other words, they will believe that having sex is more important than the risks associated with not using contraception.[147]

Abortion

Less than one year after *Eisenstadt*, the Supreme Court's landmark decision of *Roe v. Wade* held that the right to privacy extended to a woman's decision to have an abortion, but states do have an interest in protecting the pregnant woman's health and the potential human life.[148] Although only 14% of women who obtain abortions are married,[149] it did not take long for states to legislatively regulate abortions, and many of those regulations related to the pregnant women's husbands. For example, Missouri had a statute requiring spousal consent for abortions. In order to obtain an abortion, a married woman had to have prior written consent of her husband unless her physician certified that the abortion was necessary to save her life.[150] In the Supreme Court case challenging this requirement, the state argued that the law served to preserve the institution of marriage, and family status was meant to be decided by both the husband and wife together.[151] The Court disagreed because the statute effectively gave the husband veto power over the wife's decision. Donning their marriage counselor hats, the majority also noted that the decision to have an abortion should be one that occurs through an agreement between the husband and wife, but if no agreement can be reached, it is the wife whom the pregnancy most affects, and therefore, she should get the deciding vote.

States now could not require husbands' consent for abortions, so what about requiring notice to the husband? In *Planned Parenthood of Southeastern Pennsylvania v. Casey*[152] the Court tackled just that issue. Pennsylvania required that unless there was a medical emergency, a physician would not perform an abortion unless the woman provided a signed statement indicating that she had notified her husband that she was going to have an abortion. The statute allowed for exceptions such as domestic violence, where the husband was not the father, or the husband could not be located. Despite the statute's exclusion in domestic violence situations, the Court in this case zeroed in on the fear that in abusive relationships, requiring notice would effectively be a consent requirement.

Noting the historical foundations of treating a wife as a dependent entity of her husband, the majority boldly stated that "[a] State may not give to a man the kind of dominion over his wife that parents exercise over their children."[153] As the *Casey* Court noted, and empirical research has confirmed, most wives do talk to their husbands about their decision to seek an abortion, and most husbands agree with the decision.[154] Not surprisingly, being in an abusive relationship reduces the likelihood that a woman would talk about the abortion with her husband.[155]

According to the Guttmacher Institute, 27 states require counseling designed to discourage an abortion before a woman may obtain one.[156] In South Dakota, the statute requires physicians performing abortions to warn patients in writing that the abortion poses risks for "depression and related psychological distress and increased risk of suicide ideation and suicide."[157] Yet, a nationwide survey has found no difference in depressive symptoms between women who have had an abortion from those who were denied an abortion.[158] Law- psychology scholar Jeremy Blumenthal called this "emotional paternalism" because it involves the state giving women emotionally laden information meant to discourage them from obtaining an abortion.[159]

There has been some research, albeit controversial, to support South Dakota's statutory language, which demonstrates that a small percentage of women do experience some regret and mental health issues after obtaining an abortion.[160] Most, however, report experiencing positive emotions (e.g., relief) after the abortion, especially when the abortion occurs within the first trimester.[161] Those who do experience some negative emotions tended to be younger and unmarried women without children.[162] It is possible that these negative emotions stem from societally imposed feelings of guilt.

Wrongful Birth

Wrongful birth cases provide an interesting example in which parents bring a medical malpractice case against a physician who fails to conduct testing or warn about fetal problems.[163] In states that allow this type of claim,[164] the parents generally claim that they would have chosen to abort the fetus if the physician had not neglected to test or let them know about the medical condition. Kerrie Evans was one such parent who brought a lawsuit against her health care providers requesting millions of dollars because they failed to diagnose her unborn daughter's cystic fibrosis. Evans lost her case when the jurors decided that her health care providers did not deviate from the standard of care.[165] Such claims highlight the devaluing of children with disabilities as courts grapple with value differences between not having a child at all versus having one with an illness.[166] Some argue that these cases perpetuate negative stereotypes about people with disabilities and that the message they send can emotionally damage those who are living with disabilities.[167] In addition, is there an emotional trauma a parent endures who testifies in court that they would have had an abortion? What effect will there be on the child? These cases are relatively rare enough that there are no empirical studies to answer these questions.

Parental Licensing

Psychologist David Lykken boldly proclaimed that most prisoners would not be in prison if "they had been switched in the hospital nursery and sent home with a mature, self-supporting, married couple."[168] He went on to say that most of the biological parents would not have been fit to adopt someone else's baby, and the only effective way to address crime is to "require from persons wishing to birth and rear a child of their own those same minimal criteria usually expected in adoptive parents."[169] Lykken's plan would involve clerks, similar to those at the Department of Motor Vehicles, checking for a marriage license, legal age, employment, financial self-sufficiency, physical and mental capacity, and lack of violent criminal record. Babies born to unlicensed parents would be removed at birth and given up for adoption. A second unlicensed birth would require submission to a permanent contraception treatment. Lykken provides some exceptions so that single mothers could have children if they were able to demonstrate that they have adequate resources to care for a child.

Not surprisingly, Lykken's proposal elicited critiques from scholars, with all generally dismissing the proposal as legally impossible. Richard Redding, a law-psychology scholar, provides detailed Supreme Court jurisprudence demonstrating the unfeasibility of such licensure.[170] The entire plan has shadows of China's one-child policy, and that does not sit well with freedom-loving Americans. Psychologist Sandra Scarr argues that licensing is not the answer, but greater reproductive control could be. In fact, Scarr proposes that male and female contraception could become part of our drinking water and only upon deciding to take the antidote would a person become fertile.[171] This starting point of infertility, Scarr believes, will provide people (mostly women) with the ability to decide when to have children, which increases the likelihood that they will do so in a way that maximizes each child's benefit. In other words, people will not choose to take the contraception antidote until they know that they are financial and otherwise prepared. Of course, it is an empirical question whether people would behave as Scarr proposes and rationally decide when to take the antidote that maximizes their parenting abilities. Also, who would get to decide who received the antidote? Would both men and women need to take the antidote, or could it be just one member of the couple?

Conclusion

Having or not having children is no longer a mysterious occurrence seemingly controlled by outside forces. Today, individuals have options for becoming a parent or not becoming one. Scientific advancements provide seemingly endless biological options for conceiving a baby. Similarly, relatively recent advancements make it biologically possible to delay conception or end a pregnancy. Even with the scientific advancements, some persons still use adoption to bring a child into their life because they are infertile, possess concerning genetic propensities either individually or in combination with their partner, or desire to help a parentless child. No matter how a child enters a parent's life, there are lifelong psychological and legal consequences. The next chapter addresses what happens once children are born.

5

Parenthood and Other Caregiving

The satirical website *The Onion* included the following in one of its stories:

> At the end of the day, it's all I can do to drag myself home to bed. But there's always some little child telling me how much they love me, asking me to sign this or that permission slip, bombarding me with questions . . . Who are these kids?! If I didn't make $49,000 a year and happen to be married to their mother, these kids would run away from me if they saw me on the street. But because they see me as some kind of "father figure," I have to live in a fishbowl . . . I never asked for this, and I couldn't begin to tell you why my kids look up to me so much. But I guarantee you, I've never done the slightest thing to encourage it.[1]

Of course, what makes satire funny is the thread of truth running throughout that pokes fun and highlights ironic behavior. This piece takes a culturally relevant topic and describes it in a humorously irreverent way. Amid claims of children being the "center" and the "meaning for living,"[2] people generally do not glean pure happiness out of child-rearing (or any caregiving, for that matter).[3] The *Onion* piece makes us first think how utterly disrespectful and hurtful the author is being, but that initial offense likely gives way to recognition of some internal contradiction and truth.

Although the general topics of parenthood and caregiving are not always covered in family law texts, this chapter addresses the topics because the underlying desire to be a parent is so vitally important to many of the topics covered in the chapters to follow. For example, custody battles are presumably based on the core desire to be a parent.[4] Similarly, grandparent visitation rights presumably stem from some caregiving desire of the grandparents.[5] Therefore, this chapter dives into those factors that lead a person to want to parent, how modern parenting works, and some legal ramifications of parenting.

The Parenthood Mystique: Why Does Anyone Become a Parent?

This section heading is a nod to the influential Betty Friedan and her 1963 book, *The Feminine Mystique.*[6] Friedan described the results from a Smith College alumni survey she conducted in which she found that a vast majority of her classmates, despite being intellectually curious and ambitious in college, were taking on the primary role of homemaker. Friedan described the suffocating social situation as a confusing mystique of time-filling tasks that left the women largely unfulfilled. The book remained on the *New York Times* best-seller list for six weeks. It struck a chord at the time and remains a popular feminist reading today. Perhaps its popularity stems from the fact that, while the world has changed drastically since 1963, the basic concept of parenting has not. Parental status has remained largely static with a relatively similar basic understanding of the parent–child relationship.[7]

The Greek philosopher Plato provides a comparative example of what the world would look like without the standard parent–child template. In Plato's *Republic*, we see a rejection of the family as we know it. As noted earlier, Plato believed that procreation was important, especially for the best and brightest genetic lines, but he felt the Guardian class would be hindered by raising children. As a solution, Plato proposed that the wives and children be common without specific knowledge of which child belonged to which parent.[8] The 20th-century kibbutz movement in Israel provides a contemporary example of communal living where children were raised collectively without a focus on the nuclear family.[9] But to current families in the United States, such arrangements seem more like a society featured in postapocalyptic young adult novels.[10] In fact, even when there is no parent available to raise a child, the state steps in *loco parentis* to effectively act as the parents.[11] Parents' rights and abilities to raise their children are legally protected from state and other outside interference.[12] Why is there this strong pull toward family-centric parenting?

Parenthood Does Not Equal Happiness

Secret Confessions is an online confessional where people can anonymously confess about any topic of their choosing. Others can leave comments about the confessional.[13] The website also includes archives that provide confessions by month and categories of confessions such as addiction, hate, regret, and revenge.[14] The website provides a listing of the confessions that have received the most comments. A confession about someone who fantasizes about killing people and a wife who feels guilty for cheating on her husband have 74 and 73 comments, respectively.[15] A confession by "Ann" that states, "I am depressed. I hate being a mom. I also hate being a stay at home mom too!" has 2,428 comments.[16] The next closest is a confession of a woman who killed her baby and let her husband go to prison for the crime, which has 177 comments.[17] What is probably more interesting than the vast number of comments for Ann's confession of hating being a mom is the tenor of those comments. Comment after comment reaches out a cyber hug for Ann to agree with her assessment and claim that they are in the midst of their own maternal hell.[18] Facebook has a less anonymous community group called "I regret having children."[19] Only 1,391 people have "liked" the page, although presumably, being your child's Facebook friend or being concerned with how one's other friends would react, would be an inhibitor to clicking the like button. The About section of the page says, "This page is here to let all the mothers and fathers know that regretting having a child(ren) is normal and shouldn't be taboo."[20] Cheerfully Childfree is another Facebook community that touts all the benefits of not becoming a parent—or, as the website calls them, "breeders."[21]

It is true; being a parent will not necessarily make you happy.[22] In fact, there is very good scientific evidence to suggest the exact opposite, especially while you are actively parenting.[23] Still, most people choose to be parents,[24] and most would likely say publicly they would be miserable without being a parent.[25] Yet, child care is not pleasurable,[26] marital relationships generally suffer when children are added to the mix,[27] and parents are generally more depressed, with lower well-being, than nonparents.[28] Aside from biological and evolutionary reasons to have children,[29] how do we resolve this apparent incongruence?[30] Three psychological principles aid in solving this riddle: affective forecasting, cognitive dissonance, and the burden of choice.

Affective Forecasting

It turns out that people are really bad at predicting how they will feel in the future, termed "affective forecasting." Research studies demonstrate that from simple positive events like your sports team winning a big game to more significant, life-altering events like a kidney transplant and removal from dialysis, people are relatively incapable of knowing how they will react. People overestimate just how damaging and negative losses and difficulties will be and similarly overestimate how rewarding and positive accomplishments and affirmative events will be. Becoming a parent inherently involves predictions about how a person will feel in the future when his or her bundles of joy turn into needy toddlers and volatile teenagers. In general, people overestimate how happy they will be when they become parents.

Dan Gilbert, an expert on happiness and our inadequate predictions about happiness, says that we are deluded into believing parenthood will make us happy.[31] Pre-parent people imagine all the good about parenthood or, at least, expect that the good will outweigh the bad. Similarly, though post-parent people do remember the difficulties, they mostly remember the satisfaction of parenthood.[32] Gilbert cites a number of studies that contrast with these predictions and memories. There seems to be a steady decline of marital satisfaction up to the point that the children leave home; at that point, the satisfaction begins to rebound to pre-child levels. As Gilbert notes, most of parenting involves dull and hard work with little to no appreciation for it, yet as a society we continue to have children because the system is "rigged" to make us think children will bring us happiness.[33] This rigging is done to ensure proliferation because it is good for society even though it may not bring happiness for the individual. Another explanation is that we should not focus so much on happiness because it is simply how you feel at that moment; it is a mood in a cross section of time rather than the more enduring well-being.[34]

Cognitive Dissonance

Historically, as the economic value of children decreased, their emotional value seemed to increase.[35] Child labor laws restricted the economic value of children, yet parents still continued having and valuing children. Cognitive dissonance, one of the most widely cited and influential social psychological theories, provides some insights into why this might be.[36] In general, cognitive dissonance provides that people are troubled by inconsistency, and they will therefore expend psychological energy to maintain or restore consistency.[37] If a person's behaviors and attitudes do not match, dissonance occurs, and the theory predicts that the person will adjust the attitude to relieve the dissonance. Some experimental research focused specifically on cognitive dissonance in parenting by making the costs of parenting salient and manipulating the presence or absence of parental benefits.[38] By demonstrating the dissonance effect, participants were more likely to idealize parenting when they received the parent-cost without the parent-benefit manipulation.[39] In other words, higher costs of parenting lead to parents idolizing parenting and parenthood.[40] Additional research suggests that satisfaction with parenting may be attributable to the parents' outlook; specifically, the parents' communal focus seems to have a positive effect such that these parents do not experience parental caregiving as costly.[41]

The Burden of Choice

Based on the array of options at your local mall's soap and lotion store, it would seem that we can never have too many alternatives. Do you want cream or lotion? Body butter or moisturizer? Which of dozens of scents? Some choice is good; having a choice versus no choice increases intrinsic motivation and enhances performance. A number of psychological research studies have demonstrated this from choosing which puzzles to solve and for how long[42] to choices about what night to watch a movie in a nursing home.[43] Even the illusion of choice increases intrinsic motivation.[44] Assuredly, choice and autonomy are core reasons the United States exists—American revolutionaries such as John Locke fought hard to ensure our freedom of thought and action.[45]

Yet despite the American Revolution and the dizzying array of creamy items to rub on dry skin, it turns out that having too many choices can be bad. Rather than increase intrinsic motivation, having too many choices has the opposite effect. One study found that if a store displays a psychologically overwhelming 24 or 30 flavor options of jam rather than a psychologically manageable 6 options, shoppers are less likely to sample or purchase the jam.[46] A related study using chocolates rather than jams also found that participants were more satisfied with their sampled chocolates in the limited rather than extensive choice condition.[47] Similarly, when college students were given 30 versus 6 extra-credit essay topics, they were not only less likely to choose to do the assignment, but when they did do the assignment, they performed worse than those students who were provided with fewer options.[48] One explanation the authors provided for their findings was that of "regret avoidance." With more choices, participants had more opportunities to make a less-than-optimal choice. Whatever the reason, research consistently shows that more choices do not equal better. That is, more choices do not necessarily mean more positive outcomes.

Although the research described above concerned inconsequential choices compared to the decision to have a child, psychologist Barry Schwartz contends that overwhelming levels of choice and self-determination regarding parenting are oppressive rather than freeing.[49] Schwartz states, "Moreover, one is free to choose whether to have kids or not, whether to have them early or late, whether to bear them or adopt them, whether to have them as part of a traditional marriage and family or as part of any of a host of nontraditional family arrangements."[50] Schwartz argues that rather than all these freedoms leading to better well-being and higher satisfaction, we have an "explosive" growth in depression rates partly because the excess choices leads people to indecisiveness and painful uncertainty.[51] Of course, Schwartz's conclusions are based on correlations and therefore do not support causal conclusions. Additionally, Schwartz is assuming that all choices are feasible. For instance, a couple who did not have children when they were in their 20s no longer has the choice to have children early. To truly determine if it is the choice that is overwhelming, research would need to first determine what choices are viable.

Rather than aspiring toward what he sees as an infinite freedom of choices for everything around us, Schwartz argues that we should appreciate boundaries such as those we experience in language. With language, there is freedom, but it is constrained within well-defined rules. His solution is for positive psychologists to provide those boundaries by which people should live—a sort of framework that binds our lives by certain rules. Schwartz stops short in explaining where these rules should originate and who should get to write this playbook.

Can such rules have legal foundations? Should they? China's one-child policy that was in place from 1979 to 2015 provides an extreme example of the government restricting the decision to have children.[52] What role could (and should) psychologists play in writing such rules? Thinking empirically, is there a way for law psychology to approach the quandary of too many choices in parenting? Rather than liberty-restricting rules, would there be ways to nudge people into the most optimal choices for themselves without the stress of overwhelming choices? Legal scholar Cass Sunstein and economist Richard Thaler use psychological and behavioral economics theories in their book, *Nudge*, in which they advocate for libertarian paternalism and choice architecture.[53] Although Sunstein and Thaler do not suggest using nudges in the instance of choosing to become parents, they do provide evidence of the power of nudges. They note that "people will need nudges for decisions that are difficult and rare, for which they do not get prompt feedback, and when they have trouble translating aspects of the situation into terms that they can easily understand."[54] That certainly sounds like the choice to become a parent. Although the authors do not advocate for the government telling anyone what choices to make, they note that nudges can be useful when the choices are difficult. What kind of nudge would be appropriate, though? Would we want to nudge people to have fewer children? Wait to have children?

Modern Parenting

Although reproductive options were discussed in the previous chapter, it is important to note why such options may sometimes be curses rather than blessings for the modern parent. To understand, consider reproductive planning before modern medical techniques. For many centuries, the idea of planning or preventing such a "miracle" would have been ludicrous.[55] More recently, far from perfect planning and preventing relied on fertility statues and animal intestines.[56] Within the last 100 years, passive acceptance and superstitious reliance gave way to scientifically verifiable and legal methods to prevent and plan pregnancies. This life-changing event could now be timed or avoided. At the same time, children's mortality rates dropped significantly because of medical advances and compulsory education laws led to children trading dangerous work for safe classrooms. Children's lives naturally became more pampered as families were less likely to rely economically on children for agrarian or industrial labor.

Today, it is not the case that having more children is economically beneficial. Raising a healthy child in the United States from birth in 2012 to age 18 is projected to cost about $240,000,[57] or about $36.50 per day for middle-income parents. Even after adjusting for inflation, the cost of raising a child has increased 23% since 1960.[58] None of this even touches the rising costs of college tuition or of raising children with special needs. The costs include six main subcategories: housing, food, transportation, clothing, health care, and child care/education.[59] Why have the costs increased? There are lots of theories, but one common notion is that parents are simply more concerned with their children's mental and physical health than before and, basically, you get what you pay for. A Facebook post by mother and writer Bunmi Laditan reflected this difficulty.[60] She starts, "Being a modern parent is terrible. I'd give my left kneecap to have parented in the 70s or 80s when all you had to do to be considered a good mom is to remember to wind down the windows when you smoke in the car." She concludes her 467-word post about buying her children vitamins from an online vitamin specialty store by writing, "So now, I'm about to spend an electricity bill on vitamins because in 2016, you don't really love your kids if you're not a paranoid mess about their physical well-being and willing to spend a small fortune on dye-free toothpaste made in the woods that tastes like elderberry and privilege."

Indeed, family income does influence how much parents spend on raising their children. While middle-income parents of a child born in 2013 are projected to spend around $245,000, those parents who make less than $61,530 per year are projected to spend approximately $176,000.[61] Those families earning more than $106,540 per year should expect to spend slightly more than $400,000 to get their child to 18 years old.[62] These costs have contributed to the current idea that children are a luxury rather than a normal human experience,[63] with such sentiments expressed as "If you can't afford a dog, don't get a dog. If you can't afford a kid, don't get a kid."[64]

For the most part, parents are given great latitude in how they parent.[65] Much like everything else in the United States today, there is a polarization about who should become parents, when they should become parents, and how they should parent. Legal scholars Naomi Cahn and June Carbone have written extensively about this topic and focus much of their attention on the economic underpinnings of these differences.[66] Cahn and Carbone divide families into thirds based on education and economic stability.[67] The top one-third of the population who are wealthy or educated (or both) are also in stable two-parent relationships with the ability to spend time and money on their children. The bottom third are generally not marrying. Those in the middle third marry, yet divorce at high rates and are the most likely of the three groups to raise children "within multiple, unstable cohabitations."[68] Children raised in communities with a high proportion of single-parent homes are less likely to experience economic mobility—that is, the movement from poor to middle or upper class.[69] So, not only does the micro-level (within the family) have an effect, but the macro-level (other families) of the community also disadvantages the children.

The age at which people become parents is also much different, with well-educated men and women more likely to wait to have children until their 30s or 40s—once their careers are established.[70] The age of first birth has consistently increased for college-educated women, but for less educated women there has been little to no change.[71] The disparities continue, with the two-parent upper class being not only able to afford extracurricular activities for their children but also having the job flexibility to attend those extracurricular activities. A single mother working a low-wage job will struggle to be able to afford swimming lessons and would have difficulty getting her child to those lessons if she could afford them.[72] Cahn and Carbone note that without these activities for children, the class gap widens because the lower socioeconomic status children are not afforded the same types of opportunities as the "high-quality"[73] children born into wealthier families.[74]

Cahn and Carbone argue that these class differences are at the very core of our political divide in the United States,[75] referring to this divide as the "red families" and "blue families."[76] For the more conservative "red families," sexual activity is only morally acceptable within marriage, which results in earlier marriages. "Blue families" do not expect their children to be chaste until marriage because their marriage is unlikely to occur until much later in life once college and post-college schooling are completed. It also means that the definition of responsible parenting focuses on being married for red families and on having financial stability for blue families. The result is more divorce and economic instability for the red families.[77] While the more liberal and wealthier communities are waiting to get married until they have the means to financially support themselves, the more conservative and poorer communities continue to constrain sex and childbirth to marriage, which only perpetuates the cycle of early marriages.[78] This leaves us with a family law cultural divide that truly pierces the central core of belief systems. As we will see in the next section, that divide continues regarding the topic of deciding how to raise children.

Helicopter Versus Free-Range Parenting

On the spectrum of parenting, some parents hover over their children the way a helicopter hovers right before landing, whereas other parents give their children great latitude and freedoms. Colloquially, the first form of parenting is referred to as "helicopter parenting," and the second is referred to as "free-range parenting." Both forms of parenting are rooted in legal and psychological foundations, and both can lead to extreme and unintended negative outcomes.

Overinvolved parents seem to be a modern parenting phenomenon. Communications scholar Chris Segrin and colleagues have examined the helicopter parenting style, or, as they call it, "overparenting."[79] Segrin describes helicopter parenting as being developmentally inappropriate for the child's age.[80] Parents are not only providing advice but also excessive advice and overinvolvement and assistance in problem-solving. This relationship between the parents' and the child's life goes beyond involvement into enmeshment all for the apparent benefit of the son's or daughter's well-being. Segrin argues what would have been a healthy level of involvement when the son or daughter was younger becomes stunting as they turn the corner toward adulthood.[81] Although most argue that helicopter parenting is rooted in caring too much, Segrin and colleagues demonstrate that critical family environments where parents and children have negative views of one another could be breeding grounds for helicopter parenting.[82]

Most often seen and referenced as millennials, the children of helicopter parents have been studied generally in their early adulthood years when they are in college. It is not uncommon for current college students to have multiple phone calls per day with their parents; one of those phone calls is commonly the wake-up call so that the student need not rely on an alarm clock.[83] Some of this involvement seems to stem from a consumer-based perspective because of the rise of college-tuition costs and the resulting financial burdens placed on parents.[84] The research on helicopter parenting has demonstrated links between overparenting and several negative consequences for the early-adult child, including poor peer relationships and attachments,[85] poor rapport with college and advanced-degree instructors,[86] increased use of anxiety and depression medications,[87] reduced self-efficacy,[88] and stunted development.[89] Parents who view their children as needing intense parental support even report lower life satisfaction themselves.[90]

From a motivational psychology perspective, it is not surprising that helicopter parenting results in negative outcomes for the children. Psychologists Richard Ryan and Edward Deci's seminal work on Self-Determination Theory[91] provides a framework for understanding why helicopter parenting may not get the intended positive results. At the most rudimentary level, Ryan and Deci outline our three basic human needs: competence, relatedness, and autonomy. How these needs are met determines whether the person will engage actively in life and live at their optimal human functioning. Ryan and Deci explain that infants are born with an intrinsic motivation that pushes them to explore and learn. That motivation must be nurtured appropriately, or it will be interrupted and wane. Indeed, rewards and punishments based on task performance undermine intrinsic motivation because they rely on external power and control.[92] Research examining these concepts more deeply has shown that when parents or teachers support a child's autonomy rather than try to control the child's environment, that child's intrinsic motivation will be more positively nurtured. Helicopter or overparenting can interfere with a child's intrinsic motivation development. Instead of the children growing up to be the successes the parents were pushing them to be, they struggle to be fully functioning adults. It is no wonder the term *adulting* has entered our lexicon.[93] Millennials generally use the term to describe normal adult activities that they find difficult or developmentally beyond them. Developmental psychologist Holly Schiffrin and her colleagues showed in their research that many of the negative effects could be explained because helicopter parenting interferes with the child's need for autonomy and competence.[94]

Addressing autonomy and competence in children, *New York Sun* columnist Lenore Skenazy wrote about letting her 9-year-old son ride the New York City subway and bus home alone.[95] In the column, Skenazy described how her son had been begging to get to ride public transportation by himself and find his way home without a parent by his side. Skenazy not only let her son tackle this task without a cell phone but then also wrote about it in her column. She went on to describe the reactions she received from people she told about her son's experience: "Half the people I've told . . . now want to turn me in for child abuse," Skenazy wrote. Mostly, those people who questioned Skenazy's parenting were concerned about child abductions, which Skenazy explains are so rare that it is impractical to let the fear of them alter parenting behaviors. More important, she argues that being overprotective is a self-fulfilling prophecy; children who are raised thinking they cannot do anything on their own will believe it and not do anything on their own.

This simple column describing a public transportation ride started a movement referred to as free-range parenting.[96] In contrast to the reaction to helicopter parenting and the focus on the child's long-term well-being, the reaction to free-range parenting has largely focused on the legal implications. A Maryland couple caught the media's attention when they allowed their 10-year-old and 6-year-old to play alone in a local park. The Meitiv family lives in Silver Spring, Maryland, where their house is approximately one mile from a park where the children like to play.[97] On multiple occasions, the police picked up the siblings while they were walking home from the park. Suspecting neglect, the police turned the children over to Child Protective Services (CPS). The children remained with CPS for several hours until their parents were finally notified. The Meitivs were eventually cleared of all neglect charges but not before garnering national attention and sparking debate about how much range children can have before it becomes neglect.[98] Other similar instances involve parents within sight of the children or relatively close when the police intervene suspecting abuse.[99]

Although helicopter and free-range parenting are the focus of the current parenting conflict, warring views about appropriate parenting are not a modern phenomenon.[100] Indeed, recent history demonstrates a certain swinging of the pendulum from a decade of over-parenting to the next with under-parenting.[101] Overall, despite the different methods, parents are trying to provide their children with what they believe is the environment and type of parenting the child needs. Aside from true abuse cases, parents in both parenting camps are doing what they feel is best for their child and not intending harm. Should the law be more restrictive in guiding parental behaviors? Do psychologists have an important perspective on this topic that they could contribute?

As we saw earlier, psychologist David Lykken proposed a controversial parental licensure requirement with the basic premise being that, to be able to bear a child, potential parents would have to meet the same minimum requirements set forward for adopting a child.[102] The proposed licensing would be similarly granted as a driver's license with proof of marriage, legal age, monetary security, and no previous violent crimes. As described earlier, Lykken's proposal garnered some critiques and criticism. Richard Redding, for one, provides the legal arguments against Lykken's plan—such methods would be deemed unconstitutional on equal protection and due process grounds.[103] Instead, Redding proposes better outcomes through "mandatory parenting education classes in schools, tougher child abuse laws, improved child protective services, and more research on the effectiveness of public policies."[104] In other words, Redding focuses on teaching people how to parent and punishing those who do not meet minimum standards, which is generally how we have approached parenting in the United States. Such regulations require a common understanding of what is appropriate parenting. Who should decide that? Are psychologists or lawyers or both together best suited to define those standards?

As noted earlier, political leanings tend to influence core parenting outcomes,[105] which make it difficult to imagine being able to find common ground beyond the goal that parents should love their children. In other words, people can probably agree that they need to love their children; the disagreement enters the discussion when trying to operationalize what love means. Seminal work by developmental psychologist Diana Baumrind provided three typologies of parenting based on parental responsiveness and demandingness.[106] Baumrind's three types of parenting were authoritarian, authoritative, and permissive.[107] Psychologists, John Martin and Eleanor Maccoby added a fourth parenting type, rejecting-neglecting, in their work in the 1980s.[108] Most research holds that authoritative parenting is associated with the most positive developmental outcomes for the child.[109] However, without consensus about the operationalization of precise authoritative parenting practices, it will be impossible to develop a fully supported parenting class, minimum standards, or any other factor related to parenting.

Special Instances of Legal Regulations

The following five subsections address a myriad of topics that highlight the unique parent–child relationship and the resulting legal and psychological implications because of that relationship.

Family Leave

A topic not always covered in family law, but important from a social psychological view of the family, is family work-leave policies. Psychological research has clearly documented the demands of caregiving on a person's career—especially differential gender effects[110]—and the U.S. law has clear regulations. The Family and Medical Leave Act (FMLA) allows up to 12 weeks of unpaid leave per year for eligible employees and eligible reasons.[111] Eligibility generally rests on having worked at least 12 months for the employer and the employer having at least 50 employees. The leave can be used for the birth of a child or for adopting or fostering a child. An employee can also use the leave for the care of a spouse, a child, or a parent who has a serious health condition. The employee does not have to take the leave at all or all at once but can take it intermittently to best suit their needs. Once the employee returns, the employer must provide the person with his or her same job or one as close to similar as possible.

The FMLA was not enacted without contention. Congress tried to pass it in the 1980s, but the first President Bush vetoed it. Finally enacted in 1993, more than 50 million employees had taken leave by 2005.[112] A small portion (18%) are using FMLA leave to care for a new child, while the majority use it to care for their own serious illnesses or the illnesses of a family member (31%).[113] More women (58%) than men (42%) are taking FMLA leave.[114]

Although many families benefit from FMLA because employees are guaranteed the right to go back to their job, it is unpaid leave, which means some are not able to take advantage of the leave. Many other industrialized countries have paid maternity leave (and some even have paid paternity leave).[115] Some private companies do offer paid leave, and some states are requiring leave to be paid, but it is still the exception rather than the rule.[116]

California is one state that has been more proactive in requiring leave be paid when it is taken.[117] Health policy researcher Maya Rossin-Slater and colleagues examined the California system using approximately ten years of data about leave-taking and outcomes.[118] Not surprisingly, California's paid leave increased leave-taking for mothers of infants with the greatest impact on Black, noncollege-educated, unmarried, and Hispanic mothers. The researchers explained that the increased use of leave may have been because before the paid-leave option, mothers simply quit their jobs. Therefore, the paid leave increased worker continuity for those mothers who took leave and then returned to their jobs rather than quitting their jobs and needing to find a new job. Indeed, the paid family leave also increased the work hours of employed mothers with 1- to 3-year-old children.[119] The researchers explained that this increase was possibly due to the increased job continuity observed from the paid leave.

There may be a gendered underbelly of family leave. That is, the guise of making the policies gender neutral by calling them "family" rather than "maternity" leave may not have had the intended effect. When women request family leave, they are behaving in a gender-normative way, but when men request it, their request is outside the gender norms, and they can experience greater backlash.[120] Research supports this idea, demonstrating that men are more penalized for wanting to take family leave and seen as not good corporate citizens when they request to do so.[121] It seems that the "daddy bonus" (men with children earn more than men without children[122]) does not extrapolate to caring for the children.[123] Women still have more work flexibility than men do after the birth of a child.[124] It also seems that the FMLA has produced inequalities with regard to race. Although minority respondents in one study were more likely than White respondents to indicate the need for leave, they were much less likely to act on that need and take a leave.[125] Not only does leave have obvious impacts on the parents' careers, but psychologically, relationship satisfaction between parents also suffers when parents are not able to manage job flexibility after the birth of a child.[126]

Finally, what happens when women are more likely to take a leave than men after the birth of a child? One possibility is that maternity leave effectively disadvantages women for many years beyond the time they are home. Imagine the following scenario, Amy and Steve are both working parents, but financially it only makes sense for their family for one of them to take any length of family leave when their child is born. So when their child is a few days old and the other relatives have left, Steve goes back to work. Amy opts for the 12 weeks of unpaid leave and very much enjoys those three months at home with their new baby. What naturally occurs during those three months is that when the baby cries in the middle of the night, only Amy gets up because Steve must go to work the next morning. That plan makes good sense because although the FMLA protects Amy's job while she is taking her leave, there is no complementary protection for Steve's job if he underperforms because he has been up with a crying child in the middle of the night. This pattern continues not only for the middle of the night feedings, but virtually everything else about the infant's care. All during the day, Amy is the only one caring for the infant. When Steve gets home from work, he may try to engage with the baby, but the infant is likely to exhibit either a real or perceived preference for the normal caregiver, Amy.[127]

While Amy is off work, this arrangement works well, albeit likely emotionally and physically taxing on Amy.[128] Nonetheless, the real issue arises when Amy returns to work (if she ever does). At that point, the infant is three months old and now well into a routine with Mom.[129] Attempts by Steve to help could well be (or be viewed as) bumbling and interfering. It is hard to imagine even heroic efforts by Steve being able to overcome this established mother–child routine. After all, which parent will be more likely to know the pediatrician? Which parent will have set up day care? Which parent is the child accustomed to seeing in the middle of the night?

Habit, routine, and familiarity are powerful forces that are difficult to overcome.[130] Of course, none of this is an issue if one parent decides to stay out of the workforce to raise children, and despite the statistical probability that it will be the mother who does so, there are changes in the winds, with more fathers making the choice of their children over their jobs.[131] However, without an equality of paid leave for both parents who desire to remain working, are we setting up mothers to not only be the only caregiver during her leave, but the only (or strong primary) caregiver after her leave ends? If full paid leave for both parents is too financially difficult, then what about combined leave between the two parents? More flexibility to allow both new mothers and fathers to be equally involved in the infant's life could be a step in the direction of equality.

Safe Haven Laws

For some new parents, it is not work schedules that concern them when they have a baby but whether they can care for the child or even let others know that they have had a baby. Throughout the United States, all 50 states have some form of safe haven law that allows parents to anonymously leave infants at designated locations for the child to become a ward of the state without legal ramifications for the parent.[132] The stated goal is to get the babies adopted as quickly as possible and avoid infanticide or abandonment in unsafe locations.[133] In most states, leaving the child must occur early in the child's life, usually before they are one month old.[134] Generally, a safe haven is a place like a hospital or a fire station so that there are adequate supports available to care for the infant.[135] Some states also have processes in place that would allow a parent to reclaim their child if done before a termination of parental rights was performed.[136]

As noted, these laws are meant to protect very young infants. However, in 2008 for about two months in Nebraska, a safe haven law was in place that applied to any child up to the age of 18. The legislature used the word *child*, rather than *infant*, and *child* was defined elsewhere in the statutes as being anyone up to the age of 18. The well-intentioned, but largely embarrassing, law resulted in 35 older children, most over 10 years of age, being dropped off at safe haven locations by desperate parents.[137] Only one child was under the age of 5.[138] One father, a widower, dropped off all nine of his children because he could not care for them without his wife.[139] Some of those parents drove their teens from other states to take advantage of the Nebraska law; one mother drove 1,200 miles from California to drop off her 14-year-old son.[140] In an emergency session, the legislature amended the law to apply only to infants 30 days old or younger.[141] These parental reactions to the Nebraska law highlighted a larger need for services and aid to parents. Many of the parents who left their teens described the psychiatric needs of their children and their inability to pay for or provide the level of care needed.[142]

Some scholars argue that any safe haven laws are overbroad and do not address true needs,[143] and there is no systematic research about the effectiveness of safe haven laws.[144] Very few states collect data on safe haven relinquishments[145] and only about half of the statutes include efforts to inform the public the law exists.[146] Indeed, it is hard to even define effectiveness for these purposes. One option is to compare unsafe to safe abandonment—in other words, comparing how many infants are abandoned in safe havens versus abandoned in unsafe locations such as dumpsters.[147] It seems that even in states with active public campaigns, abandonments in unsafe locations still occur.[148] New Jersey cleverly advertises its safe haven law as "No Shame. No Blame. No Names,"[149] yet one baby was abandoned near one of these signs rather than in a designated safe location.[150] It seems the well-intentioned laws may not be well tuned to actual human behavior. Perhaps the public campaigns could take a lesson from other public campaigns, such as health campaigns promoting appropriate behavior through persuasive messaging. For example, research on public health campaigns finds the most successful ones take a global approach and focus on the individual's behavior nested within the larger social construct.[151]

Parental Responsibility Laws

As the quick revocation of the Nebraska Safe Haven law exemplified, once a child is a teenager, it seems the time for deciding not to be a parent has long passed. The time for the law to not place blame on parents has also passed. Parental responsibility laws generally are those laws that hold parents civilly and criminally responsible for the delinquent behaviors of their children. The laws can be categorized into three different types: parental civil liability, contributing to the delinquency of a minor, and parental involvement laws.[152] Every state has at least one form of these laws.[153] Historically and today, parental responsibility laws speak to the greater notion of child welfare, the role of the family in society, and the role the state plays when it steps in to act for the parents.[154] These laws are not as widely supported by the public, and by juveniles themselves, as the political pundits and policy makers would argue.[155] The laws are, however, prevalent in media stories about juveniles.[156] In fact, national media sources depict the notion of parental responsibility and blame the parents in stories about juvenile crime.[157]

Under common law tort principles of negligence, parents can be held civilly liable and required to pay for the damages their children commit if the parents themselves were negligent and that negligence led to the child's behavior. In other words, the person injured by the child or his or her representative (the plaintiff) would be required to establish the parents' "duty, breach, causation, and damages."[158] This means that there must have been a causal connection between the parent's behavior and the harm the plaintiff suffered.[159] As an alternative to the difficulty a common law tort claim poses, all states have legislatively created parental liability statutes that can apply to either negligent or intentional actions of the juvenile. These statutes effectively impose strict liability (i.e., liability without the need for negligence or intent) on the parents, because they allow a victim of a juvenile crime to bring a civil case against the parents of the juvenile because they are the parents.[160] There is no defense of carefulness or state of mind on the part of the parent. This vicarious liability imposed on the parents allows the plaintiff an easier case to prove than in the common law tort case, but the trade-off is generally low recovery limits. For example, in Alabama, parents are liable for "actual damages sustained," limited to $1,000 for any "intentional, willful, or malicious" acts that the juvenile commits.[161]

The second form of parental liability, contributing to the delinquency of a minor, does not exist in common law. Criminal state statutes governing this concept are not restricted to only parents, but parents easily fall into the law's purview. A parent, or any adult, who encourages or aids in a juvenile's delinquent behavior can be charged with contributing to the delinquency.[162] These laws require that the parent (or another adult) act intentionally. Generally, this crime is considered a misdemeanor, but some states consider it a felony in certain circumstances.[163] The classic example case is a drug-dealing parent using his or her child to deliver or hold the drugs for him or her.[164]

The third and final form of parental responsibility laws is the most nebulous and broad. These laws, referred to as parental involvement laws, require parents to pay for the cost of their delinquent child's care, participate in court hearings, enroll in parenting classes, pay fines, do community service, and engage in many other activities.[165] Parents are guilty by being a parent of a child who has committed a status (i.e., illegal because of the juvenile's age, such as a curfew violation) or delinquent offense. When Nevada was enacting its statute, the legislators noted that the law was meant to address not only the "offending youth, but the dysfunctional family as well."[166] Although the punishment possibilities are broad, the enforcement of these laws is spotty at best.[167]

Many psychological theories and research certainly point to the importance of parental influence. Early in the 1900s, G. Stanley Hall was advancing parental responsibility in directing children in positive rather than detrimental behaviors, especially during the "storm and stress" of the teenage years.[168] Others throughout the past century have also promoted the important role parents play in raising law-abiding children, and empirical research is clear that the type of parenting a child receives is a predictor for the type of child and teenager he or she will be. The rift between the psychological research and the laws, however, is that even if the parent-to-child behavior predictive models were perfect, there is no evidence to suggest that punishing parents will provide the desired results.[169] No empirical research has examined the effectiveness of these laws. In fact, even an Ohio Court of Appeals case noted the lack of empirical research: "The data permit no firm conclusions as to whether parental responsibility laws are efficacious."[170] Ironically, in the absence of data, the Ohio court decided to rely on the city's unsupported claims that the laws were effective and therefore the court held the ordinance was a valid exercise of the city's police power. Clearly, more psychological research is needed on the topic of parental responsibility laws to move beyond public opinion and into empirically testing their effectiveness and utility.

Grandparent Involvement

Recent Census Bureau statistics detail that grandparent-headed households have increased in the past few decades.[171] With the general aging in our society of people living longer,[172] there is an opportunity for more grandparent involvement and primary caregiving by grandparents.[173] Extenuating circumstances, such as parental drug abuse, imprisonment, and child maltreatment, contribute to the grandparent involvement. Unfortunately, research suggests that grandparents who are raising their grandchildren suffer more health problems than do grandparents not raising their grandchildren,[174] potentially because they do not prioritize self-care activities.[175] The grandparents also face legal hurdles, especially if they are raising their grandchildren without formal legal custody, which can lead to difficulties consenting to the child's medical treatment and educational needs.[176] Most of the research in this area has focused on grandparent well-being, with only a few studies examining the impact on the children.[177] In one such study, grandchildren were interviewed about the experiences being raised by their grandparents or great-grandparents. Although the grandchildren expressed disappointment and other negative emotions about their own parents, most expressed appreciation and enthusiasm toward their grandparents.[178] Historically, there has been a lack of resources for grandparents in this situation, but there is some movement to provide financial and other support.[179] In addition, this is an area where psychological research could provide empirical insights. For example, are there unique needs of grandparents raising grandchildren that the child welfare system should be addressing to truly meet the best interests of the child?[180] What about the unique needs of the children being raised by their grandparents?

Legal Paternalism in Educating Children

The idea that the law should act as this supreme decision maker is referred to as "legal paternalism."[181] Under this approach, the law restricts a person's freedom for his or her own good. In a variety of instances, we already have a great deal of legal paternalism in our society.[182] Seatbelt laws are a good example of the law telling us what is best for us and protecting us from ourselves.[183] On the extreme end are laws against suicide, which is the ultimate way to harm oneself.[184] Some scholars argue that paternalism increases rather than diminishes freedoms because protecting someone now will lead to later abilities to make more decisions.[185] Family law is built on a foundation and history of legal paternalism. For example, the marital restrictions described earlier proscribe certain marriages because the law deems them unfit and knows better than the individuals.

For parents, one area of legal paternalism is in how their children are educated pursuant to compulsory education laws or homeschool curriculum requirements. Every state has required school attendance, with most requiring that attendance to start by the age of 6 or 7 until at least age 17 or 18.[186] Similarly, if a family chooses to homeschool, then they are subject to homeschool legal requirements that are state specific. These requirements generally relate to matters such as the topics taught, record keeping, and required number of days per year the children participate in instruction at home.[187] The compulsory education and homeschool requirements demonstrate that the government is paternalistically involved in family decisions about children's education. Not everyone supports the educational requirements in the United States with one movement calling for the unschooling of children.[188] Unschooling focuses on self-directed education with the children directing the topics and activities. Not surprising, empirical research is lacking on the differential outcomes for children who are unschooled.

Conclusion

Having overcome the biological access to parenting described in the previous chapter, we have examined here modern parenting and the reasons a person would want to become a parent. Psychological principles, such as affective forecasting, cognitive dissonance, and burden of choice, aid in understanding the paradox of parenting difficulties and the desire to parent. Because the idea of childhood and adolescence is culturally and historically relative,[189] parenting is too. This relativism is obvious in comparing helicopter parents to free-range parents. Although both ends of the parenting spectrum can be within the legal range of acceptable parenting, both also can have negative and unintended consequences. Yet legal regulations of parenting, such as those exemplified in parental responsibility laws, are untried and untested. And legal regulations of family leave, safe haven laws, and grandparent involvement open some glaring issues that also can lead to unintended consequences for the entire family.

6

Dissolution of Marriage

If you look at any family law casebook, the chances are quite good that the majority of the book addresses divorce and its ramifications. As described at the outset of this book, the door to the family home is mostly closed until some triggering event opens it. Divorce is one such event. Before a couple is married and during their marriage, they can choose to divide their money and property as they like. They can have one checking account where all their money intermingles, and there are no requirements that one spouse receives a certain amount of money each month from the other spouse. Lydia McGuire of Nebraska learned this when she brought a case in the 1950s against her husband, Charles McGuire, for not providing for her in a way that matched his financial abilities.[1] Charles was particularly frugal, as evidenced by Lydia's complaint that they had not been to a movie in 12 years, their house did not have indoor plumbing, and she was not given money to buy clothing or household furnishings. The Nebraska Supreme Court responded to Lydia's complaints and lack of creature comforts by noting that the "living standards of a family are a matter of concern to the household, and not for the courts to determine."[2] Although the court's disdain for Charles was clear, it nonetheless held that public policy required them to not intervene in the matter because the marriage was intact.

This all changes when a marriage is terminated. A divorce not only severs a marriage but introduces judicial regulation.[3] Just as the beginning of a friend relationship will not create legal ramifications, the ending of one will not either. Want to join a new book club and leave your old one? No problem. The law does not care. Not true with divorce. This chapter addresses how and why marriages end, judicial regulation of divorce, the legal rationalizations for dividing and distributing financial resources, and the psychological effects of these legal interventions.

Dissolution of an Intimate Relationship

Psychology researchers have investigated the way relationships dissolve and why. For the most part, the characterizations focus on the process of dissolution and the stages or phases individuals pass through as they move toward full dissolution. For example, in one of the first conceptualizations of relationship dissolution, Paul Bohannan focused on six phases of a divorce that start with the emotional divorce and end with the psychological divorce.[4] Social psychologist and communication scholar Steve Duck focuses on the process of dissolving a relationship and what he characterizes as the four stages involved in the process.[5] These four stages are labeled intrapsychic, dyadic, social, and grave-dressing. In the beginning, the focus is on the partner's behavior and how dissatisfying it is. The next stage focuses on confronting the partner to discuss the issues. The third, or social stage, announces the breakup to other people. And, finally, in the fourth and final stage the focus is on accounting for and describing the breakup. Although other researchers may develop specific stages for divorce, most agree that a divorce should be thought of as a process rather than an event.[6] Yet, even if the stages seem clear from a researcher's standpoint, Duck notes that a couple in the middle of a relationship dissolution can be largely unaware.[7] In fact, many are unaware that they were going through the stages of a dissolution until after the breakup has occurred.[8] Therefore, current research focuses on the process rather than on clearly delineated phases or stages that are not representative of the fluidity and messiness in real life.[9]

A dissolution of a marital relationship inherently requires a person to make predictions about what he or she will want in the future. For example, a mediation to decide a custody arrangement would require the parties to think about the kind of relationship they want with their child in the future and how they will feel with that arrangement. As discussed earlier, this is called affective forecasting, and it relates to people's (in) ability to predict how they will feel in the future.[10] In general, people are poor at accurately predicting how they will feel in the future. Because of focalism (i.e., focusing on only one event), they may overestimate or underestimate how negative or positive they will feel because of the divorce. They are also likely to believe that those feelings will last much longer than they are likely to because of another cognitive bias referred to as impact bias, which is the tendency for someone to overestimate the duration and intensity of their predicted feelings.[11] Affective forecasting is a particularly important psychological concept for family law attorneys and mental health experts to understand because it helps to provide a context for understanding the expected emotional response to a dissolution of a relationship compared to the actual emotional response.

Marriage Dissolution

The law as it relates to marriage dissolution, like the law as it relates to marriage generally, is largely state-defined.[12] As noted earlier, restricting federal involvement in marriage law allows the states to mold to local norms more easily and allows for more experimentation.[13] That means that aside from a few constants, the law of marriage dissolution in one state will look very different than the law of marriage dissolution in another state.[14] Attorney Joseph Steinberg says that "divorce may well be the most sensitive social barometer in our community. It reflects changing social values with amazing speed."[15]

No matter the legal requirements, current estimates indicate that approximately 50% of marriages end in divorce, with that number being higher for second and third marriages.[16] Although divorces are common today, true divorces were once reserved only for the wealthy. U.S. law, although not universally so restrictive, also has a history of constricting divorce. In particular, one restriction in obtaining a divorce was the requirement that there be some sort of fault demonstrated by one party.

Fault Versus No-Fault Divorce

Until a few decades ago, most divorces in the United States had to be based on the fault of one of the parties. Without the fault of one party, the court was unable to grant a divorce. Some states allowed for less restrictive means, such as in 1933 when New Mexico allowed divorce on the grounds of incompatibility.[17] For many states, however, the spouse bringing the divorce had to prove some specified wrongdoing of their spouse such as adultery, drunkenness, drug addiction, cruelty, desertion, or nonsupport.[18] Many of these faults were gender-based, such that the allowable basis for a man bringing a divorce was different from a woman. For example, a woman was permitted to bring a divorce action against her husband for a lack of financial support. A man was not permitted such a recourse.[19] Similarly, a man could bring an action against his wife if he learned that before they were married she had been sexually involved with another man. Such non-chaste behaviors were not an allowable cause of action against husbands.[20]

Until 1967 in New York, adultery was the only allowable wrong that constituted a fault for divorce. This resulted in a strange go-around where couples colluded to create adultery so that they could divorce. There is even evidence of "adultery rings" where women were hired to pretend in court as if they had been involved in adultery with the husband so that the couple could divorce.[21] Other states allowed additional grounds beyond adultery, such as cruelty. In those states, the courts could apply a liberal definition to encompass mental distress that virtually every married person could claim.[22] The requirement of fault—meant to discourage divorces—had the unintended effect of making the process a charade. Some scholars estimate that as many as 90% of divorces were collusive in the fault-requirement era.[23] Such unintended effects resulted because lawmakers failed to consider human behaviors and desires.[24]

The fault system also included defenses the "faulty" spouse could bring to defeat the divorce petition. For example, an abandoning spouse could claim the abandonment was in response to physical abuse. The fault then could be transferred to the other spouse. One such defense, recrimination, had quite the tautological effect. With recrimination, the defense is that while the defendant spouse was indeed a bad spouse, the petitioning spouse was also quite bad. This accusation of someone who has accused you is the grown-up, legal version of "I know you are, but what am I?" The effect under fault requirements was comical because if neither party was innocent then the judge could deny the divorce. The spouses' two wrongs might not have made a right, but they apparently made a marriage that could not be legally broken. In one such case from the 1950s, the court noted that "the fact that married people do not get along well together does not justify a divorce . . . Testimony which proves . . . [the parties are] unsuited for each other . . . is insufficient to sustain a [divorce] decree."[25] Clearly, the law failed to consider human behavior in the instance of recrimination.

In 1969, California was the first state to enact a divorce statute that allowed couples to divorce without proving one had been at fault. All 50 states have similar statutes now that have removed the fault requirement or added a no-fault option.[26] This relatively new no-fault option allows a couple to agree their marriage is over, and—to use the new terminology enacted by California—dissolve their marriage.[27] In the decade following the legal change from fault to no-fault divorce, researchers examined behaviors and attitudes of those affected by the law. For example, psychology professor Stanley Mazur-Hart examined divorce rates in Nebraska using a time-series quasi-experimental design.[28] Being quasi-experimental, the study lacked random assignment to groups, but Mazur-Hart utilized the naturally occurring groups of divorces before and after the no-fault divorce legislation. The research demonstrated that the allowance of no-fault divorces had no significant effect on the overall divorce rate. More nuanced and specific evaluation of the data revealed that allowing no-fault divorces was related to an increased rate of divorces for Blacks, people over 50 years of age, and couples married longer than 25 years. Some research suggested that men were more likely than women to file for divorce under the no-fault system as compared to the fault system,[29] perhaps because men were no longer required to bring an unchivalrous claim against their wife as they would have needed to under the fault system.[30] Legal scholar Thomas Marvell also used a time-series and cross-sectional design but broadened his sample to 38 states.[31] With the additional states, Marvell compared the growth rates for divorce before and after the implementation of no-fault divorce. Finding limited support that the divorce rates increased in some states under their new no-fault laws, Marvell cautioned that the results were not entirely clear and that if there was an increase, it was quite minor. Other researchers confirmed these findings, but all are restricted by the quasi-experimental nature of the research, so we are left without true causation explanations.[32]

Separations (and Waiting Periods)

Sometimes referred to as a "limited divorce" or a "divorce from bed and board," a legal separation was common before no-fault divorces were an option.[33] A legal separation allowed the couples to live apart, although they were not allowed to remarry. Currently, state laws vary on the requirements of separations before divorces, with many mandating a separation before the couple can divorce. They range from 60 days to 3 years, with longer time requirements generally waived or reduced if both parties agree to it. The idea behind these waiting periods is that the couple will have an opportunity to try out the divorce and see what it will feel like to be separate from their spouse before the legal decree of divorce is final. They are also meant as a legislative discouragement of divorce. In contrast, there is also a movement to allow for quick and inexpensive divorces. For example, Sacramento, California, has a One Day Divorce program that not only significantly cuts the time but also the cost of divorce for low-income eligible parties.[34]

Unfortunately, until quite recently, there was a dearth of research on couples who are separated. Often, separated and divorced are lumped together into one category for research purposes without distinguishing the categories.[35] The research specifically on separations mostly focused on the impact of the separation on the children rather than the couple directly.[36] This focus makes sense because the impact of the divorce on the children is often a primary concern,[37] and continued stress after divorce is often related to child-rearing issues.[38] But a separation is a unique time with unique stressors and has a separate impact from divorce.[39] There is a distinctive level of loneliness and adjustment to having less attachment to an ex-partner that goes beyond co-parenting conflict issues.[40] Indeed, the risk of suicide may be greater during separation than divorce for younger males,[41] and the risk is exacerbated by the legal negotiations, financial strains, and adjusting to new social networks that can be common during a separation[42] and create psychological distress.[43] Self-compassion, being kind to one's self, seems to serve as a protective factor for those undergoing a separation.[44] People with higher self-compassion during their separation also had less divorce-related stress.[45] An ability to cope with this stress seems to even have biological bases.[46] Certain people seem to have an elevated risk of poor physiological outcomes that may even be related to their genes. Psychologist Karen Hasselmo and her colleagues examined this genetic association by focusing on respiratory sinus arrhythmia as a way to assess cardiac response in a sample of recently separated adults.[47] In simplified terms, people who were short allele carriers who also reported high levels of emotional distress seemed to be more vulnerable to negative outcomes.

Despite the trauma surrounding separations, the law often requires waiting periods between separation and finalization of the divorce. Elena Moore, a sociologist who specializes in family relationships, examined how these waiting periods impact the separated couples and the way the couples defined their new boundaries.[48] Although Moore's study included only separating couples who had children, some of her findings would likely be applicable even if there were no children involved. For example, there was much uncertainty surrounding the couple's preseparation home and who should be able to stay in it and who should leave. The separation period made the uncertainty about the home linger and contributed to additional conflict between the separated couple.[49] Despite some therapists recommending separation as a trial divorce, no empirical research seems to address that notion. Granted, couples amid marital conflict are unlikely to volunteer for a randomized controlled trial assigning them to stay to together or to separate. Nonetheless, even correlational research in this area is lacking. By combining couples who are separated or divorced into one group, researchers are losing what may be different for those times in a person's life. Future research should focus more specifically on the nuanced differences between those who are separated and those who are divorced. Additionally, because some states still have waiting periods for a divorce, the impact of such waiting periods is an especially important topic for researchers to examine.

Annulment

Using the technical definition, an annulment is not an ending of a marriage because for an annulment to take place, the marriage must have been defective such that the marriage did not truly exist—it is null. As highlighted earlier, an annulment can occur when the marriage is void because of some barrier that is in place. Per the Catholic Church's doctrine, annulments are the only permissible way to dissolve a marriage that still permits remarriage of either person in the future.[50] The Catholic Church encourages the use of experts in determining the validity of marriages for discerning if an annulment is appropriate; psychiatrists and psychologists are often called on for such purpose.[51] For example, the parties must have due discretion or due competence of judgment to marry, and several mental illnesses would interfere with such capacity.[52] Mental illness is not required for an annulment, however. Being confused or immature could interfere with the required due discretion or due competence required for a valid marriage under canon law.[53] The church tribunal relies on a psychological expert to opine whether the parties to the marriage had the level of diligence and competence the church requires for the marriage to be valid. This situation creates a unique melding of religion, law, and psychology, yet there is very little empirical examination of the topic. Future research could usefully examine the psychological testimony in a similar way that such testimony has been examined in other situations. For example, should these determinations be left to only clinical judgment or should there be standardized assessment instruments involved? Should special training and certification be required for an expert to provide their testimony on the issue? If so, what type of training would make someone qualified in this sphere?

Dividing Property

When a marriage is intact, how the couple divides their resources is a matter of their own personal choice and not for the courts. If a husband wants his man cave to sprawl throughout the basement while his wife has no personal space for herself, that is legally fine. Similarly, a wife can completely control the couple's finances with no input from the husband. In contrast, when a couple divorces, the door to the family home swings open for the court to make those determinations that Lydia McGuire wanted them to do for her while she was still married and without indoor plumbing.[54] When couples divorce, they must divide their resources and decide future terms of support (i.e., alimony or maintenance). This division of property results in a great deal of state intervention for matters that would be left private in an intact marriage.

Not surprisingly, court-ordered property divisions have changed over the past few decades. Also not surprisingly, historically the law governing property division favored men more than women. Women were rarely property owners or income generators, and any property they did have was most likely also in their husband's name.[55] The common law approach to property division focused on which member of the couple owned what. Dividing property between a traditional breadwinning husband and homemaker wife meant there was very little to give the wife. Some states followed a community property system that treated all property acquired during the marriage as equally owned by both members of the marriage.[56] Today, the law has attempted to equalize the treatment of the parties in common law states. Specifically, the courts now attempt to distribute property in an equitable way between the divorcing spouses no matter who technically owned or acquired the property. There are therefore minimal differences now between community property and common law states when it comes to property divisions in a divorce. How the actual division occurs, however, is dependent on state law, and so long as the court can confirm that the division is equitable, the division is generally open to negotiations between the parties. With the determination being equitable (i.e., fair) rather than equal (i.e., same division) there is room for bias to creep in. Property division at divorce raises two primary psychological bias considerations: physical touching and perceived association. The former relates to the parties' potential bias, while the latter relates to the judge's potential bias. Unfortunately, general property law and the specific topic of property division are relatively neglected topics in law-psychology research.[57]

Physical Touch, the Endowment Effect, and Value

Do you value this book more while you are reading it and holding it than when it is sitting on your shelf? Maybe. As described earlier regarding surname choices, the endowment effect is the notion that people prefer and value objects that are owned by them[58] over objects not owned by them.[59] The longer an item is owned, the higher the endowment effect.[60] Researchers have even found the effects with primates.[61] Some research suggests gender differences in the endowment effect.[62] Potentially important in the context of property division, men were less susceptible to the endowment effect when the item in question was incongruent with their identity, meaning that when the item was not tied to their identity they did not exhibit the endowment effect.[63] And the emotions of regret and disappointment impact the endowment effect, such that these negative emotions moderate the valuation of an object. Objects associated with negative emotions are seen more negatively to the point of canceling or reversing the endowment effect.[64]

Additionally, simply touching (or even thinking about touching) an object leads to feelings of increased ownership of that object.[65] The research on touch and object ownership is mostly from the consumer psychology literature and generally focuses on the importance of consumers touching the items they consider purchasing.[66] From the results of a series of four experimental lab studies, Joann Peck and Suzanne Shu concluded that touching an object increased feelings of perceived ownership and valuation of that object.[67] Later related research showed that even haptic imagery of the items increased feelings of ownership in the same way that touching the object did.[68] In fact, when the participants more vividly imagined touching the objects, they had greater perceptions of control and feelings of ownership.[69] These studies used simple objects such as coffee mugs, Slinkys, mechanical pencils, and blankets.

These researchers were not focused on a divorce setting but, rather, on how their findings were important to in-person and online retailers. However, combining the "mere touch" with the "endowment effect" research, it seems likely that physical objects a person can touch will result in increased perceived ownership and valuation compared to nonphysical objects. In a divorce, the two largest sources of property are generally the house and retirement pensions. Of the two, the house is more tangible, yet the retirement accounts may be more valuable. Does the endowment effect differentially influence the divorcing spouses? This is especially important because the person who gets primary custody of the children will also likely receive the house.[70] Are retirement accounts undervalued because they are not physically present the way a house is and they represent future money as opposed to money owned currently? In fact, for some that money may not be truly accessible for many years into the future. Indeed, for the cash poor, future money may not have the same value as current because they have an immediate need for liquid assets. Empirical research in this area could help to determine if these cognitive biases interfere with divorcing spouse's property division requests and end up disadvantaging some spouses more than others.

Perceived Association

Potential bias is not only a concern for the spouses; the judges involved are also susceptible to letting it color their decisions.[71] In a series of three studies, psychologists James Beggan and Ellen Brown demonstrated how a third party can be influenced by noncausal associations when determining ownership of a target object. Although the researchers' intent was not to inform judges' decision making in a divorce setting, their first study employs a vignette focused on a divorcing couple. In their vignette, Beggan and Brown describe a divorcing couple who enjoys watching movies and therefore decided the TV and VCR should stay together and not be divided between the spouses. The study participants decided who should get to keep the TV and VCR. The researchers manipulated the association with the objects by showing pictures of the husband, wife, or neither with the TV and VCR. The simple difference of having the spouse pictured with the item resulted in participants providing higher ratings of ownership. Therefore, third-party decision makers attributed more ownership based on physical proximity to the item—a factor not important in determining ownership.[72]

Stereotypes have also been shown to influence judgments of ownership. Sarah Malcolm and her colleagues studied both children's and adults' judgments of ownership in a series of three experiments.[73] Malcolm's study was not focused on divorcing couples, instead, the experiments focused on relatively inconsequential items and the participants made ownership judgments based on a vignette-like story. The results demonstrated that children and adult participants favored group stereotypes over first possession in their judgments of ownership.

These two studies taken together illustrate that there could be inherent biases in the way others view ownership and who is deserving of retaining property from the marriage. Again, the goal is to divide the property in an equitable way, but cognitive biases could distort the way certain items are valued. To use the house and retirement pension discussed in the last section, in a heterosexual marriage, which spouse is likely to be more associated with each? Gender stereotypes would suggest the house is more associated with the wife and the retirement pensions with the husband.

Property distributions are unlikely to simply hand the wife the house and the husband the retirement pensions, but it is possible for these biases to leak into the way the parties and the judge view what is an equitable division. What if one spouse stayed out of the workforce to manage the couple's home and family? Will this increase perceived association with different types of property? Empirical research is needed to extend the laboratory experiments into more property division issues, and like much of the research described in this book, more ecologically valid settings would help to determine if these biases are improperly influencing property division.

Spousal Support (Alimony)

Spousal support, commonly referred to as alimony, is an agreement that upon divorce the spouse with more economic means will support the spouse with less for some specified time. Courts generally focus on both the receiving spouse's need and the providing spouse's ability to pay.[74] It will come as no surprise to readers of this book that gender-norm changes have shifted the role of alimony. Historically, when women's access to property ownership and employment were restricted, alimony was an important way to maintain the wife's status upon divorce.

The rise in female employment and the feminist movement brought with them the view that there was less of a need and desire for alimony—and certainly not a gender-specific need. In fact, the Supreme Court addressed a gender-specific alimony scheme in 1979. The case, *Orr v. Orr*[75] resulted from the divorce of an Alabama couple, William and Lillian Orr. William challenged an order to pay alimony because at the time, the Alabama statute imposed alimony obligations only on husbands. The Court noted that the fact that the statute discriminated against men rather than women did not protect it, and it used an intermediate level of scrutiny, noting that "[c]lassifications by gender must serve important governmental objectives, and must be substantially related to achievement of those objectives."[76] The Court held the statute was an unconstitutional equal protection violation because gender is not an accurate proxy for need.[77]

Without gender as a proxy, courts generally look to the earning potential of the alimony-receiving spouse and the length of the marriage.

Although permanent alimony is possible, most courts now only allow limited alimony that lasts a few years to enable the alimony-receiving spouse time to rehabilitate his or her economic condition and become self-supportive. Alimony today is most prevalent when one spouse has stayed out of the workforce to maintain the couple's home and children. So, although intended to be gender-neutral, given that women are generally the ones to stay at home in a one-salary couple, it is infrequently granted to men and is part of a larger issue of gender and inequality.[78]

Although alimony has garnered considerable legal and public discourse, empirical research has not followed. A recent search of the term *alimony* in the main psychological research database yielded only 28 articles from academic journals. The following sections outline a twofold empirical focus on alimony. First, empirical research is needed to examine the social and psychological factors that contribute to alimony decisions. Second, empirical research is needed to examine the social and psychological outcomes for those former spouses who receive (and provide) alimony.

Spousal Support Decisions

Unlike child support—discussed in the next chapter—spousal support is not as cleanly regulated; spousal support decisions are generally left up to the discretion of the court, and reasons for awarding alimony are as varied as the reasons for divorce.[79] Instead of well-defined formulas, judges are expected to make alimony orders that are just and equitable,[80] yet there is no clear theory of why modern family law still includes alimony awards.[81] Lacking a coherent theory, resulting alimony awards are unpredictable and inconsistent.[82] Unfortunately, statutory guidelines, when they exist,[83] and judicial decisions about alimony seem to rest on outdated principles of marriage and are potentially influenced by the cognitive biases discussed earlier. This results in seemingly capricious decisions in one of the most litigated areas in family law.[84]

State statutes provide guidelines to the court. In Florida, for example, the statute allows courts to award alimony to either party to be "a bridge-the-gap, rehabilitative, for a set duration, or permanent."[85] Not only are the reasons for awarding alimony varied, but courts are also to consider several factors in making their spousal support decisions.

Some of those considerations include the standard of living established during the marriage, the length of the marriage, the age of each party, the emotional and physical condition of each of the parties, the financial resources of each party, and their earning capacities.[86] The courts will also consider the parties' contribution to the marriage, such as homemaking and career building of one of the parties.[87]

Despite the death of fault divorce, 22 state statutes include adultery of either spouse in the court's alimony determination decision.[88] For example, in North Carolina when a court is determining "the amount, duration, and manner of payment of alimony," the statute indicates that the court shall consider marital misconduct, which includes adultery.[89] In fact, either spouse in North Carolina can request a jury trial to determine marital misconduct.[90] Likewise, Georgia law will not allow an adulterous spouse to receive an alimony award if it is demonstrated by a preponderance of the evidence that the adultery was the cause of the divorce.[91]

Not only does fault creep into alimony decisions, but so, too, do notions of support obligations. Alimony almost always ends upon the remarriage of the receiving spouse, whether the remarriage will have a financial impact or not,[92] as it is viewed as a "material change in circumstances." Cohabitation does not necessarily have the same effect. Some jurisdictions treat romantic cohabitation the same as marriage, while others do not. As such, there is an unspoken assumption that marriage comes with financial support and that, therefore, continued alimony is not necessary when someone remarries. One problem is that such a conclusion can only be logical if the reason for awarding alimony was merely the need of the recipient and not also the payer's ability to pay, but some empirical research suggests that the ability to pay is a strong predictor for alimony amounts.[93]

What then should the judge consider in modifying an alimony award upon remarriage or cohabitation? The statutes provide some guidance, but such discretion may open the judge's decision making to bias. For example, in Tennessee, there is a rebuttable presumption to suspend alimony when the new third party is contributing to the support of the alimony recipient.[94] But does it matter how much support that new third party is able to provide? Imagine a divorced couple who had significantly different earning histories prior to their divorce, with Pat earning significantly more than Chris. Upon their divorce, Chris is awarded alimony. Chris begins cohabitating with Jessie while still receiving alimony. How much support will Jessie need to provide for the judge to view it as a material change and therefore suspend alimony? Will the amount of the original alimony award matter? Based on the cognitive bias of anchoring, that original alimony amount will likely matter. Anchoring is often discussed in relation to juror decision making or negotiations. A dollar figure or other number provides an anchor for future dollar figures or numbers. If a plaintiff's attorney says the plaintiff deserves $1 million as opposed to $10 million, the jurors will be anchored to the initial amounts and their awards will be lower because of the lower initial amount. We know judges are just as susceptible to anchoring as laypeople are.[95] Therefore, the initial alimony amount is likely to serve as an anchor to how much support Chris needs, even if the initial award was based more on Pat's ability to pay. Therefore, if the initial alimony award was high, Jessie will need to be able to provide a commensurate level of support for the judge to conclude it is reasonable to suspend the initial alimony. Of course, the anchoring effect is not unique to alimony modifications and likely is also an influential factor in initial alimony decisions. Recipients' "need," in the eyes of the court, may be colored by the amount of their initial request.

Because alimony is open to such a wide level of discretion and is awarded for a variety of reasons, it is ripe for deeper and more theoretical empirical examination. Although anchoring as a bias was highlighted earlier in decisions surrounding alimony modifications, there are likely many other cognitive biases that influence a judge's alimony decisions[96] and the parties' requests. Additionally, with calls to standardize alimony and make it more like child support,[97] empirical research is needed to understand the impact alimony has on those paying and receiving it, which is the topic of the next section.

Providing and Receiving Spousal Support

In our society, money represents power. The exchange of money between people necessarily is an exchange of power. When that exchange is taking place in the context of a divorce, deep emotions can overshadow reason.[98] Combine that with many marriages involving spouses of different genders who approach negotiations and their roles in marriage differently from each other. For example, Judith McMullen argues that because women are likely to self-blame when their marriage fails, they will be poorly equipped to successfully negotiate for alimony.[99] Indeed, some research confirms that after a divorce, men increase their financial standard of living while women decrease theirs.[100] Insomuch as there is an inequality, should an alimony decree take into account the gender wage and training gaps as a way to address societal inequalities independent of the marriage? What impact would that have both psychologically and legally?

Alimony creates a financial tie between two people who do not want to be affiliated with each other. As discussed earlier, sometimes the door to the family home is opened, and alimony is a good example of an event that further opens that door.[101] While a couple is married, it is their decision on how much money each person contributes and accesses. If one of them wants to voluntarily reduce his or her income to pursue a passion, the couple can discuss and decide on their own without any outside interference. Not so once alimony is involved. As noted previously, an alimony modification can occur when there is a significant change in circumstances. In addition to the previous situation where there was a potential for decreased need, there are also instances when the alimony can be modified because of an increased need or a decrease or increase in ability to pay. Generally, courts are willing to lower an alimony amount when a person loses a job with no fault of his or her own or becomes disabled. Courts are split, however, on more elective changes in circumstances. Take Patrick Meegan, for example, who voluntarily left his job as a sales executive to join a Catholic monastery to become a priest.[102] The court found that Patrick did not quit his job to avoid paying alimony but did so in good faith and that an alimony reduction was appropriate. In contrast, voluntarily taking an early retirement does not guarantee an alimony modification.[103] Even in the sales executive–priest case, where the court allowed the alimony modification, it was the court that was deciding whether a career change was allowed, which exemplifies how alimony metaphorically further opens the door to the family home.

For spouses receiving alimony, not only are they financially tied to their former spouse, but they are likely dependent on that support. Yet, we know very little about the emotional consequences of receiving alimony.[104] Legally, enforcement of alimony falls far below that of child support. Whereas federal and state laws aim to ensure child support obligations are fulfilled, no such similar enforcement is present with spousal support.[105] Empirical research attention is similar to legal attention with a great deal focused on child support and very little examining alimony decisions and impacts.[106] What research has been done is focused on what situations lead to alimony awards and not the personal implications for those awards on the person receiving and paying the award.[107]

Alternative Dispute Resolution and Divorce

Even though the court must still be involved to provide the final dissolution decree, many divorcing couples work out their divorce in a form of alternative dispute resolution (ADR). Indeed, some argue that going to court should be a last resort and attorneys should be ethically obligated to inform their clients of ADR options, especially when children are involved.[108] There are good reasons to support such obligations. For one, procedural justice research suggests that ADR will be especially beneficial in providing parties with a voice in the process such that they will feel more involved and satisfied with not only the process but also the outcome.[109] When children are involved, the importance of ADR is even more pronounced because the traditional zealous advocacy of a client's rights may not be in line with the best interests of the children.[110] As we will see, divorced parents often have some sort of shared custody or visitation rights and need to be able to communicate and work together in raising their children. If the divorce is processed through the traditional adversarial system, then the couple has likely been involved in a lengthy, public battle that is sure to leave them, and potentially the children, scarred. Psychologist and divorce mediator Jeffrey Zimmerman argues for the importance of ADR in divorce by analogizing how absurd it would be to expect other pairs of people in a bitter lawsuit, such as surgeons and patients or airplane pilots and passengers, to then work together.[111] Yet, we expect ex-spouses to work together in raising their children after some extremely bitter lawsuits. The following paragraphs detail some alternatives to the contentious, adversarial system approach to divorce.

A collaborative divorce shifts the paradigm of an adversarial divorce by focusing on the family's needs and reducing the litigious nature of divorce.[112] In fact, the attorneys sign an agreement to only pursue the case outside of the courtroom, with the understanding that they will resign from the case if it cannot be settled without going to court.[113] Not only are the attorneys and spouses collaborating; the process can also employ a collaboration of multidisciplinary experts. For example, a financial expert can be called on to aid in predicting ramifications for certain financial divisions.[114] Similarly, a mental health expert is part of the team to coach the parties on the best communication strategies, how to manage emotions, and ways to facilitate better functioning.[115] In fact, the term used for the mental health expert in a collaborative divorce is a *divorce coach*.[116] One way to think about it is that the attorneys are focusing on the legal needs, and the divorce coach is focusing on the psychological needs. In highly contentious divorces, two coaches can be involved so that each member of the couple has a coach to help guide and encourage collaboration.[117] The beginnings of collaborative divorce were only a few decades ago, in 1990, but the movement has grown into an international organization with more than 5,000 members.[118]

Despite the widespread interest and calls for more ADR in matrimonial law,[119] there is a shortage of empirical research on the effectiveness of collaborative divorces. One study, as part of the Collaborative Divorce Project, is worth noting. Clinical psychologist Marsha Kline Pruett and her colleagues performed an evaluation of 161 couples who had been randomly assigned to receive a collaborative divorce intervention.[120] The intervention included a variety of services for the divorcing couple, including psychoeducational parenting classes, co-parenting consultation, and mediation-focused sessions. The researchers gathered additional information from the attorneys, case files, and school teachers of the children involved. The parents involved in the collaborative divorce indicated a significantly more positive experience with the divorce than those in the comparison group. Additionally, the collaborative divorce couples reported experiencing less conflict and were less likely to need custody evaluation services than those couples not receiving collaborative divorce services.

Pruett and her colleagues' research suggests that collaborative divorces can have positive outcomes, but the true focus is on the process of divorce. Some commentators have noted that focusing on the process can have the unintentional effect of continuing to disadvantage women and dependent children in the financial outcomes of divorce.[121] In fact, because a collaborative divorce focuses on maintaining relationships, and generally women are predisposed to value relationships more than men, collaborative divorce could exacerbate women's worsened financial outcomes.[122]

Integrating mediation into a divorce is another popular ADR response. Mediation involves a neutral third party to help resolve disputes, with mediators often being either attorneys or mental health experts.[123] Mediation is meant to empower the parties to negotiate agreements rather than induce an adversarial fight with attorneys negotiating separately from the parties or having a judge make the decisions. Mediation, therefore, focuses on self-determination of the parties by making them active participants in resolving their dispute.[124] Trained mediators provide structure for the discussions but do not make decisions for the parties. Although mediation has a long history, it was first used with divorce around the 1970s.[125] Today, many states now require mediation when there is a custody dispute involved in the divorce.[126] Although on its surface this requirement seems to be about protecting the children in the middle of a custody dispute, some scholars believe much of the emphasis with ADR responses has been on efficiency above all other matters.[127]

Some research suggests that mediation fosters creativity, such that the mediation agreements address more issues than the original claims brought to the mediation.[128] But there is little research comparing the different types of mediation, such as multiple mediation sessions versus a single session or court-connected versus community-based.[129] Additionally, there are concerns of power differentials during a mediation that could influence both the process and the outcome.[130]

Research examining mediation has generally been focused on either the participants' satisfaction with mediation or the impact the mediation had on the family going through the divorce.[131] For the first question, research evidence suggests that divorcing parties are more satisfied with a mediated rather than a litigated divorce, but that difference may be influenced by the party's gender.[132] Professors of psychology Robert Emery and Melissa Wyer randomly assigned 40 separated couples to either mediation or litigation to determine child custody.[133] Their study found that those families going through mediation reached agreements quicker than did those in the adversarial system. But the experience was different for mothers compared to fathers, with mothers feeling like they had lost more and won less in the mediation group compared to those in the litigation group.[134] Mothers also experienced greater psychological distress in the mediation group as compared to those in the litigation group and compared to fathers in either group.[135] The researchers replicated their study a few years later with a larger sample size of 35 mediation families and 26 litigation families.[136] Again, they found a reduction in time for the mediation group and the same pattern of satisfaction for the mothers and fathers.[137] Examining outcomes one year after mediation versus litigation, psychologists Katerine Kitzmann and Robert Emery found there were no statistical differences between the parent–child relationships for children whose parents obtained a divorce through mediation versus litigation.[138] Among other scales, the parents completed an inventory focused on rating the quality of their relationship with their child and the child's behavior problems. Parental participation in mediation did not directly impact child behaviors or parent–child relationships; however, as demonstrated in other research on conflict resolution style, parents who cooperate and compromise during divorce decision making compared to hostile and angry parents are more likely to have children who demonstrate positive behaviors.[139]

The notions behind collaborative divorce and mediation rest on principles from social psychological research on conflict resolution. Since the 1950s, following World War II, social psychologists have focused on alternatives to war and conflict. Social psychologist Muzafer Sherif's most famous study, the Robber's Cave, provided early evidence that intergroup conflict occurs when there is competition for limited resources.[140] Called Robber's Cave because the study took place at an Oklahoma state park by that name, the field experiment randomly assigned twenty-two 12-year-old boys to one of two groups. The groups were kept separate and encouraged to bond as a group until the competition phase. During the competition phase, the two groups were intentionally pitted against each other to fight for limited resources—prizes, food, and trophies. The animosity between the groups escalated quickly to the point that the researchers had to physically separate the two groups. Although the study was limited in several ways, it supports the idea that hostility increases when groups compete over scarce resources.

In a traditional adversarial divorce, the spouses are pitted against each other to divide their limited resources. Based on the research by Sherif and other conflict research, mediation and collaborative divorce reset the premise that divorcing couples need to compete over limited resources. Instead, the parties are included more in the process, which provides them with voice and therefore is likely to increase feelings of procedural fairness[141] and decrease negative conflict.

Conclusion

Family law scholars Harry Krause and David Meyer write, "Lasting marriage is the goal . . ."[142] But is that still true today? Despite the rhetoric that today's marriages are in a recent demise, the idyllic image of suburban marriage is more a creation of the post–World War II era than a true, sustained way of life. At the turn of the 20th century, women worked outside the home, and divorces were common.[143] We are now into the next century, and women again work outside the home, and divorces are again common. Has the law lagged in responding to the social status changes of marriage? Removing the fault requirement seems one step in the direction of moving away from the old view of divorce that focused on the need for an iniquity to dissolve the marriage, but are there other ways the law can respond to the pendulum swings? Similarly, as marriage becomes less common and people, especially women, remain single longer,[144] should family law be more expansive and focus on family-like relationships? Without marriage, and therefore divorce, a social requirement, does this open the door to thinking about a new form of law that addresses intimate relationships outside marriage?

Unfortunately, a marriage dissolution does not only impact the divorcing couple but also impacts the children of that marriage. The next chapter addresses children of divorce and ripple effects on their lives from the legal and psychological dissolution of a marriage.

7

Child Custody, Visitation, and Support

WikiHow is marketed as the website that tells you "how to do anything." The opening page says, "We're trying to help everyone on the planet learn how to do anything. Join us."[1] One such how-to page is "How to win a custody battle."[2] The wiki page provides four main sections, each with at least five subsections. The four main sections—with cartoon drawings of parents and children—are (1) Analyzing your situation, (2) Obtaining helpful evidence, (3) Being on your best behavior, and (4) Going to court. Under the section on obtaining helpful evidence, the first suggestion is to "gather evidence that you are a good parent." Some suggested pieces of evidence include pictures of the parent with the children to show involvement in the child's life, receipts for special-need items (e.g., therapy, wheelchairs), and testimony from neutral parties about great parenting skills. Similarly, the page suggests gathering evidence to use against the other parent. Some recommended evidence includes whether the parent has a criminal history, history of missing important days or events for the child, or history of excessive physical punishment. The site also suggests the parent "scour" social media to find "a picture of the other parent drunk and at a party" and to save or print that photo.

As noted earlier in the book, a couple who is not married or who are in an intact marriage does not have to abide by any legal requirements for how they spend or intermingle their money. Similarly, a couple who is not divorced has great latitude in deciding how to raise their children, how much time and money each parent will spend on the child, and whether they get drunk at a party. Upon divorce, the metaphorical door to the family home is opened, and the couple must come to legal agreements about how to divide their time and resources. And, as the wikiHow page demonstrates, their private behaviors can become fodder for courtroom discussions and potential reasons for custody determinations.

The current chapter addresses many of the topics described on the wikiHow page and other legal matters surrounding custody and visitation decisions. Additionally, the chapter addresses the wide variety of research that has examined the outcomes for the couple and children involved in the divorce and the ways in which divorce law can either improve or negatively impact those effects. Finally, the chapter addresses visitation requests by nonparents and a new area of family law: pet custody.

Historical View of Custody and Visitation

One of the hottest contested and recently evolving components of a divorce involves custody of the children.[3] This area of family law has been particularly influenced by the social status of men and women. Early common law provided the fathers with sole custody because of the paternalistic focus that viewed children as their father's property.[4] In the late 1700s, U.S. courts began to consider the needs of the children and the parental qualifications to supply those needs.[5] In the first-known appellate case concerning child custody, the court granted custody to the mother, citing the father's temper and little to no property ownership or home.[6] In addition, the mother had moved in with her own father, and she and the child were being properly cared for by him. By the mid-1800s, judges were relying on the "best interest" standard by looking at what would be best for the child's well-being.

What judges presumed would be best sometimes trailed into what we now see as unconstitutional. For young children, judges applied the "tender years" doctrine, assuming the mother was the best caregiver for young children. Boys who were older were generally placed with their fathers based on the assumption they would be better off with a parent of the same sex. By the 1970s and 1980s, states no longer allowed sex to be a deciding factor because such reliance would violate the Equal Protection Clause.[7] Careful study reveals, however, that the departure from relying on sex may have been more symbolic than actual. Psychology researchers Laura Santilli and Michal Roberts compared divorce cases before and after the Alabama Supreme Court ruled the tender years doctrine unconstitutional in *Devine v. Devine*.[8] It found no significant differences between the number of fathers requesting custody or the number of fathers granted custody before and after *Devine*.[9]

As discussed in Chapter 4, the race of the parents and the child was an acceptable basis in deciding the best interest of the child until the 1984 Supreme Court case of *Palmore v. Sidoti*.[10] The Florida court had originally held the child's best interests would be served granting custody to the father. The court reasoned that because the White mother was co-habituating with a Black man, the child would be vulnerable to social stigmatization. The Supreme Court recognized the existence of racial prejudices but concluded that "[p]rivate biases may be outside the reach of the law, but the law cannot, directly or indirectly, give them effect." The Court held the lower courts' decision was a violation of the Fourteenth Amendment, which means race should not be a consideration for a custody decision.

Sexual immorality and sexual orientation were also once fodder for custody-deciding courts. Adultery by a parent was used as evidence against parental fitness. Today, parental sexual immorality is only important as it relates to and affects the children.[11] And, until recently, homosexuality was presented as a lack of moral character or as bringing social stigma to the child. Even before *Obergefell v. Hodges* found the Fourteenth Amendment requires recognition of same-sex couples,[12] psychological evidence was mounting against using sexual orientation as a deciding factor in child custody disputes. Psychological research on the topic demonstrates that being raised by a gay or lesbian parent is not detrimental to children.[13]

Although the legal landscape is clearer for same-sex parents after *Obergefell*, there are still some difficult decisions left undecided, particularly when there is one biological parent and one adoptive parent. For example, a lesbian couple decides to have a child using artificial insemination. In a heterosexual marriage, statutes such as Minnesota §257.56 designate the "husband" as the putative "father." Statutory language meant to protect against sperm donors claiming parental rights now could have the effect of interfering with a lesbian parent who wants joint custody upon divorce. In fact, that exact scenario played out in Tennessee when a legally married lesbian couple, Erica and Sabrina Witt, filed for divorce a few years after conceiving a child by artificial insemination. At the time of the delivery, the couple lived in Tennessee before *Obergefell*, and before Tennessee recognized same-sex marriages. Therefore, only the biological mother's name, Sabrina, was placed on the birth certificate. When the couple filed for divorce, Sabrina claimed Erica did not qualify under the artificial insemination statute because the law used the term *husband*. The court disagreed and read the terms of the statutes in a gender-neutral way and thereby recognized Erica's parental rights. Tennessee and Minnesota are not alone in using gender-specific terms in their statutes concerning putative parents,[14] which means further legislation and court decisions are likely in this area as family law continues to adjust to same-sex relationships.

Religion, too, can be tricky in custody disputes because religions often have tenets related to child-rearing and parental behaviors are difficult to untangle from the religious beliefs. As established in *Wisconsin v. Yoder,* parents have constitutionally protected rights related to their free exercise of religion and their children.[15] Although *Yoder* focused on compulsory education for Amish children, the case is often cited in reference to parents' rights regarding the education of their children outside traditional school settings. Additionally, courts cannot favor one religious tradition over another and must be careful to avoid bias against religious beliefs. As such, courts attempt to focus on a parent's religious conduct only if it harms the child emotionally or physically.[16] Past cases often involved Jehovah's Witnesses, whose faith prohibited certain medical care, such as blood transfusions, for their children.[17] Family lawyer Warren Camp notes that the current religious tension in child custody disputes is with the Islamic faith.[18] According to Camp, Islam is one of the fastest growing religions in the United States, and the rate of Muslims divorcing is similar to that of the general population. In addition, Shari'a law dictates the father always retains legal custody while the mother generally retains physical custody for children until they are between 7 and 12 years old at which time their father will have both physical and legal custody.[19] Shari'a law also requires the child to be raised Muslim to fulfill its best interest standard.[20] Courts have been mixed in how much they are willing to support the Shari'a requirements.[21] Citing the general bias and discrimination against Muslims, Camp argues a need for self-regulation of bias and careful attention to the specific needs of this faith among lawmakers.[22] Considering the changing U.S. demographics and continued potential for bias, Muslim divorce and custody is an area ripe for psychological research especially research related to stereotyping and bias.

Historically, judges rested their custodial decisions on several factors legally unavailable to them today. Early common law provided the fathers with sole custody. The best interest of the child standard then was used to grant sole custody usually to the mothers and excluded parents who did not fit the societal standards of the time. Each of these shifts represents distinct social philosophies about parenting and lay understanding of developmental psychology. Today, judges often rely on outside expertise to help determine the best interest of the children. The next section addresses these outside experts.

Best Interest Standard and Psychological Experts

Although custody decisions are usually worked out by the parties without formal judicial involvement,[23] one of the major changes from no-fault divorce was that judges in contested custody cases could focus on the best interest of the children rather than the fault of one of the parents.[24] Despite general guidance in some state statutes,[25] best interest is a nebulous concept, and judges generally want clear standards. Mental health experts such as psychologists or psychiatrists are frequently called on to help judges determine what is in the best interest of the child when custody is contested. As is often the case with legal standards, there is no exact mirrored psychological standard.[26] Just as the *Diagnostic and Statistical Manual of Mental Disorders* (*DSM-5*) does not have an entry for *insane*, it similarly does not have an entry for *best interest*. As such, there are serious concerns about a psychologist providing expert opinions in a custody dispute, especially in providing an opinion about the ultimate issue of which parent should have custody.[27] Therefore, psychological experts must enter this arena carefully and rely on best practice standards.[28]

In 2010, the American Psychological Association (APA) provided 14 guidelines for mental health experts involved in custody decisions.[29] The 14 guidelines are organized into three main topics: purpose of a custody evaluation, preparing for the evaluation, and conducting the evaluation. In the purpose section, the guidelines focus on the welfare of the child, the child's psychological needs, and the potential fit with the parents. Specifically, the guidelines encourage focusing on the "skills, deficits, values, and tendencies relevant to parenting attributes and a child's psychological needs" rather than on a general personality assessment of the parents.[30] In preparing for an evaluation, the guidelines direct experts to gain relevant knowledge about the laws and research on families, maintain impartiality, understand cultural differences, and avoid conflicts of interest. For conducting the evaluation, the guidelines recommend the basic business practices of doing the evaluation in a timely manner, obtaining informed consent, and maintaining appropriate records. In terms of the substantive advice about the evaluation, the experts are directed to gather information from multiple sources outside the immediate family involved in the custody dispute, such as school records and extended family. Additionally, the expert should only provide an opinion based on a sound evaluation that acknowledges the limitations of psychological tests. Finally, the guidelines indicate that not all evaluations will result in a custody recommendation and should only end with a recommendation if it can be based on sound psychological data.

Before the APA developed its guidelines, James Bow and Francella Quinnell examined a sample of 52 child custody reports.[31] The reports ranged from 5 to 63 pages long with a mean of 24 pages (SD =17) and took between 2 and 88 hours to complete.[32] All experts reported conducting individual interviews with all the parents or parental figures, and most also did psychological testing on those parents (90.4%). Children older than 5 years of age were almost always interviewed (92.3%), but the reports only included psychological testing (e.g., personality tests, IQ tests, and child perceptions of parent scales) with one-third of the children.[33] Of the reports, 94% included a specific custody or visitation recommendation.[34] In a separate study, attorneys reported supporting custody evaluators making ultimate recommendations about custody.[35]

As the APA guidelines indicate, contested custody cases are high stakes and emotionally charged. They also often involve opposing experts, which, unfortunately, can create what Linda Nielsen refers to as a "woozle."[36] Much like the Winnie the Pooh story about Pooh and his friends being frightened by the footprints of a woozle, which were their own footprints, Nielsen argues that social science research on custody has been distorted and misguided by those making custody recommendations and decisions.[37] For example, Nielsen explains that this can happen when a particular research study is repeatedly cited while other studies are ignored. The more the study is cited, the more credible it seems even if it was not that credible of a study.[38] Similarly, Nielsen notes that researchers also distort research by not acknowledging the limitations of their studies when they are talking about their research with the media and other nonresearchers.[39]

The American Judges Association's publication *Court Review* published a point-counterpoint set of pieces concerning the potential for harmful effects from child custody evaluations.[40] Ira Turkat, a clinical psychologist, began the article series by noting that he knew of no empirical research supporting positive outcomes from child custody evaluations.[41] Turkat argued that despite the APA guidelines and evaluators' professionalism, some children are being harmed by the very custody evaluation meant to attend to their best interests. The harm, Turkat argued, is mostly because these evaluations—and opposing experts hired to refute them—take financial resources from the family while intruding unnecessarily into private family matters and exposing those involved to diagnostic errors. To support his arguments, Turkat surveyed 101 divorced individuals who had personally paid for a custody evaluation. He asked these individuals if the custody evaluation had any negative or harmful effects on their children and whether the evaluation made any of their children's lives worse.[42] Additionally, he asked his respondents if they felt their children would have been better off if they had not spent the money on the custody evaluation. Although the survey did not provide any information about who did the evaluations or differentiate between respondents who received the custody arrangement they were requesting from those who did not,[43] the results overall suggest that around one-fifth to one-quarter of respondents felt the custody evaluation had negative or harmful effects on the children and made the children's lives worse.[44] Of the respondents, 65% indicated that their children would have been better off if the family's money had not been spent on the custody evaluation.

The counterpoint presented by two other clinical psychologists, Jonathan Gould and Allan Posthuma, focused on the fact that most evaluations are used as settlement tools that protect families from the burdens and additional financial costs of an in-court battle.[45] They also encouraged the judges involved in ordering a custody evaluation to carefully consider who will be doing the evaluation and the specific questions the judge wants answered by the evaluation. Both recommendations, they said, decrease unnecessary intrusion and increase the value of the evaluation. This point-counterpoint set of articles demonstrates that reasonable people can disagree about the value of psychologists being involved in child custody disputes and that these areas are ripe for psychological empirical study.

Another contentious issue is whether the children should be interviewed as part of the custody evaluation. As understanding of child development has increased, the general belief is that children should be consulted, but doing so raises both a psychological and a legal question. The psychological question relates to how the children should be questioned. The legal question is what weight the child's responses should be given.[46] Based on the empirical research they reviewed, Karen Saywitz and her colleagues provide ten principles for interviewing children in a custody dispute situation. These ten principles focus on using an age-appropriate setting and explanations for the interview, building rapport, engaging the child in fully considering the positives and negatives of various options, and avoiding suggestive techniques.[47]

Ultimately, child custody evaluations are an area in need of additional sound empirical research both about the evaluation process itself and about custody arrangements more generally.[48] Although the field has developed a great deal from 1975 when Robert Mnookin declared the process of deciding custody was no better than a coin flip,[49] the field still has a way to go. Even those experts who provide testimony are often uncomfortable with the way the court uses their expertise,[50] often because the court has not been clear in what they wanted from the expert.[51] Random control trials are clearly outside the realm of possibility; however, there are other viable alternatives of inquiry that could inch us closer to a better system for the impacted children and their parents. For example, better judicial training on the topic of child custody—especially as it relates to psychological testimony and recommendations—could enable judges to make more informed decisions without inappropriate reliance on expert testimony.

Types of Custody Arrangements

Judges today have two basic options from which to choose when determining custody: sole custody or some form of shared custody. Although not a presumption, there is growing support for the norm of shared parenting.[52] Because custody has both legal and physical components, these two options are then subdivided further such that one parent may have physical custody while the other has legal custody, or the parents may share legal custody. The language describing these arrangements has changed in recent years. Today, we talk more of decision-making authority rather than of legal custody and of parenting time instead of physical custody.[53] As fathers became more involved in child-rearing and mothers more involved in the monetary support of the family, the one-parent assumption evolved into more frequently shared or joint custody arrangements.[54]

Psychologists Daniel Kahneman and Amos Tversky's prospect theory tells us that people hate losing more than they like winning.[55] The joint custody option lets both parents feel like they have not lost their custody rights,[56] but is it in the best interest of the child? Some evidence suggests that joint custody helps maintain as closely as possible the predivorce family status because the child is not forced to choose one parent over the other and the parents both get to be involved.[57] However, joint custody asks two people who have decided they cannot be married to co-parent, which on its face seems a difficult mission. Perhaps because of this, research suggests joint custody arrangements are more frequent and more beneficial for parents with less conflict than those with greater strife.[58] Indeed, some even advocate that joint custody or shared parenting should only be agreed on by the parties rather than ordered by a judge,[59] even to the point of legislatively removing the authority from judges to grant joint custody.[60]

Joint custody can be accomplished in different ways. One option is for the child to live primarily with one parent, with parenting decisions shared between the parents and child visitation with the other parent. Another option keeps the shared decision making and involves the child moving between the parents' homes. How frequently the child moves between the homes is also variable. Some agreements have the children spending weekdays with one parent and weekends with another. Some agreements have children switching between parents on a monthly, weekly, and even daily basis.[61] An area of research debate, there is still no clear consensus concerning overnight stays for very young children with the nonprimary parent.[62] Nonetheless, research does suggest that children's adjustment is better in joint versus sole custody arrangements.[63]

One relatively new option places the child's needs truly at the center. Referred to as the "bird's-nest" version of co-parenting, the parents are the ones who move in and out of the home where the child resides.[64] Like a nest for baby birds, the children stay in the family home while the parents set up two separate homes for themselves and rotate their time and living arrangements around where the child is. The children can then maintain their neighborhood friendships, as they will remain in one place rather than two.[65] Because of the newness of this option, empirical research is relatively nonexistent. Vanessa Hurwitz examined the idea in her dissertation by interviewing seven families that had set up nesting arrangements.[66] The parents she interviewed all indicated strong support for nesting and felt it had been a positive experience for their family.[67] And, in case the opening to this chapter sparked your interest in wikiHow pages, yes, there is a wikiHow page on implementing a bird's-nest custody arrangement.[68] The page breaks down the process into six steps and includes the following warning: "If you opt to stay with relatives or friends as your home away from home, expect it to be challenging. You'll be subjected to criticism, advice, and disbelief from people who think you should either get back together or have nothing to do with one another again. It's probably best to avoid such sharing arrangements."[69] Such a warning demonstrates the newness of nesting and the lack of social acceptance of it yet.

Some of the types of custody options have been examined empirically, but many, such as nesting, have not and are ripe for psychological inquiry. Of course, truly comparing custody situations empirically would require random assignment of the families to the different custody options and many other ethically and practically impossible tactics.[70] But there are ways statistically to control for rather than manipulate variables even if it would be only scraping the surface of the innumerable potential influencing factors that likely have an impact on child and family outcomes after a divorce.[71]

Child Support

Just as intact families can decide how much time the parents spend with their children, so, too, can they decide how much money to spend as long as they are providing for basic support needs and not being neglectful. Not so with divorced families or families where there is a court order of child financial support. Unlike alimony discussed in the previous chapter, child support is highly regulated and formulaic. Starting in the mid-1970s, the federal government began requiring the states to adopt child support guidelines to be eligible for federal funding. Pursuant to Title IV of the Social Security Act, each state must establish guidelines and review them every four years to ensure the guidelines result in appropriate child support amounts.[72] The resulting child support awards should be predictable and consistent. However, the federal government does not dictate what those guidelines are to be; rather, it encourages each state to experiment to find the best tactic for that state. Although child support enforcement is generally handled at the state and local level, 18 U.S.C. §228 allows federal enforcement when the payer is delinquent on payments for more than one year or exceeding $5,000. A violation of this law is a criminal misdemeanor punishable with fines or imprisonment up to six months.[73]

Despite the flexibility afforded by the federal government in developing child support guidelines, most states have adopted a formula that considers the income shares of both parents (the "Income Shares" standard). The basic idea is that the child should benefit economically from both parents, and it should be the same proportion as if the parents lived together.[74] According to the National Conference of State Legislatures, the remaining states use one of two other models. In the "Percentage of Income" model, the custodial parent's income is not considered. Instead, a percentage of the noncustodial parent's income is used to calculate monthly child support payments. In the "Melson Formula," the calculation is like the Income Shares standard but considers both parent's basic needs in addition to the children's. Because it is possible to rely on the formulas for child support calculations without imposing dollar-amount ceilings, the very wealthy can be ordered to pay several thousand dollars per month in child support. For example, former National Football League (NFL) Dallas Cowboys player Deion Sanders was ordered to pay $10,550 in monthly child support for his three children.[75] To put that into perspective, Sanders was to pay $42,200 per child, per year in child support—a dollar amount only a couple thousand dollars less than the median yearly income for U.S. workers.[76] Of course, extremely high child support requirements are likely to be the rare exception with the more likely occurrence being child support that feels overly burdensome for the payer parent and inadequate for the recipient parent.

Even when parents are ordered to pay child support at much lower rates than NFL football players, there are often still feelings of resentment and concerns over financial ability to pay.[77] Some research suggests a positive correlation between visitation and paying child support, such that as visitation increases, so, too, does paying child support.[78] Other research has not found a significant relationship between either visitation frequency or visitation quality and support payments.[79] In a longitudinal study, a sense of control in the upbringing of the child was strongly related to paying child support.[80] Similarly, the more satisfied the parent is with the custody arrangement, the more support they were willing to pay.[81] Clearly, this research demonstrates that psychological factors outside ability to pay impact how compliant a person is with his or her child support orders.

The Impact of Divorce on Children

In addition to the financial and logistic impact of custody, visitation, and financial support, children of divorce can also experience psychological impacts on their well-being. Behavioral scientist Paul Amato and his colleague have done two meta-analyses focused on children's postdivorce well-being.[82] A meta-analysis is a statistical technique that allows researchers to combine and summarize results across studies to describe a common effect.[83] Prior to their first meta-analysis, individual studies produced inconsistent results regarding the negative effects of divorce on children, with some demonstrating serious negative effects for children of divorce and others finding no effects of divorce.

In their first meta-analysis, their sample of 92 studies conducted from the 1950s to the 1980s included both children who were living in single-parent homes because of separation or divorce and children who were in two-parent, intact families. Altogether, there were 13,000 children combined in the reviewed studies. The studies also needed to include at least one quantitative measure of well-being. These measures of well-being focused on the following variables: academic achievement, conduct, psychological adjustment, self-concept, social adjustment, mother–child relations, father–child relations, and other.[84] Two-thirds of the studies found that children of divorce had lower well-being scores than did children from two-parent homes, but the effect sizes were generally quite modest, making some of them statistically different but perhaps not practically so.

Ten years later, Amato published an update to his 1991 meta-analysis focusing on the 67 studies published in the 1990s that also had similar measures of well-being.[85] According to Amato it was necessary to do such an update because it allowed the examination of a possible societal shift toward more acceptance of divorce, which meant the possibility of less marital discord than in the past to push couples to the point of divorce. The 2001 results closely mirrored the 1991 results but demonstrated that the gap between children of divorce and children of intact families widened during the 1990s compared to the 1980s, with children of divorce showing slightly worse overall psychological well-being.[86] The authors theorize that the worse outcomes for children of more recent divorces could be because divorces are happening more frequently for people who are only mildly dissatisfied in their marriages. In other words, fewer couples are waiting until their marriages become truly discordant to seek a divorce. These divorces are more difficult on the children because they happen without as much warning and the children's lives are disrupted by the divorce rather than the parental discord leading up to a divorce. The authors also believe that the general economy of the 1990s could have played a role because two-parent homes benefited more than single-parent homes during the economic expansion of the 1990s.

Because of these potential negative outcomes, courts have attempted to ameliorate the situation by ordering parent education programs. These programs focus on teaching parents about children's adjustment to divorce and the importance of maintaining a low level of conflict. Some states mandate these courses, whereas others only encourage them, and some states offer the courses online.[87] In Florida, for example, the course is required, but there are offerings online.[88] There are nine modules in a four-hour course covering divorce as loss, parental role, developmental stages, communication, abuse, legal concepts, visitation, and additional help.[89] Upon completing the course, the divorcing parent receives a certificate. One study involved systematically examining 28 such programs in a meta-analysis.[90] The study results demonstrate that most of the programs were four to nine hours in length and had an overall positive effect for participating parents. In fact, parents who participated in a divorce parenting education program compared to those who did not were 50% better on outcome measures such as co-parenting conflict, parent–child relationships, child well-being, parent well-being, and relitigation.[91] In addition, some promising research suggests that children experiencing divorce can be taught better coping skills that, in turn, reduce emotional and mental health problems for the children.[92] Some of this skill building even effects change long term.[93]

Although previous research suggested that children of divorce had greater risks for negative mental health outcomes such as depression, recent research suggests that parents' own depression may confound this relationship.[94] Still, it seems that the best predictor of positive child adjustment following a divorce is the parents' psychological well-being and the quality of the parent–child relationship. As such, an important research focus for determining how children will do postdivorce is how the parents are coping and the type of conflict and conflict resolution style that are present.[95] Only a few longitudinal studies have been published that focus on the divorcing partners' subjective well-being.[96] In a meta-analysis of those studies, divorce was a mild negative event with subjective well-being increasing after the divorce.[97] An additional meta-analysis showed that a person's social relationships following a divorce serve as an insulating factor against negative postdivorce adjustment.[98] Of course, as the marriage landscape continues to develop and change, so, too, should the research examining the impacts on children of divorce or nonmarital dissolution. For example, are there different effects for children of nonmarried couples who decide to dissolve their relationship? Does the legal involvement required to dissolve a marriage make matters better or worse for the children (and the couple)?

Grandparent Visitation

By the late 1980s, all 50 states had passed legislation permitting grandparents and other nonparents the right to petition for visitation rights, generally when there was a death of a parent or a divorce.[99] Some of these statutes were quite broad and gave sweeping rights to nonparents. One such law was in the state of Washington, which allowed "any person" to petition for visitation rights "at any time," and the court was to grant such visitation when it served the best interest of the child.[100] The statute garnered the U.S. Supreme Court's attention in *Troxel v. Granville*, after a mother appealed a lower court's granting of generous visitation to her children's paternal grandparents.[101] In a plurality opinion, the Court focused on the "breathtakingly broad" statutory language that permitted a court to order visitation to anyone, even over the objections of a fit parent.[102] Indeed, the Court noted the custodial parent's own assessment of his or her child's needs took a backseat to the determination by the Court. But, the Court failed to rule on the validity of the statute and instead focused on the fact that it had been unconstitutionally applied to this mother. As such, states were left to determine if their statutes were appropriately deferential to parents when they granted nonparents the right to petition for visitation.[103] At this point, there is not a clear consensus among the states of how to legally handle nonparent visitation, with states' political cultures contributing to the type of statute they have.[104] States generally require a showing by the grandparents or other interested parties that permitting visitation is in the best interest of the child or prohibit visitation if the child will be harmed. But what will suffice for such a showing? Can general psychological research meet such an evidentiary standard, or is case-specific clinical psychology testimony necessary?

From the psychological view, the laws are well-intentioned efforts to increase the number of caring adults in a child's life,[105] which is widely regarded as important and beneficial. Nonetheless, laws forcing parents to defend their definition of family and who should be involved in their child's life unavoidably divert resources away from the child and infringes on the parent's constitutional right to raise the child as the parent sees fit.[106] Tammy Henderson examined 65 appellate cases from 1986 to 2001 where grandparents had successfully petitioned for court-ordered visitation with their grandchildren.[107] Henderson's research focused on the legal precedence, constitutional elements, and reasons for granting visitation.[108] The vast majority of the decisions rested on the idea that the grandparent visitation would be in the best interest of the child.[109] Oftentimes, there were extenuating circumstances, such as an incarceration or deployment of a parent, such that the grandparent wanted to ensure a connection with his or her side of the family in the absence of the parent.

One interesting research question regarding grandparent visitation that has not been examined is whether a "grandparent bias" exists. National statistics confirm that most judges are of grandparent age.[110] State legislators are too.[111] Does that influence their desire to ensure grandparents retain visitation with their grandchildren? A correlational study could examine judges' and legislators' attitudes toward grandparent visitation and compare those who are grandparents to those who are not and even control for those who have children who are divorced or other factors that would traditionally open the family to grandparent visitation petitions.

Pet Custody

If you have made it this far in this book, then you know that the backdrop of family law is ever evolving and has drastically changed in the past several decades. With those changes come new areas and sometimes those areas are sort of surprising. Pet custody disputes would likely more than surprise our great-grandparents who viewed pets as more utilitarian than childlike.[112] According to one survey of family law attorneys, pet custody disputes have been increasing in recent years.[113] Not surprisingly, dogs and cats were most often the targets of the disputes.[114] Although some judges are not inclined to use their court's resources to decide matters involving family pets, there are those judges who recognize the important physical and emotional role of pets in their guardian's lives.[115] Courts are even providing pet visitation orders and hearing arguments to change pet custody decisions.[116] Some couples write prenuptial agreements to address future pet parenthood in the event of a breakup.[117] But, from a strictly legal perspective, pets are property, not children.[118] Just as judges do not consider who might be the best caregiver for the family lawnmower or what would be in the best interest of the flat-screen TV, they should not consider such for a pet, but they do, and the public often thinks they should.[119] Alaska was the first state to enact pet custody legislation.[120] In its law, decisions about ownership or joint ownership of a pet are to take into account the well-being of the pet.[121] If that sounds familiar, it is because it is very similar to the best interest standard used for making child custody decisions. As psychology understands more about the influence of pets on physical and emotional health and as the field of animal rights develops,[122] we may see even more states take a similar path. What is yet to be seen is if this will also lead to pet custody evaluations, pet support payments, and visitation rights for pet grandparents!

Conclusion

In their *Behavioral Sciences and the Law* special issue on Families, Divorce, Custody, and Parenting, Gregg Herman and Randy Otto note that "[p]arents and children involved in circumstances in which there is considerably less agreement and more acrimony face an even more difficult time."[123] Herman and Otto go on to describe the challenges mental health professionals, judges, and lawyers face as they attempt to determine what is in the best interest of the child when there is a custody dispute. Unfortunately, these difficult decisions are also being made in a what some call a "flawed" system because of the weaknesses and contradictions within the system.[124] This system must decide highly personal and private issues such as how to divide a child's time between parents and between parents and other potential caregivers such as grandparents. These decisions that have long-term impacts on all parties involved are made using the nebulous guiding principle of the best interest standard that seems to invite bias and stereotypes. Unfortunately, there is no wikiHow page for legal professionals and psychologists involved in this area of family law. But with increased psychological research on key aspects of these topics, lawyers, judges, and mental health care professionals will be better positioned to positively influence and fairly decide custody matters.

8

Intimate Partner Violence, Child Maltreatment, and Elder Maltreatment

David Pelzer describes his childhood as one that involved his mother punching him, forcing him to drink ammonia, burning him on the gas stove, and trying to force him to eat a soiled diaper.[1] Pelzer said he feared for his life while living with his abusive mother. He described in detail one incident that involved his mother stabbing him in the stomach with a knife and the need for him to clean his own infected wound. The abuse finally ended when David was 12 years old and was sent to a foster family. Jeanette Walls's childhood was very different from Pelzer's but still dysfunctional.[2] In her recounting of her childhood, there are stories of poverty resulting from her parents' mismanagement and squandering of finances. The family moved frequently and often did not have enough to eat. Although not physically abusive to her children, the mother told the children that her life would have been easier if she did not have them, and both parents' behaviors were erratic and irresponsible toward their children. These descriptions are from *A Child Called It* and *The Glass Castle*, respectively. Both books were *New York Times* best sellers, with millions of copies sold. There is a voyeurism appeal with these stories[3]—just as the metaphorical door to the family home opens when abuse is present, societally we seem to want to peer inside. It is not hard to name many other popular books and movies about family violence. In fact, Amazon.com lists 30,926 results for books using the search term "child abuse."[4]

Despite the general principles of parental autonomy and privacy, domestic violence and child maltreatment invite police, lawyers, social workers, and judges into the family. This is an area of family life where the door to the family home is thrown wide open, allowing government intervention. Because the topics of domestic violence, child maltreatment, and elder maltreatment are covered well in many other sources within the psychology of victims, the current chapter describes the topic generally and then highlights some areas that are less likely to receive psychological empirical attention. In the intimate partner violence section, the focus is on special domestic violence courts. In the child maltreatment section, the focus is on corporal punishment, obesity as a form of neglect, and termination of parental rights. In the elder maltreatment section, the focus is on informal caregivers and mandatory reporting.

Intimate Partner Violence

Not surprisingly, attitudes concerning, and definitions of, what constitutes domestic violence have changed over time. Historically, violence between spouses was considered a private family matter.[5] Using today's definitions, the Centers for Disease Control and Prevention report that one in four women and one in nine men have experienced some form of intimate partner violence.[6] Although intimate partner violence can impact any race and socioeconomic status, racial and ethnic minorities and those with lower household incomes are disproportionally more likely to experience it.[7] The deleterious impacts of intimate partner violence on the direct victims and the children in the home are immense and clearly documented.[8] And batterer treatment programs are generally ineffective.[9] Likewise, battered woman syndrome is a well-established psychological topic within the area of intimate partner violence and covered well other places.[10]

The past few decades have seen legal and psychological attention to the new movement toward specialty courts, also known as problem-solving courts.[11] These courts take a therapeutic jurisprudence approach to addressing a legal issue such as is the case with drug courts, mental health courts, and domestic violence courts.[12] Domestic violence specialty courts utilize a collaborative and multidisciplinary approach to cases of intimate partner violence that recognizes the unique dynamic of this type of crime.[13] A goal of these therapeutically infused courts is to hold the defendants accountable while also recognizing the needs of both the defendant and the victim. They also serve the state's needs by being specialized and efficient.[14] The research is promising on their success of reducing rearrests for those who participate in a domestic violence specialty court as compared to defendants processed through a traditional court.[15]

A Salt Lake City special domestic violence court built its court with the help of battered women advocates.[16] Focusing on the stakeholders involved with the court, sociologist Rekha Mirchandani examined how the court was different from a nonspecialized court. Two differences, Mirchandani noted, were that most of the court officials were female and that rather than an adversarial approach, the court used a consensus-building approach.[17] The judge actively engaged with both the victim and the offender during the hearings, discussing not only the case but also their personal lives. Examining the perspective of the professional stakeholders (e.g., lawyers, judges, social workers) involved, Mirchandani interprets her findings as demonstrating that the Salt Lake City specialized domestic violence court has been able to address the traditional patriarchal legal responses in domestic violence cases. For example, the stakeholders described a heavy emphasis on male dominance from a cultural perspective while also requiring the defendants to take responsibility for their actions.

Criminologist Angela Gover and her colleagues examined a specialized domestic violence court in Lexington County, South Carolina, by observing cases and interviewing defendants, victims, judges, law enforcement, a prosecutor, a mental health counselor, and a battered woman's shelter advocate.[18] The observations revealed collaborative efforts by the court, often before the hearings began, with the court personnel all working together to process the case. Both victims and offenders reported a high rate of satisfaction with the specialized court. They also reported the court provided them an opportunity to tell their story and treated them with dignity and respect—all important procedural justice components.

Taken together, the empirical studies of specialized domestic violence courts demonstrate the courts are reducing recidivism and attending to the needs of victims and offenders that are unique because of an intimate relationship. There is certainly room for additional research into these courts that could identify strengths and weaknesses to ensure that they adequately address the important issues of domestic violence. For example, domestic violence offenders have a high rate of attrition in their psychological treatment programs, and the ones at highest risk for reoffending are also at highest risk for dropping out of their programs.[19] Would there be a way for the special courts to decrease the treatment attrition, or are there already programs in place that do a good job with decreasing attrition that should be implemented more widely?

Child Maltreatment

All states have intricate statutory schemes addressing child maltreatment. Yet, research has repeatedly demonstrated that personal biases will influence responses and what the believed outcomes should be. Criminology provides a wealth of information about the effectiveness of police policies and statutory schemes meant to address domestic violence and child maltreatment. The psychological research is clear and voluminous that there are deleterious mental health outcomes for those involved in domestic violence or child maltreatment. It is also an area where the professional division between law and psychology is pronounced. Many states include psychologists in their mandatory reporting of child abuse laws,[20] but the attorney–client privilege is seen as restricting attorneys from divulging abuse information unless death or substantial bodily harm is reasonably certain.[21]

Although parents have great latitude in how they raise their children, a limit occurs when abuse or neglect is involved. Neglect generally refers to the failure to provide for basic needs, while abuse can involve physical, sexual, or emotional maltreatment. Statutes provide definitions of maltreatment, and extreme cases like that described in the introduction of this chapter are easy to see as abuse. The line, however, is not always clear, and there are certainly historical and cultural biases at work.[22] It is no surprise that, historically, child abuse did not always garner government interference. As described earlier, child reverence is a modern phenomenon, and plenty of examples abound of how children were more traditionally treated similarly in some ways to slaves by their parents and employers.[23]

Awareness and concern about child abuse came to the public forefront about 20 years prior to intimate partner violence. Although the first documented U.S. case of child maltreatment was in the 1870s,[24] it was not until the 1962 publication by pediatrician Henry Kempe and his colleagues that the law took shape against child maltreatment. Published in the *Journal of the American Medical Association*, Kempe's article documented what he called battered child's syndrome, which he supported with his research that found hundreds of children who were severely injured by their parents.[25] Soon thereafter, federal legislation provided guidelines for states to address child abuse.[26] Inspired by Kempe's work, empirical research on child abuse flourished.[27] Today, child abuse is still considered a serious public health concern in the United States, with estimates suggesting one in four children experience abuse at some point in their lives.[28]

Children who have been maltreated have an elevated risk for insecure attachment,[29] and recent meta-analyses demonstrate that maltreatment also results in negative neurobiological consequences such as cognitive processes,[30] decreased gray matter,[31] and neural responses.[32] Psychologist Cathy Spatz Widom studied police and court records to determine if children who had been maltreated were at a higher risk for later criminal behavior.[33] Widom started with the court records of 908 children who had been sexually or physically abused or neglected between 1967 and 1971. She obtained a matched sample of children who had not been abused, on characteristics such as gender, age, ethnicity, and socioeconomic status. Widom then compared across a 15- to 20-year period the police records for these two groups of children and found that those who had been abused were significantly more likely to have been arrested for a violent crime. Perhaps explaining the increased criminality, Widom and her colleagues also found the children who had been abused were significantly more likely to have mood disorders and antisocial personality characteristics.[34]

The severe and negative consequences of abuse clearly carry throughout a child's life; similarly, the economic consequences are also far-reaching. One study estimated the financial costs for a nonfatal child abuse case as $210,012 in health care costs, productivity losses, child welfare costs, criminal justice costs, and special education costs.[35] The same study estimated that, in one year, the United States had $124 billion in costs related to child abuse.[36] There is not enough room in this book to describe even a sampling of all the research and legal responses to clear situations of abuse and neglect. Instead, the following two sections address particular gray areas of abuse and neglect: corporal punishment and obesity as neglect. The final subsection addresses the state's involvement in terminating parental rights because it represents the most extreme form of government involvement within the family. Although child witnesses could emerge during a child maltreatment case, the topic is not covered in this chapter because it is addressed well on its own in other places.[37]

Corporal Punishment

Courts have held that parents have a constitutional right to use corporal punishment in disciplining their children insomuch as that corporal punishment is reasonable.[38] State statutes generally require the punishment to be reasonable and not excessive. What, then, is reasonable? In his book on the topic, founder and director of the Family Research Laboratory at the University of New Hampshire Murray Straus defined corporal punishment as "use of physical force with the intention of causing a child to experience pain but not injury for the purposes of correction or control of the child's behavior."[39] But the fields of both law and psychology struggle with a perfect definition. Corporal punishment is a hotly debated topic by scholars and parents.[40] Psychologist Christopher Ferguson differentiates corporal punishment from spanking in his meta-analysis, saying spanking is "relatively mild physical punishment using an open hand on the buttocks or extremities" while corporal punishment is a broader class of behaviors that includes "hitting with an object, such as a switch, shaking, pushing, slapping the face, etc."[41] In contrast, developmental psychologist Elizabeth Thompson Gershoff's meta-analysis included spanking as a form of corporal punishment.[42]

In addition to the debates about how to define corporal punishment are the debates about the impact of spanking and corporal punishment. Gershoff concluded from her meta-analysis that, although corporal punishment did result in immediate child compliance, it was also related to ten undesirable outcomes such as a higher short- and long-term likelihood of delinquent and antisocial behavior and mental health issues.[43] Developmental psychologist George Holden questioned whether additional context would be necessary to fully understand the implications of Gershoff's meta-analysis. For example, Holden noted that there was nothing in the studies examined or Gershoff's treatment of them that reflected learning theory or socialization research. In other words, the punishments were taken out of context and not examined in relationship to what else was happening in the child's life. For the purpose of learning theory, Holden noted that it would be important to know if the corporal punishment was applied consistently and that, for the purposes of socialization, it would be useful to know if there was additional yelling that occurred at the same time as the corporal punishment that might exacerbate the negative impact. Finally, Holden argues that to understand the full impact of corporal punishment, the child's perspective should not be ignored. Holden argues that we do not know whether children remember what they had done wrong to warrant the punishment or if they only remember the punishment because it has such extreme physical and emotional impacts on the child. Diana Baumrind and her colleagues also had concerns with the Gershoff meta-analysis, including that corporal punishment was not isolated from other harsh parenting that could be the true reason for the negative outcomes.[44]

In Ferguson's meta-analyses, he focused on longitudinal studies that examined the effects of corporal punishment and spanking.[45] His results were initially similar to Gershoff's, but when he used a more nuanced statistical methodology, the impact of spanking and corporal punishment on negative outcomes was quite minimal. Ferguson recommended that psychologists be more careful in explaining the subtleties of the impacts of corporal punishment and spanking on any long-term negative outcomes.

Two divisions within the American Psychological Association (APA) released a task force report concerning physical punishment of children.[46] Division 7 (Developmental Psychology) and Division 37 (Society for Child and Family Policy and Practice) examined empirical research and legal regulations related to physically punishing children. The task force concluded that parents and others should be advised not to use any form of physical punishment on children. The task force also proposes that the APA become more actively involved in discouraging physical punishment and in educating the public about the long-term negative effects of physically punishing children.

Despite the psychological discouragement of physical punishment and programs aimed to prevent corporal punishment in homes,[47] there are laws that still allow school systems to impose corporal punishment on their students.[48] Corporal punishment is a classic example of the three competing voices from law, psychology, and the public. U.S. law allows it, psychology is cautiously concerned about its use,[49] and by a 2–1 margin the public supports it.[50] Although there are countries that have outlawed the practice,[51] in the United States we hold tight to our privacy and child-rearing rights,[52] and with most of the public believing it to be an appropriate disciplinary technique, the law is unlikely to change.

Obesity as Neglect

The United States has one of the highest rates of childhood obesity in the world, making it what many call a public health crisis.[53] Analogous to the way the law responds to underfed children, the law has responded both civilly and criminally toward parents who have morbidly obese children.[54]

One concern with attaching responsibility and blame to the parents of obese children is that the society is ignored as a contributing factor, and it is well documented that healthy foods and activities are more difficult for lower socioeconomic status individuals to obtain.[55] Based on a public opinion survey by Jayson Lusk and Brenna Ellison, agricultural economists, the public seems to ignore the social context in which childhood obesity occurs.[56] Using a national representative sample of almost 800 people, Lusk and Ellison asked respondents to indicate a list of seven entities that were primarily to blame, somewhat to blame, or not to blame for obesity in the United States. The entities were government policies, restaurants, grocery stores, food manufacturers, farmers, parents, and the obese individuals themselves.[57] Although 80% felt that individuals were primarily to blame for obesity, with only 14% somewhat to blame and 6% not to blame, parents were the next most likely entity to be rated as primarily to blame (59%). The public is not alone; as Deena Patel states in her *Family Court Review* article, "[d]o little kids steal their parent's car keys and drive themselves to McDonald's? No. That is why the state should intervene if a child is morbidly obese . . ."[58]

Law-psychology scholars Jenny Reichert and Monica Miller used attribution theory to examine mock jurors' desire to punish parents for medical neglect of obese children. Reichert and Miller provided college student samples in their two studies with a trial summary that described a mother of an obese son that an expert either described as having the genetics from his father to be overweight or no information about genetics. The participants then rated whether they believed that the mother was guilty of medical neglect and whether she should receive a sentence that was very high, low, or somewhere in between.[59] Most of their participants did not believe the mother should be found guilty of medical neglect, and there were no statistical differences based on their manipulated variables. Reichert and Miller concluded that the external factors, such as the case facts, were less influential in their participants' decision making than the internal factors, such as the participants' attribution of responsibility and other individual differences. They also conducted a third study focused on whether their participants would support legislation that would allow prosecution of parents who let their children become obese and what their thoughts were on such legislation. Despite the lack of support for specific prosecutions in their first two studies, participants were more likely to support general legislation on prosecuting parents of obese children. Such general versus specific disconnect is not abnormal, especially as it relates to parental responsibility;[60] however, it does suggest there could be a disconnect between wanting to blame the parents and actually punishing parents when their children are obese. Of course, whether the public would support such laws is only a piece of the important research that could be done on this topic. Important empirical research to be done could examine whether such regulations would have a positive impact on parental behaviors that would also positively impact the children's actions. Because there is not a clear path between the law and the child's actions, it is hard to know what kind of impact such laws would have.

Termination of Parental Rights

When other efforts have failed, a termination of parental rights (TPR) is within the power of the family court. TPR decisions stem from both legal and psychological decision making. Similar to custody decisions, psychologists are called on to help the court make predictions about whether the risks present at the time of the abuse are still present and likely to continue and impact the best interest of the child.[61] A TPR permanently severs the parent–child legal relationship. As such, the courts do not take the process lightly, and the Supreme Court has held that the Due Process Clause of the Fourteenth Amendment requires the State must prove their TPR case by at least clear and convincing evidence,[62] which requires the trier of fact to find that the evidence is substantially more likely than not. The entire process is one of balancing the constitutional rights of the parents and the best interest of the child.

Every state has a statutory scheme focusing on specific parental behaviors or how impractical reunification will be.[63] The Adoption and Safe Families Act of 1997 (ASFA) was a cultural shift from focusing on the reunification of children with their birth parents to a focus on the health and well-being of the children. This federal legislation required the states to pass complementary legislation to continue to receive federal funds for child welfare. One of the major changes in the law was the requirement that states move to a TPR when a child had been in foster care 15 out of the last 22 months,[64] which can be challenging if the parents and family need extensive and lengthy services.[65] There are some allowable exceptions, such as if the child is in kinship care, the state has not done what it needed to do to attempt reunification, or if a TPR truly would not be in the best interest of the child.[66] Additionally, if the child is unlikely to be adopted, there is little incentive for the courts to press toward a TPR. This means older children are more likely to age out of the system without being adopted,[67] which creates a new set of issues for these emerging adults who were raised in foster care.[68]

Similar to the guidelines provided by the APA for custody evaluations,[69] the APA also has guidelines for evaluations in child protection matters.[70] The 14 guidelines are divided into the following three categories: orienting guidelines, general guidelines, and procedural guidelines. The orienting and general guidelines speak more to the standards of professional conduct and the purpose for performing such an evaluation. The procedural guidelines are the crux of the evaluator's responsibilities, and they focus on the ways to approach the evaluation. Included in this process is the admonition for psychologists to use appropriate and multiple methods of data gathering to address the court's questions, use clinical or assessment data to inform their conclusions, and provide answers to the court's questions only when they have sufficient data.[71]

Some research conducted not long after the implementation of ASFA demonstrated that attorneys and guardians ad litem (GALs) involved in TPR cases may overly rely on a parent's court plan compliance independent of the fit and appropriateness of that court plan.[72] The research first surveyed attorneys and GALs and asked them to think about one of their current potential TPR cases and to indicate the importance of different factors. These respondents indicated that a lack of court plan compliance was given considerable weight in their decision to pursue a TPR.

Following this first study, the researchers created a mock case description and manipulated how well a single mother, described as either mentally retarded or clinically depressed, had complied with the court plan. In addition, they also manipulated how well the court plan was matched to the needs of the parent, with either a narrow or overly broad court plan. For example, in the overly broad plan for the clinically depressed mother, she was ordered to meet with a psychiatrist two times per week, take prescription antidepressants, attend parent training classes two times per week, take anger management classes, and attend parent support group meetings two times per week.[73] The narrowly focused plan required the mother to meet with a psychiatrist twice per week and take prescribed medication. Almost 150 attorneys and Health and Human Services (HHS) workers participated in the study by reading the case description and then indicating whether they would recommend a TPR for the mother, which they were most likely to do if the mother was described as not being compliant with her court plan. None of the other manipulations mattered statistically, and in their open-ended responses, almost half of the respondents expressly indicated that their reasons for recommending or not recommending a TPR were based on the mother's court plan compliance. These results are concerning given the high stakes of a TPR case and that families involved in TPR cases are overwhelmingly of lower socioeconomic status,[74] have mental health problems, and are struggling with alcohol and drug abuse,[75] all of which make meeting broad court plans even more challenging. Therefore, what seems like a neutral and objective standard—court plan compliance—may be less unprejudiced than it seems. Again, the described research was with attorneys and HHS workers. Would psychologists participating in a TPR evaluation be similarly distracted by court plan compliance? It is unclear but would be an interesting future research study. Related, is there underlying bias in the formation of the court plans? It is certainly possible that parents with less social capital end up with more extensive court plans because the court is attempting to provide more services and supports, but as the previously mentioned research indicates, such expansive court plans can have unintended consequences.

Elder Maltreatment

Although not uniquely a family law topic, elder maltreatment is frequently a family issue because perpetrators of elder abuse are most often family members.[76] States address elder maltreatment similarly to the way they address child maltreatment.[77] In fact, some elder maltreatment statutes are mirrored exactly off their child maltreatment statutes. Although efficient to model the elder maltreatment laws after the child maltreatment laws, it is unsuitable in at least three ways. First, children do not generally have the financial resources that older adults have,[78] making financial abuse nonexistent for children but one of the most prevalent for older adults.[79] Second, older adults have reached the age of majority for consensual sexual activity, so there is no set age that is appropriate to forbid sexual activity similar to the way statutory rape and child sex abuse statutes are written. Third, and what is discussed further in the sections that follow, are issues related to neglect that can be ambiguous if the older adult refuses care or it is unclear that someone has assumed caregiving responsibilities. These neglect ambiguities are amplified in light of mandatory reporting laws.

Informal Caregivers Assuming Responsibility

It may seem difficult to imagine that someone would not know they were a caregiver and not understand how to provide appropriate care. But take Lee Peterson as an example. Lee argued he was not his mother's caregiver and therefore could not be criminally responsible for her death.[80] Lee and his brother, James, shared a home with their 82-year-old mother and had agreed that, because Lee worked long hours outside the home, James would be the one to take on the responsibility of caring for their mother. Unfortunately, their mother's condition became quite dire in the last months of her life—paramedics found her lying in human waste with extensive bedsores and dying from a ruptured colon.[81] Despite Lee's claim that he had not assumed the caregiving responsibility, the court held that Lee had a legal duty to oversee the care his brother was providing and ensure his brother was not abusing or neglecting their mother. Lee and his brother, James, were found guilty of aggravated manslaughter.

Dale and Janice Simester argued the neglect statute in their state required them to have medical and psychiatric knowledge a lay person would not have.[82] Janice's 74-year-old uncle lived with the Simesters, and testimony at trial suggested he was "grumpy" and had a "bad odor about him,"[83] which the Simesters argued made it difficult for them to ascertain how bad his condition was in his final weeks of life. Medical testimony at their trial described the victim as severely dehydrated, covered in dried urine and feces, and in renal failure. Medical testimony indicated that his physical condition, including a bedsore that had penetrated to within one inch of his hip bone, would have taken one to two weeks to develop. The court, therefore, was unsympathetic to their defense that they did not know the nature of the victim's physical or mental condition and found them guilty of criminal neglect of an elderly person.

As one final example, Theresa Sieniarecki lived with her mentally and physically declining mother who died from malnutrition and infection complications following her refusal to accept medical assistance.[84] Theresa testified that most of the caregiving burden fell on her rather than her siblings who lived nearby, but she did not see herself as her mother's caregiver, and she did not want to interfere with her mother's right to refuse medical care. The court noted that anyone in Theresa's position would have known they had assumed a caregiving role and that her mother was incompetent to make medical decisions. The court sentenced Theresa to 22 months in prison for the neglect of her mother.

Taken together, these cases suggest that courts believe people know when they are a caregiver to an older adult and know how to provide appropriate care. Consider how different it is to become a caregiver for an infant as compared to an older adult. When a person becomes a parent either by having a baby or adopting a child, there is an event that makes it clear there is a new parent–child relationship. It would be difficult for parents of a newborn baby to argue they did not know they were the caregivers for the baby. Yet, with older adults, there is often a slow progression toward caregiving. Sometimes a fully competent adult moves in with adult children out of convenience or for economic reasons. In fact, sometimes the older adult moves in to help with the caregiving of children. Although there may be a clear health event that brings about a new living situation, research shows that is not always the case and they are often entered into without intending them to be long term.[85]

In addition, study participants imagining themselves in a variety of living situations with older adults who need some form of help were not as attuned to their legal responsibilities as the courts in the previously described cases assumed people would be.[86] In fact, it is possible that hindsight bias could be playing a role in court decisions,[87] such that once an elderly person has died, it becomes easy to conclude that something went wrong and someone had failed his or her duty of care. Looking backward, it is hard to miss all the warning signs that may not be as clear in the present.

Mandatory Reporting

All states encourage or require people in certain professions (e.g., nurses, physicians, teachers, social workers) to report suspected child abuse. Although not always the case with intimate partner violence situations, generally there is a presumption of victim competency and freedom to decide whether to report the abuse.[88] In contrast, many elder maltreatment laws mimic the response to child maltreatment by incorporating mandatory reporting requirements. Imposing mandatory reporting on older adults forces them into the same *parens patriae* framework of child maltreatment statutes and effectively disempowers them without consideration for their privacy and autonomy.[89] This is especially troubling given that some states set their qualifying age as young as 60 years old.[90] Additionally, there are three practical complications with mandatory reporting of older adult maltreatment. First, far fewer people generally come in regular contact with older adults than with children because there are no compulsory education requirements for older adults. In addition, many of the signs of abuse can present as normal aging.[91] Second, mandatory reporting statutes presume incompetence or inability of the victim to be able to report. For children who have not reached the age of majority, this makes sense, but for the heterogeneous population of older adults, the logic is less clear. Indeed, research demonstrates that competent older adults would know to report abuse and many say they would do so.[92] Third, unlike child maltreatment statutes, older adult maltreatment statutes generally include self-neglect as a form of maltreatment and include self-neglect as a mandatory reporting trigger.[93] Certainly, self-neglect could be symptomatic of an underlying mental or physical condition that should be reported and addressed, but self-neglect can also be part of a well-considered, competent desire to die.[94] In contrast to child maltreatment, older adult maltreatment is a relatively neglected area of empirical psychological research, but there is a slow movement to turn more attention to older adult issues.[95]

Conclusion

Domestic violence is commonly not given wide attention in family law texts and is often addressed in separate courses and texts on the topic,[96] but the topics addressed in the current chapter are uniquely family-oriented. Intimate partner violence, child abuse, and elder maltreatment can and do occur outside a family unit, but the ramifications are different when they occur within a family. And, as this chapter has highlighted, psychological research and practice have been foundational in each of these areas of law. In an effort to stretch this area, this chapter provided new foci on topics such as obesity as child neglect and the problems with mandatory reporting of elder abuse.

Conclusion

Closing the Door to the Family Home

As we metaphorically shut the door to the family home with the ending of this book, what can we say collectively that psychology offers family law? Of course, there is the obvious counseling and clinical evaluations, but hopefully this book has opened readers' eyes to the virtually endless ways psychology is, and can be, influential in addressing some of the most difficult and debated family law topics of today and the family law of the future. In some areas, psychological researchers have been actively involved in making empirically sound policies that make the lives of family members better, while in other areas it seems the research has led to more confusion. Still other areas have been neglected entirely and seem ready for careful research examination. One constant seems clear—the concept of a family and the way the law treats families continues to evolve, and psychology can help guide and explain these evolving standards.

The Family Law Education Reform (FLER) Project was a combined effort of law academics and practitioners to address the gap between family law courses and what a lawyer needs to practice family law.[1] Among their recommendations was that family law courses emphasize the need to be able to interact with an interdisciplinary team that includes psychologists and social workers. The report encourages law professors who teach family law courses to embrace the social sciences and to take family law beyond the analytical.[2] Because traditional family law classes almost exclusively focus on appealed litigated cases it gives the impression that litigation in family law is the most common and most important activity a family law attorney will undertake.[3] Yet much of family law practice today does not involve litigated cases, and a family law attorney needs to have a vast array of skills beyond articulating legal arguments in the courtroom. The FLER report emphasized that the past 20 years in family law has seen a sharp increase in the need for family law attorneys to be able to work cooperatively with professionals from social science fields and to think beyond the legal arguments into the emotional and human side of family law matters.[4] The FLER recommended a greater focus on topics such as Alternative Dispute Resolution and domestic violence. Additionally, the report recommended placing family law within the macro context of race, class, gender, age, and power.[5] As such, it emphasized recruiting the next generation of family law attorneys from undergraduate students with backgrounds in psychology or other social sciences because that background would well prepare someone for family law work.[6]

In contrast to what the FLER project indicates law students need, legal scholar Catherine Ross notes that texts on family law include very little social science, which she says does not reflect how important it is for this area of law.[7] Ross also notes that it is time for an updating of classic family law texts to reflect the immense changes within family law that have occurred in the past several decades.[8] Because many of the well-used texts were first editions in the 1970s, the content reflects family law scholarship and practice from that time. But, Ross argues that family law texts should also include information about nonlegal issues such as emotional contexts that assist family law attorneys in understanding and communicating with professionals from other fields that will be integral to their family law practice. Although the current text is not meant to replace a traditional family law text, it does provide supplemental materials that speak to the needs that Ross and the FLER identify.

In addition to supplementing more traditional family law texts with topics the FLER project highlighted as important considerations, the current book set out to articulate psychological research ideas. Family law is a neglected area of law psychology research, yet there are innumerable ways that empirical research could inform and improve systems. Throughout this book those ideas have been highlighted, and new research questions posed. Just as the FLER project encouraged a new crop of family law students, one goal of this book is to encourage a new crop of law psychology researchers to focus their attention on areas within family law that are wide open to empirical inquiry. Combined, the hope is that this book expands the topics addressed in family law courses and by family law scholars and the topics of inquiry in law psychology.

Still, as noted in the introduction to this book, there is no unifying family law theory. There is no simple way to bring all the topics together in a cohesive unit. And, the topics that fall under the umbrella of family law continue to broaden. Family law remains a perfect fit for law psychology inquiry because the law will continue to make behavioral assumptions about people who want to be married, stay married, get out of a marriage, and deal with the aftermath of an ended marriage. There are also behavioral assumptions about raising children and caring for aging parents. Hopefully this book has provided some insights into some of those areas and has provided a gateway to more empirical research. That empirical research can inform the behavioral assumptions the law makes about families, but also the professionals involved in family law decisions such as social workers, judges, lawyers, and psychologists.

It should be noted that the current book has taken a decidedly domestic approach and neglected international comparative law issues. Yet, as technology advances and ease of travel shrink the world and blur the lines between countries, the laws and cultures of other nations are bound to have an impact on U.S. family law even more. Kidnapping across international borders raises questions about the potential harm to the children.[9] Yet, as demonstrated by the comparison of helicopter versus free-range parenting described earlier, harm to children is not easily defined, even within the United States. The area of international comparative family law is sure to be even more important and influential in the decades to come and a fertile area for empirical examination.

The introductory chapter of this book ended with a quote from Carl Schneider and Lee Teitelbaum, so it is fitting to end the book with another quote from the same authors. In their article about empirical scholarship in American law, they note,

> Few areas of law affect human beings as often, as directly, as momentously as family law. Few areas have been so much debated and reformed. Debate and reform have been animated by deep and angry convictions about how people should treat each other, and how the law should treat people. But family law has been restructured with so little information about the way people live and think and about how the law works that

> we have little reason to suppose that the reforms can accomplish their purpose. This cannot be right.[10]

It is hopefully clear from the current book how much human psychology is intertwined within family law. A main goal was for the chapters of this book to bring vividness to the way people live and think in the family home and to provide encouragement to look to psychology to examine and even resolve the thorniest of family law issues. When the door to the family home is opened by the law and there is government intrusion within the family, there will be an impact. Psychology research can help determine if that impact is a necessary and beneficial intervention or if it is more likely to be a negative intrusion that leaves some or all of the family members worse off than before.

ACKNOWLEDGMENTS

I first want to thank the students who took my Psychology and Family Law course, where I began thinking through how I would put these ideas down into a book. Each of those students (Tiffany Bodem, Danielle Schunk, Nathaniel de Leon, Lindsey Wylie, Lori Hoetger, and Brandon Hollister) provided insights that influenced different areas throughout the final product. I especially thank my three graduate students, Lori Hoetger for letting me borrow her casebook (I need to return that!), Katherine Hazen for her tireless wizardry getting my footnotes into appropriate *Bluebook* order or hunting down citations for me, and Emma Marshall who went down many a rabbit hole to find me the perfect citation. Thank you to my other past and present graduate students, Lindsey Wylie, Leroy Scott, and Josh Haby, who patiently waited on me returning e-mails and their papers while I was working on this book. As you know, graduate students are the reason I do what I do, so I hope my neglect did not lead to a kerfuffle in any of your lives.

This book was the brainchild of Linda Dermaine, and I am very proud to be a part of her Psychology and Law series—thank you for the invitation. Thank you to Jennifer Robbennolt for her encouragement along the way and the book example she and Valerie Hans co-authored. NYU publisher Jennifer Hammer is not only encouraging but also patient. She patiently put up with my never-ending need for more time. I also greatly appreciate the detailed responses my two anonymous reviewers provided that guided my finalizations of this project.

I also want to thank Professor Emeritus Alan Frank for introducing me to family law and for being the most compassionate law professor I have ever known. Alan is one of my greatest influences in the way I approach teaching. My high school psychology teacher, Ms. Twyla Humphrey Preising, formally introduced me to psychology, and in her Advanced Placement U.S. History class, she also taught me how to study. The other two people who are my greatest academic influences are Alan

Tomkins and Vicky Weisz. As I always say, Alan can see in me my capabilities long before I can see them in myself and Vicky pushes me along, encouraging me as I feel like I stumble toward my next goal. They teach me not only about academics but also about family life and continue to be an example to me.

Personally, I must thank Sean Self, Angela Highsmith, and Angel Self. As three dear friends I've known more decades than I'd like to admit, Angela, you encouraged me along the way to get this done, Sean, you made me feel so guilty that I was not getting it done sooner, and, Angel, you provided me online retail therapy respite. My Grace Group—Amanda Gonzales, Suzan Lund, and Jenny Keshwani—thank you for asking me about this book and praying for me to get it finished. I thank our nannies, Ms. Colleen, Ms. Jennifer, Ms. Isabella, and Ms. Becca—you helped hold our family together long before I started this book and for that I'm forever grateful. To my bridesmaids, Beth Bargeron, Lori Hart, Lisa Denton, and Carrie Bootcheck, who, more than 20 years ago, helped me navigate my own legal change in status from single to married. Jennifer Groscup, for among innumerable other things, thank you for introducing me to *Unbreakable Kimmy Schmidt*—I turned the mystery crank for 20 minutes at a time and finally got this book done. And Amy Mitchell—from the agricultural library to running marathons to encouragement texts when I was writing—you are my family I have chosen even if you do think I work too much.

Finally, I thank my legal family. My parents demonstrate that some marriages that last more than fifty years can be both passionate and companionate. Their faith in God and our family is my cornerstone. To my husband, Adam, and our daughter, Mabry, you are my favorite idea generators and proofreaders. Thank you for putting up with me talking about needing to write and for doing more than your fair share to keep our family going. Indeed, I have found the ones my soul loves.

For better, for worse, here's my book. —EB

NOTES

INTRODUCTION

1 MARK COSTANZO & DANIEL KRAUSS, FORENSIC AND LEGAL PSYCHOLOGY (3rd ed., 2018).

2 Craig Haney, *Psychology and Legal Change: On the Limits of Factual Jurisprudence*, 4 L. & HUM. BEHAV. 147 (1981).

3 Stephen Parker & Peter Drahos, *Closer to a Critical Theory of Family Law*, 4 AUSTL. J. FAM. L. 159 (1990) (asking whether family law should even be considered a discrete area of law). The authors are describing Australian family law, but most of their points could be directed at U.S. family law as well.

4 Karen S. Adam & Stacey N. Brady, *Fifty Years of Judging in Family Law: The Cleavers Have Left the Building*, 51 FAM. CT. REV. 28 (2013).

5 PEW RESEARCH CENTER, THE DECLINE OF MARRIAGE AND RISE OF NEW FAMILIES (2010).

6 D. KELLY WEISBERG & SUSAN FRELICH APPLETON, MODERN FAMILY LAW: CASES & MATERIALS (4th ed., 2010).

7 BRIAN BIX, THE OXFORD INTRODUCTIONS TO U.S. LAW: FAMILY LAW (Oxford University Press 2013).

8 JENNIFER K. ROBBENNOLT & VALERIE P. HANS, THE PSYCHOLOGY OF TORT LAW (New York University Press 2016); MICHEAL J. SAKS & BARBARA A. SPELLMAN, THE PSYCHOLOGICAL FOUNDATIONS OF EVIDENCE LAW (New York University Press 2016).

9 Weisberg & Appleton, *supra* note 6, at 1.

10 Vivian Hamilton, *Principles of U.S. Family Law*, 75 FORDHAM L. REV. 31 (2006).

11 Bix, *supra* note 7.

12 Bix describes this as backward- versus forward-looking focus and exemplifies the tension with permanent alimony seeming appropriate and just. *Id.*

13 *Id.*

14 JUDITH C. AREEN, CASES AND MATERIALS ON FAMILY LAW (6th ed., Foundation Press 2012).

15 Mary E. O'Connell & J. Herbie DiFonzo, *The Family Law Education Reform Project Final Report*, 44 FAM. CT. REV. 524 (2006).

16 Neil S. Grossman & Barbara F. Okun, *Family Psychology and Family Law: Introduction to the Special Issue*, 17 J. FAM. PSYCHOL. 163 (2003).

17 Steven Breckler, *From the Executive Director: What Everyone Needs to Know about Psychology*, PSYCHOL. SCI. AGENDA (March 2012), www.apa.org.

18 APA Divisions, AM. PSYCHOL. ASS'N (AUG. 18, 2018, 11:18 AM), www.apadivisions.org.

19 *About APA: Society for General Psychology*, AM. PSYCHOL. ASS'N (May 20, 2016, 5:32 PM), www.apa.org.

20 *About APA: American Society for the Advancement of Pharmacotherapy*, AM. PSYCHOL. ASS'N (May 20, 2016, 5:37 PM), www.apa.org.

21 *About APA*, AM. PSYCHOL. ASS'N (May 20, 2016, 5:40 PM), www.apa.org.

22 Robbennolt & Hans, *supra* note 5; Kevin W. Boyack, Richard Klavans, & Katy Borner, *Mapping the Backbone of Science*, 64 SCIENTOMETRICS 351 (2005); John T. Cacioppo, *Psychology Is a Hub Science*, 20 OBSERVER 5 (2007).

23 Boyack et al., *supra* note 22.

24 Robbennolt & Hans, *supra* note 8.

25 James R. P. Ogloff, *Two Steps Forward and One Step Backward: The Law and Psychology Movement(s) in the 20th Century*, 24 L. & HUM. BEHAV. 457 (2000).

26 *Id.*

27 Mark A. Small, *Legal Psychology and Therapeutic Jurisprudence*, ST. LOUIS U. L.J. 675 (1993).; Lindsey E. Wylie, Katherine P. Hazen, Lori A. Hoetger, Joshua A. Haby, & Eve M. Brank, *Four Decades of Psychology and Law: A Content Analysis*, 115 SCIENTOMETRICS 655 (2018).

28 Ogloff, *supra* note 25; Jennifer Skeem, President, AM. PSYCHOL. & L. SOC., Presidential Address at Am. Psychol. & L. Soc. Annual Conference: Innovating Psychology & Law: Tackling Bigger Problems, More Proactively (Mar. 2014); Eve M. Brank, *Elder Research: Filling an Important Gap in Psychology and Law*, 25 BEH. SCI. & L. 701 (2007).

29 See generally Eugene Borgida & Erik J. Girvan, *Social Cognition in Law*, in APA HANDBOOK OF PERSONALITY AND SOCIAL PSYCHOLOGY: ATTITUDES AND SOCIAL COGNITION (Eugene Borgida & John Bargh eds., 2010) (demonstrating the use of social-cognitive principles within legal scholarship and further note that it is the teams of interdisciplinary researchers that are producing the most depth in their analyses).

30 Bix, *supra* note 7, at 19.

31 *Id.*

32 Robert E. Emery et al., *'Bending' Evidence for a Cause: Scholar-Advocacy Bias in Family Law*, 54 FAM. CT. REV. 134 (2016).

33 Clare Huntington, *Essay: The Empirical Turn in Family Law*, 188 COLUM. L. REV. 227 (2018).

34 *Id.* at 303.

35 Evidence-based medicine is an approach meant to optimize decision making by using research evidence. Guyatt et al., *Evidence-based Medicine: New Approach to Teaching the Practice of Medicine*, 268 J. AM. MED. ASS'N. 2420 (1992).

36 PHILIPPE ARIES, CENTURIES OF CHILDHOOD: A SOCIAL HISTORY OF FAMILY LIFE (Robert Baldick trans., Vintage Books 1960).

37 Deborah J. Anthony, *A Spouse by Any Other Name*, 17 WM. & MARY J. WOMEN & L. 187, 189 (2010).

38 Gayle Kaufman, *Do Gender Role Attitudes Matter?: Family Formation and Dissolution Among Traditional and Egalitarian Men and Women*, 21 J. FAM. ISSUES 128 (2000).

39 John Lande & Forrest S. Mosten, *Family Lawyering: Past, Present, and Future*, 51 FAM. CT. REV. 20 (2013).

40 JOANNA L. GROSSMAN & LAWRENCE M. FRIEDMAN, INSIDE THE CASTLE: LAW AND THE FAMILY IN 20TH CENTURY AMERICA 1 (Princeton University Press, 2011).

41 *Id.*

42 *Id.*

43 Carl E. Schneider & Lee E. Teitelbaum, *Life's Golden Tree: Empirical Scholarship and American Law*, 2006 UTAH L. REV. 53, 89 (2006).

CHAPTER 1. BARRIERS TO MARRIAGE

1 Kathy Landin, *15 of the World's Weirdest Marriages, 'I Now Pronounce You . . . What?!,'* THE FW, http://thefw.com; also, *Roller Coaster of Love: The Weirdest Cases of People Marrying Inanimate Objects*, HUFFPOST COMEDY (May 25, 2011, 5:12 AM), www.huffingtonpost.com.

2 The animals ranged from a dolphin to a snake and a goat.

3 That is, the person marries him- or herself (also known as sologomy). One featured person, Liu Ye, married a foam cutout of himself. He said he did so as a way to express his "dissatisfaction with reality."

4 Erika La Tour Eiffel was once in a long-term relationship with a bow and married the Eiffel Tower.

5 Sasjkia Otto, *Woman Getting Married to Fairground Ride*, THE TELEGRAPH (Aug. 5, 2009, 7:00 AM), www.telegraph.co.uk.

6 *Id.*

7 Relevant to the surname discussion in the next chapter—the article indicated that after the wedding took place Miss Wolfe planned to change her last name to that of Weber—the ride's manufacturer. *Id.*

8 Marriage can be defined as a legal and as a social institution. Early American colonies modeled marriage on English ecclesiastical marriage. The church provided divine blessing for the marriage and stood in for the crown for legal recognition. Justin T. Wilson, Note, *Preservationism, or The Elephant in the Room: How Opponents of Same-Sex Marriage Deceive Us into Establishing Religion*, 14 DUKE J. GENDER L. & POL'Y 561, 579 (2007). The New and Old Testaments reference the words *marriage*, *husband*, and *wife* more than 500 times. However, five themes have been identified: companionship, intimacy, husbands love and sacrifice and wives submit, spouses are different but equal, and through the partnership, each spouse should strive to overcome immorality. Mary Fairchild, *What Does the Bible Say About Marriage?: Why Marriage Matters in Christian Life*, ABOUT RELI-

GION, http://christianity.about.com. For example, the Book of Genesis describes the first wedding: "Then the Lord God made a woman from the rib he had taken out of the man, and he brought her to the man. The man said, 'This is now bone of my bones and flesh of my flesh; she shall be called 'woman,' for she was taken out of man.' For this reason a man will leave his father and mother and be united to his wife, and they will become one flesh." *Genesis* 2:21–24 (New International Version).

9 *See, e.g.*, NEB. REV. STAT. § 42–104 (2016). Common law marriages are governed by a different set of requirements.

10 Lawrence A. Frolik & Mary F. Radford, *'Sufficient' Capacity: The Contrasting Capacity Requirements for Different Documents*, 2 NAELA J. 303, 316 (2006); Edmunds v. Edwards, 287 N.W.2d 420 (Neb. 1980) (holding that a cognitively impaired man had sufficient capacity to understand the meaning of the marriage contract at the time of his marriage to another patient at the state institution).

11 U.S. CONST. AMEND. X.

12 Labine v. Vincent, 401 U.S. 532, 538–39 (1971).

13 *In re* Burrus, 136 U.S. 586, 593–94 (1890).

14 The Supreme Court relied on the penumbras of the Bill of Rights to justify the right to privacy in family decision making. Griswold v. Connecticut, 381 U.S. 479 (1965). The Court has also relied on the Due Process and Equal Protection clauses of the Fourteenth Amendment and the First Amendment freedom of association to justify interfering with state regulation of marriage. See Loving v. Virginia, 388 U.S. 1 (1967) and Zablocki v. Redhail, 434 U.S. 374 (1978).

15 See Prince v. Massachusetts, 321 U.S. 158 (1944); Meyer v. Nebraska, 262 U.S. 390 (1923); and Pierce v. Society of Sisters, 268 U.S. 510 (1925).

16 Santosky v. Kramer, 455 U.S. 745, 770 (1982) (Rehnquist, J., dissenting).

17 For example, Justice Kennedy argued, "When homosexual conduct is made criminal by the law of the state, that declaration in and of itself is an invitation to subject homosexual persons to discrimination both in the public and in the private spheres" without reliance on social science research that demonstrates the statement to be true. Lawrence v. Texas, 539 U.S. 558, 575 (2003).

18 MICHAEL GROSSBERG, GOVERNING THE HEARTH: LAW AND THE FAMILY IN NINETEENTH-CENTURY AMERICA (The University of North Carolina Press 1988).

19 Michael Grossberg, *Guarding the Altar: Physiological Restrictions and the Rise of State Intervention in Matrimony*, 26 AM. J. LEG HIST 197 (1982).

20 1959 WASH. SESS. LAWS 736.

21 JOANNA L. GROSSMAN & LAWRENCE M. FRIEDMAN, INSIDE THE CASTLE: LAW AND THE FAMILY IN 20TH CENTURY AMERICA 40 (Princeton University Press 2011). It is beyond the scope of this chapter, but interesting research on social support and people with epilepsy found that marriage may serve as a buffer for the negative impact of epilepsy on self-reported health status. John O. Elliott, Christine Charyton, Peter Strangers, Bo Lu, & J. Layne Moore, *The Impact*

of Marriage and Social Support on Person with Active Epilepsy, 20 EPILEPSY AND BEHAV. 533 (2001).

22 For example, before 2007, a woman under 50 years of age wishing to be married in Montana was required to have a rubella blood test. Today, the test is still required, but brides can opt out. MONT. CODE ANN. § 40-1-203 (2015). Mississippi repealed its blood test requirement in 2012. MISS. CODE ANN. § 93-1-5 (2012).

23 Presumed incapacity from young age is still a barrier to entering marriage and is discussed in the next section.

24 As recently as the middle of the 20th century, a Pennsylvania statute prohibiting the issuance of marriage licenses to parties who are "of unsound mind" was struck down. F.A. Marriage License, 4 Pa. D. & C.2d 1 (1955).

25 SANFORD N. KATZ, FAMILY LAW IN AMERICA (Oxford University Press, 2nd ed. 2014).

26 M.C. Dransfield, Annotation, *Mental Capacity to Marry*, 82 A.L.R.2d 1040 (1962). In fact, the Florida Bill of Rights for Persons with Developmental Disabilities provides that such individuals have the right to education and training in sex education, marriage, and family planning. FLA. STAT. ANN. § 393.13(3)(d) (2010).

27 *See* MASSACHUSETTS DEP'T OF HEALTH & HUMAN SERV., HEALTHY RELATIONSHIPS, SEXUALITY AND DISABILITIES: RESOURCE GUIDE (2014) (providing a list of resources for educators, parents, and individuals on sexuality and relationships for individuals with cognitive impairments) and TERRI COUWENHOVEN, TEACHING CHILDREN WITH DOWN SYNDROME ABOUT THEIR BODIES, BOUNDARIES, AND SEXUALITY (Woodbine House 2007).

28 The Racial Integrity Act of 1924 made it illegal for a White person to marry anyone who was not White or Native American. VA. CODE ANN. §§ 20–57, 20–58, 20–59 (1924).

29 Robert A. Pratt, *Crossing the Color Line: A Historical Assessment and Personal Narrative of Loving v. Virginia*, 41 HOWARD L. J. 229 (1998).

30 Different from many other laws related to marriage, miscegenation laws were a U.S. creation. Harvey M. Applebaum, *Miscegenation Statutes: A Constitutional and Social Problem*, 53 GEO. L. J. 49, 49–50 (1964).

31 Loving v. Virginia, 388 U.S. 1, 6 n. 5 (1967) (Alabama, Arkansas, Delaware, Florida, Georgia, Kentucky, Louisiana, Mississippi, Missouri, North Carolina, Oklahoma, South Carolina, Tennessee, Texas, and West Virginia).

32 KARL E. TAEUBER & ALMA F. TAEUBER, NEGROES IN CITIES: RESIDENTIAL SEGREGATION AND NEIGHBORHOOD CHANGE (Aldine Publishing, Co., 1965).

33 Specifically, support increased for the desegregation of schools. Herbert H. Hyman & Paul B. Sheatsley, *Attitudes Toward Desegregation*, 211 SCI. AM. 16 (1964).

34 David M. Heer, *Negro-white Marriage in the United States*, 28 J. MARRIAGE & FAM. 262, 264–66 (1966).

35 *Id.* at 263.

36 Pratt, *supra* note 29, at 236; PETER WALLENSTEIN, TELL THE COURT I LOVE MY WIFE: RACE, MARRIAGE, AND LAW—AN AMERICAN HISTORY (Palgrave Macmillan 2002); PETER WALLENSTEIN, RACE, SEX, AND THE FREEDOM TO MARRY: LOVING V. VIRGINIA (University Press of Kansas 2014).

37 Loving, 388 U.S. at 2.

38 *Id.* at 12.

39 *Id.*; The Supreme Court opinion noted that the state argued that "scientific evidence is substantially in doubt and, consequently, [the] Court should defer to the wisdom of the state legislature . . ." The state relied on "physical, biological, genetic, anthropological, cultural, psychological and sociological point[s] of view" to argue that "in the absence of any uniform rule as to consequences of race crosses, it is well to discourage it except in those cases where . . . it clearly produces superior progeny, and that the Negro-white and Filpino-European crosses do not seem to fall within the exception." Brief for Appellee at 41–42, Loving v. Virginia, 388 U.S. 1 (1967) (No. 395) 1967 WL 113931.

40 Dorothy L. Martelle, *Interracial Marriage Attitudes Among High School Students*, 27 PSYCHOL. REP. 1007, 1008 (1970) (hypothesizing that "[i]t is probably a safe assumption that disapproval of interracial marriage within the white community is nearly unanimous . . .").

41 The poll in 1958 asked about "marriages between white and colored people," and from 1968 to 1978 the wording was "marriages between whites and nonwhites." Frank Newport, *In U.S., 87% Approve of Black-white Marriage, vs. 4% in 1958*, GALLUP (July 25, 2013), www.gallup.com.

42 DAPHNE LOFQUIST, TERRY LUGAILA, MARTIN O'CONNELL, & SARAH FELIZ, U.S. DEP'T OF COMMERCE, HOUSEHOLDS AND FAMILIES: 2010, 2010 CENSUS BRIEFS, at 17 (2012), www.census.gov.

43 Yanyi K. Djamba & Sitawa R. Kimuna, *Are Americans Really in Favor of Interracial Marriage? A Closer Look at When They Are Asked About Black-white Marriage for Their Relatives*, 45 J. BLACK STUD. 528 (2014).

44 388 U.S. at 12.

45 *Id.*

46 Griswold v. Connecticut, 85 S.Ct. 1678 (1965).

47 At issue in this case was a Wisconsin statute that restricted residents from marrying unless they can prove that their noncustodial children "are not then and are not likely thereafter to become public charges." The Court relied on the Equal Protection Clause with support from the Due Process Clause of the Fourteenth Amendment, holding that "when a classification interferes with a fundamental right, it cannot be upheld unless it is supported by a sufficiently important state interest and is closely tailored to effectuate interests." Zablocki v. Redhail, 98 S.Ct. 673, 675, 682 (1978).

48 Califano v. Jobst, 98 S.Ct. 95 (1977).

49 135 S.Ct. 2584 (2015).

50 Baker v. Nelson, 191 N.W.2d 185 (1971).

51 Brief for Appellant at 11–19, Baker v. Nelson, 93 S.Ct. 37 (1972) (No. 71–1027).
52 Baker v. Nelson, 93 S.Ct. 37 (1972).
53 Bowers v. Hardwick, 106 S.Ct. 2841 (1986).
54 Romer v. Evans, 116 S.Ct. 1620 (1996).
55 Baehr v. Miike, 910 P.2d 112 (1996).
56 HAW. CONST. ART. 1, § 23.
57 Defense of Marriage Act, 28 U.S.C. § 1738C (1996).
58 Baker v. State, 744 A.2d 364 (Vt. 1999).
59 VT. STAT. ANN. TIT. 15, § 8 (2009).
60 Lawrence v. Texas, 123 S.Ct. 2472, 2484 (2003).
61 Goodridge v. Dep't of Pub. Health, 798 N.E.2d 941 (Mass. 2003).
62 *In re* Marriage Cases, 183 P.3d 385 (Cal. 2008).
63 Varnum v. Brien, 763 N.W.2d 862 (Iowa 2009).
64 Lewis v. Harris, 908 A.2d 196 (N.J. 2006); N.J. STAT. ANN. § 37:1–28 (2007).
65 United States v. Windsor, 133 S. Ct. 2675 (2013).
66 Hollingsworth v. Perry, 133 S.Ct. 2652 (2013).
67 Proposition 8 came about because of a May 2008 California Supreme Court case holding that limiting marriage to opposite sex couples was unconstitutional. *In re* Marriage Cases, 183 P.3d 385 (Cal. 2008).
68 135 S.Ct. 2584, 2594 (2015).
69 Brief of the Am. Psychological Ass'n et al. as Amici Curiae Supporting Petitioners, Obergefell v. Hodges, 135 S.Ct. 2584 (2015) (Nos. 14–556, 14–562, 14–571, 14–574), 2015 WL 1004713.
70 *Id.* at 4–5.
71 135 S.Ct. at 2601.
72 As noted earlier, until recently same-sex marriage was an additional barrier.
73 Common law limited marriage to males aged 14 years and older and females aged 12 years and older, with many statutory schemes following the differential age regulation until the Supreme Court struck down a Utah statute that set adulthood for females at 18 years and for males at 21 years based on equal protection. Stanton v. Stanton, 95 S.Ct. 1373 (1975). Ohio still provides differential age requirements for marriage with the minimum legal age with parental consent being 18 for males and 16 for females. Both males and females must be 18 without parental consent. OHIO REV. CODE ANN. §§ 3101.01, .02, .03, .03, .05 (2015). Arkansas sets the minimum age at 16 for females and 17 for males. ARK. CODE ANN. § 9-11-102 (2015).
74 Parental consent is required in Alaska (ALASKA STAT. ANN. § 25.05.171 (2016)), Arkansas (ARK. CODE ANN. § 9-11-102 (2015)), Colorado (COLO. REV. STAT. § 14-2-106(1)(a)(I)(2009)), Idaho (IDAHO CODE ANN. § 32.202 (2016)), Louisiana (LA. CHILD CODE ANN. art. 1545 (2016)), Maine (ME. REV. STAT. tit. 19-A, § 701(3) (2011)), Nevada (NEV. REV. STAT. § 122.025 (2015)), New Jersey (N.J. STAT. ANN. § 37:1–6 (2013)), Ohio for females (OHIO REV. CODE ANN. § 3101.03 (2012)), and Oklahoma (OKLA. STAT. ANN. Tit. 43 § 3 (2016)). Parental

and judicial consent are required in Arizona (ARIZ. REV. STAT. § 25–102 (2016)), Connecticut (CONN. GEN. STAT. § 46b-30 (2016)), and Kansas (KAN. REV. STAT. ANN. § 23–2505 (2016)). Judicial consent and/or parental consent is needed in Georgia (GA. CODE ANN. § 19-3-37 (2006)), Hawaii (HAW. REV. STAT. § 572–1 (2013)), Iowa (IOWA CODE § 595.3 (2016)), Kentucky (KY. REV. STAT. ANN. § 204.210 (2016)), Massachusetts (MASS. GEN. LAWS ch. 207, § 25 (2016)), Minnesota (MINN. STAT. ANN. § 517.02 (2016)), Mississippi (MISS. CODE ANN. § 93-1-5 (2016)), Montana (MONT. CODE ANN. § 40-1-213 (2015)), Ohio for males (OHIO REV. CODE ANN. § 3101.03 (2012)), Texas (TEX. FAM. CODE ANN. § 2.102 (2009)), and Vermont (VT. STAT. ANN. tit. 15 § 8 (2009)).

75 Lynn D. Wardle, *Rethinking Marital Age Restrictions*, 22 J. FAM. L 1 (1983–1984); Kathleen E. Kiernan, *Teenage Marriage and Marital Breakdown: A Longitudinal Study*, 40 POPUL. STUD. 35 (1985); Arland Thornton & Linda Young-DeMarco, *Four decades of trends in attitudes toward family issues in the United States: The 1960s through the 1990s*, 63 J. MARRIAGE & FAM. 1009 (2001).

76 Diana B. Elliott et al., *Presentation at the Population Association of America: Historical Marriage Trends from 1890–2010: A Focus on Race Differences*, SEHSD WORKING PAPER NUMBER 2012–12 (May 3–5, 2012), www.census.gov; Julia Alanen, *Shattering the Silence Surrounding Forced and Early Marriage in the United States*, 32 CHILD. LEGAL RTS. J. 1, 5–6 (2012) (providing a perspective on forced marriages outside the law).

77 PHILIPPE ARIES, CENTURIES OF CHILDHOOD: A SOCIAL HISTORY OF FAMILY LIFE (Robert Baldick trans., Vintage Books 1960).

78 Meryl Hartstein, *Is 60 the New 40?*, HUFF/POST 50: THE BLOG (Nov. 11, 2015, 12:36 PM), www.huffingtonpost.com; Galanty Miller, *40 Is the New 20*, HUFFPOST COMEDY: THE BLOG (July 9, 2015, 4:31 PM), www.huffingtonpost.com.

79 Grossberg, *supra* note 19.

80 "A group health plan and a health insurance issuer offering group or individual health insurance coverage that provides dependent coverage of children shall continue to make such coverage available for an adult child until the child turns 26 years of age." The Patient Protection and Affordable Care Act, 42 U.S.C.A. § 300gg-14(a)(2010).

81 ERIK H. ERIKSON, CHILDHOOD AND SOCIETY (2d ed., WW Norton & Company, Inc., 1963).

82 It should be noted that one of the common critiques of Erikson's theory is that there should be less emphasis on the sequential nature of the stages and focus more on the processes that could occur throughout the lifetime.

83 Rand D. Conger, Ming Cui, Chalandra M. Bryant, & Glen H. Elder, *Competence in Early Adult Romantic Relationships: A Developmental Perspective on Family Influences*, 79 J. PERS. & SOC. PSYCHOL. 224 (2000).

84 Jeffrey Jensen Arnett, *Emerging Adulthood: The Theory of Development from the Late Teens Through the Twenties*, 55 AM. PSYCHOL. 469 (2000).

85 *Id.* at 471–472.

86 *Id.*

87 Rand D. Conger et al., *Competence in Early Adult Romantic Relationships: A Developmental Perspective on Family Influences*, 79 J. PERS. & SOC. PSYCHOL. 224 (2000).

88 Mason G. Haber & Charles A. Burgess, *The Developmental Context of Emerging Adults' Sexuality and Intimate Relationships: A Critical Perspective*, in SEX IN COLLEGE: THE THINGS THEY DON'T WRITE HOME ABOUT 65 (Richard McAnulty, ed., 2012).

89 Gretchen Livingston, *Four-in-ten Couples Are Saying "I Do," Again: Chapter 2: The Demographics of Remarriage*, PEW RESEARCH CENTER (Nov. 14, 2014), www.pewsocialtrends.org.

90 Research that has examined adolescent decision making with regard to marriage has done so within the context of teen pregnancy. *See, e.g.*, Naomi Farber, *The Significance of Race and Class in Marital Decisions Among Unmarried Adolescent Mothers*, 37 SOC. PROBL. 51 (1990).

91 Laurence Steinberg et al., *Are Adolescents Less Mature than Adults?: Minors' Access to Abortion, the Juvenile Death Penalty, and the Alleged APA 'Flip-Flop'*, 64 AM. PSYCHOL. 583 (2009).

92 Hodgson v. Minnesota, 110 S.Ct. 2926 (1990).

93 Exceptions to the two-parent requirement included the presence of parental abuse or neglect or a court order indicating that the minor is "mature and capable of giving informed consent." MINN. STAT. Ann. §§ 144.343(2)-(6)(2004).

94 Brief for Am. Psychological Ass'n et al. as Amicus Curiae Supporting Appellees, Hodgson v. Minnesota, 110 S.Ct. 2926 (1990) (No. 88–805).

95 125 S.Ct. 1183 (2005).

96 Brief for Am. Psychological Ass'n & Mo. Psychological Ass'n as Amicus Curiae Supporting Respondent, Roper v. Simmons, 125 S.Ct. 1183 (2005)(No. 03–633).

97 Steinberg, *supra* note 88, at 584. *See also* Roper v. Simmons, 125 S.Ct. 1183, 1224 (2005) (Scalia, J., dissenting).

98 *Id.* at 586. (noting that many states require a waiting period and counseling for all women seeking abortions). Thirty-five states require women receive counseling before an abortion, 27 of those states also require a waiting period of at least 24 hours. Counseling only: Alaska (ALASKA STAT. ANN. § 18.05.032 (2016)), California (CAL. HEALTH & SAFETY CODE § 124180(2016)), Connecticut (CONN. GEN. STAT. §§ 19a-116, 19a-601 (2016)), Delaware (enforcement permanently enjoined by court) (DEL. CODE ANN. tit. 24, § 1788 (2016)), Florida (FLA. STAT. ANN. § 390.025 (2016)), Maine (ME. REV. STAT. ANN. tit. 22 §§ 1597-A(2)(C), 1599-A (2016)), Nevada (NEV. REV. STAT. § 442.252 (2015)), and Rhode Island (R.I. GEN. LAWS § 23-13-21 (2016)). Both: Alabama (ALA. CODE § 26-21-4 (2016)), Arizona (ARIZ. REV. STAT. ANN. § 36–2152 (2016)), Arkansas (ARK. CODE ANN. § 20-16-1703 (b)(1) (2015)), Georgia (GA. CODE ANN. § 31–9A-3 (2016)), Idaho (IDAHO CODE ANN. § 18–609A (2016)), Indiana (IND. CODE ANN. § 16-34-2-1.1 (2016)), Kansas (KAN. STAT. ANN. § 65–6704 (2016)),

Kentucky (KY. STAT. ANN. § 311.725 (2016)), Louisiana (LA. REV. STAT. ANN. § 40:1299.35.5.2 (2016)), Massachusetts (enforcement permanently enjoined by court)(MASS. GEN. LAWS ch. 112 § 12S (2016)), Michigan (MICH. COMP. LAWS ANN. § 333.17015 (2016)), Minnesota (MINN. STAT. ANN. § 145.4242 (2016)), Mississippi (MISS. CODE ANN. § 41-41-33 (2016)), Missouri (MO. REV. STAT. § 188.028 (2014)), Montana (enforcement permanently enjoined by court)(MONT. CODE ANN. § 50-20-106 (2015)), Nebraska (NEB. REV. STAT. § 71–6903 (2016)), North Carolina (N.C. GEN. STAT. § 90–21.82 (2015)), North Dakota (N.D. CENT. CODE § 14–02.1–03.1 (2015)), Ohio (OHIO REV. CODE ANN. § 2919.12 (2016)), Oklahoma (OKLA. STAT. ANN. tit. 63 § 1–740.2A (2016)), Pennsylvania (18 PA. CONS. STAT. § 3205 (2016)), South Carolina (S.C. CODE ANN. § 44-41-330 (2016)), South Dakota (S.D. CODIFIED LAWS § 34–23A-56 (2016)), Tennessee (TENN. CODE ANN. § 39-15-202 (2016)), Texas (TEX. FAM. CODE ANN. § 171.012 (2015)), Utah (UTAH CODE ANN. § 76-7-305 (2015)), Virginia (VA. CODE ANN. § 18.2–76 (2016)), West Virginia (W. VA. CODE ANN. § 16–2F-3 (2016)), and Wisconsin (WIS. STAT. ANN. § 253.10 (2016)).

99 NAT'L DIST. ATTORNEY'S ASS'N, STATUTORY COMPILATION REGARDING INCEST STATUTES (2013).

100 Immediate family meaning ascendants, descendants, and siblings.

101 Hanan Hamamy et al., *Consanguineous Marriages, Pearls and Perils: Geneva International Consanguinity Workshop Report*, 13 GENET. MED. 841 (2011).

102 *State Laws Regarding Marriages Between First Cousins*, NAT'L CONFERENCE OF STATE LEGISLATURES (2010), www.ncsl.org; Sarah Kershaw, *Shaking off the Shame*, N.Y. TIMES (Nov. 25, 2009), www.nytimes.com.

103 ARIZ. REV. STAT. ANN. § 25–101 (2016); In Illinois the age restriction is 50 years of age with a similar waiver if a party to the marriage is sterile. 750 ILL. COMP. STAT. ANN. 5/212 (2016).

104 FLA. STAT. ANN. § 826.04 (2016).

105 N.C. G.S. § 51–3 (2013). WANT OF CAPACITY; VOID AND VOIDABLE MARRIAGES.

106 ME. REV. STAT. ANN. tit. 19-A, § 701 (2016).

107 Israel v. Allen, 577 P.2d 762 (Colo. 1978).

108 ALA. CODE § 13A-13–3 (2016).

109 KY. REV. STAT. ANN. § 530.020 (2016).

110 The fourth degree would be a first cousin. LA. CIV. CODE ANN. art. 90 (2016).

111 MICH. COMP. LAWS §§ 551.3, 551.4 (2016); N.J. STAT. ANN. § 37:1–1 (2016); R.I. GEN. LAWS §§ 15-1-2, 15-1-3 (2016); S.C. CODE ANN. § 16-15-20 (2016).

112 MICH. COMP. LAWS § 551.3 (2016).

113 *Id.*

114 MONT. CODE ANN. § 40-1-401 (2015) (also includes step family). S.D. CODIFIED LAWS § 25-1-6 (2016).

115 UTAH CODE ANN. § 76-7-102 (2015).

116 TENN. CODE ANN. § 39-15-302 (2016).

117 N.C. GEN. STAT. ANN. § 14–178 (2016).

118 750 ILL. COMP. STAT. ANN. 5/212.

119 *But see* State v. John M., 894 A.2d 376, 394, 95 (Conn. 2006) (striking down the incest statute because it violated guarantees of equal protection, "We can conceive of no rational basis for that distinction . . . between stepfathers who have intercourse with their stepdaughters and stepfathers who have intercourse with their stepson . . .").

120 ARIZ. REV. STAT. ANN. § 25–101; 750 ILL. COMP. STAT. ANN. 5/212 (2016).

121 MASS. GEN. LAWS Ch. 272, § 17 (2013); TEX. PENAL CODE ANN. § 25.02 (2015). To note, the Texas statute refers to contact between the "genitals of one person and the mouth or anus of another person with the intent to arouse or gratify the sexual desire of any person" to be deviate sexual intercourse.

122 Hamamy, *supra* note 101.

123 David P. Schmitt & June J. Pilcher, *Evaluating Evidence of Psychological Adaptation: How Do We Know One When We See One*, 15 PSYCHOL. SCI. 643 (2004).

124 EDWARD WESTERMARCK, THE HISTORY OF HUMAN MARRIAGE (Macmillan and Co., 1891); CLAUDE LEVI-STRAUSS, ELEMENTARY STRUCTURES OF KINSHIP (Beacon Press, 1969). Of course, Sigmund Freud is famously known for arguing that incest would not be such a taboo if there were not the urges toward incest.

125 Katz, *supra* note 25.

126 R. Chris Fraley & Michael J. Marks, *Westermarck, Freud, and the Incest Taboo: Does Familial Resemblance Activate Sexual Attraction?* PERSON. & SOC. PSYCHOL. B. (2010). *But see* Daniel E. Lieberman, THE EVOLUTION OF THE HUMAN HEAD (Harvard University Press, 2011).

127 Jan Antfolk, Debra Lieberman, & Pekka Santtila, *Fitness Costs Predict Inbreeding Aversion Irrespective of Self-involvement: Support for Hypotheses Derived from Evolutionary Theory*, 7 PLOS ONE (2012).

128 123 S. Ct. 2472 (2003).

129 Lowe v. Swanson, 663 F.3d 258 (6th Cir. 2011).

130 Ashley P. Turner, *Incest, Inbreeding, and Intrafamilial Conflict: Analyzing the Boundaries of Sexual Permissiveness in Modern North America*, 12 SEX. & CULT. 38 (2007).

131 In fact, there are cases of accidental incest from sperm donor kids—the *New York Times* did a story about 100-kid cluster. Jaqueline Mroz, *One Sperm Donor, 150 Offspring*, N.Y. TIMES (Sept. 5, 2011), www.nytimes.com.

132 Toni Falbo & Letitia Anne Peplau, *Power Strategies in Intimate Relationships*, 38 J. PERS. & SOC. PSYCHOL. 618 (1980).

133 Mary J. Phillips Green, *Sibling Incest*, 10 FAM. J.: COUNSELING & THERAPY FOR COUPLES & FAM. 195 (2002).

134 Johannes Kinzl & Wilfried Biebl, *Long-term Effect of Incest: Life Events Triggering Mental Disorders in Female Patients with Sexual Abuse in Childhood*, 16 CHILD ABUSE & NEG. 567 (1992).

135 Potter v. Murray City, 760 F.2d 1065, 1070 (10th Cir. 1985).

136 98 U.S. 145 (1878).

137 *Id.* at 166.

138 However, note that polygamy was repudiated by the Church of Latter Day Saints (LDS) when Utah became a state (LDS is the modern name for the Mormon Church).

139 Hannah Parry, *Polygamist Reality TV Star Kody Brown Divorces His 'Official' Wife so He Can Marry Youngest of His Four 'Brides,'* THE DAILY MAIL (Feb. 3, 2015, 1:38 PM), www.dailymail.co.uk.

140 UTAH CODE ANN. § 76-7-101 (2016).

141 Erin Alberty, *Police Probe 'Sister Wives' Stars for Polygamy*, THE SALT LAKE TRIBUNE (Sept. 28, 2010, 11:48 AM), http://archive.sltrib.com.

142 Jonathan Turley, *Brown Family Challenges Utah's Polygamy Law*, RES IPSA LOQUITUR (July 13, 2011), https://jonathanturley.org.

143 Brown v. Buhman, 2016 U.S. App. LEXIS 6571 (10th Cir. 2016).

144 This text uses the generic term of *polygamy* to refer to both polygyny (i.e., one man with multiple wives) and polyandry (i.e., one woman with multiple husbands).

145 Alean Al-Krenawi & John R. Graham, *A Comparison of Family Functioning, Life and Marital Satisfaction, and Mental Health of Women in Polygamous and Monogamous Marriages*, 52 INT. J. SOC. PSYCHIATR. 5 (2006).

146 Melissa H. Manley, Lisa M. Diamond, & Sari M. van Anders, *Polyamory, Monoamory, and Sexual Fluidity: A Longitudinal Study of Identity and Sexual Trajectories*, 2 PSYCHOL. SEX. ORIENTAT. & GEN. DIVERS. 168 (2015).

147 Nicole Graham, *Polyamory: A Call for Increased Mental Health Professional Awareness*, 43 ARCH. SEX. BEHAV. 1031 (2014).

148 GERI WEITZMAN, JOY DAVIDSON, & ROBERT A. PHILLIPS, NAT'L COAL. SEXUAL FREEDOM, WHAT PSYCHOLOGY PROFESSIONALS SHOULD KNOW ABOUT POLYAMORY (2009–2010).

149 Emily H. Page, *Mental Health Services Experiences of Bisexual Women and Bisexual Men: An Empirical Study*, 4 J. BISEXUALITY 137 (2004).

150 Weitzman et al., *supra* note 148.

151 Pamela J. Kalbfleisch, *Deceptive Message Intent and Relational Quality*, 20 J. LANG. & SOC. PSYCHOL. 214 (2001).

152 Blair v. Blair, 147 S.W.3d 882 (Mo. Ct. App. W. Dist. 2004).

153 *In re* Marriage of Meagher & Maleki, 131 Cal. App. 4th 1, 9 (Cal. Ct. App. 2005) *citing* Marshall v. Marshall, 212 Cal. 736, 738 (Cal. 1931) (stating that the fraud must go to the essence of the marital agreement).

154 *Meagher*, 131 Cal. App. 4th at 7.

155 Wolfe v. Wolfe, 378 N.E.2d 1181 (Ill. App. Ct. 1979). *See also In re* Marriage of Farr, 228 P.3d 267 (Colo. App. 2010).

156 Kerry Abrams, *Marriage Fraud*, 100 Calif. L. Rev. 1 (2012).

157 8 U.S.C. § 1186a (2016).

158 Abrams, *supra* note 150, *citing* Nina Bernstein, *Could Your Marriage Pass the Test?*, CITY ROOM BLOG (June 11, 2010, 8:45 PM), http://cityroom.blogs.nytimes.com (describing instances where questions about the color of toothbrushes and whether their microwave is stationary or has a revolving plate).

159 Pratikshya Bohra-Mishra & Douglas S. Massey, *Intermarriage Among New Immigrants in the USA*, 38 ETHNIC & RACIAL STUD. 734 (2015).

160 *Several Indians, Indian Americans Indicted in Massive U-Visa, Marriage Fraud in the US*, THE AMERICAN BAZAAR (May 19, 2016), www.americanbazaaronline.com.

161 Some scholars do suggest obtaining a legal order of voidness would decrease potential confusion.

162 Grossman, *supra* note 21.

163 Jill D. Duba & Richard F. Ponton, *Catholic Annulment, an Opportunity for Healing and Growing: Providing Support in Counseling*, 31 J. PSYCHOL. & CHRIST. 242 (2012).

164 Michael Grossberg, *Balancing Acts: Crisis, Change, and Continuity in American Family Law, 1890–1990*, 28 IND. L.J. 273 (1995).

165 Maynard v. Hill, 8 S. Ct. 723, 729 (1888).

CHAPTER 2. LEADING UP TO MARRIAGE AND FAMILY

1 MARTHA T. ROTH, LAW COLLECTIONS FROM MESOPOTAMIA AND ASIA MINOR (2nd ed., Scholars Press, 1997).

2 *Id.* at 107.

3 *Id.*

4 *Id.* at 113.

5 *Id.* at 101.

6 James Henry Breasted, *The First Through the Seventeenth Dynasties*, in ANCIENT RECORDS OF EGYPT, VOL 1 (University of Illinois Press, 2001).

7 *Proverbs* 22:6 (English Standard Version).

8 43 ELIZ. 1, C. 2, § VI (1601); 39 ELIZ. 1, C. 3, § VII (1597); 18 ELIZ. 1, C. 3, § 1 (1576).

9 Plato, REPUBLIC, (C.D.C. Reeve, trans., Hackett Publishing Co. 3rd ed., 2004).

10 John R. Gillis, *Marriages of the Mind*, 66 J. MARRIAGE & FAM. 988, 988 (2004).

11 Only a few years ago no unmarried couples were eligible to receive health insurance benefits, but that is changing, and some employers are providing insurance benefits to domestic partners. Most of the change, however, has been propelled by the same-sex marriage proponent rather than the cohabitating heterosexual couples. Lexis Explanation IRC Sec 1(a) *Married Individuals Filing Joint Returns and Surviving Spouses.*

12 The Bachelor (ABC television broadcast Mar. 25, 2002.) *About the Bachelor*, ABC, http://abc.go.com (last visited May 22, 2016).

13 Julie Wayne, *How Many 'Bachelor' and 'Bachelorette' Couples Actually Make It?*, WETPAINT (May 23, 2016, 5:30 PM), www.wetpaint.com.

14 Jaclyn Hendricks, *'The Bachelorette' Is All a Lie*, NEW YORK POST (July 22, 2015, 9:42 PM), http://nypost.com.
15 *See* William R. Jankowiak & Edward F. Fischer, *A Cross-cultural Perspective on Romantic Love*, 31 ETHNOLOGY 149 (1992).
16 Martin King Whyte, *Choosing Mates—the American Way*, 29 SOC'Y 71 (1992).
17 *Id.* at 71.
18 *Id.* at 71. Of course, many immigrant groups brought arranged marriage traditions with them to the United States with some resulting in child abuse charges when under age brides are committed to older men. *E.g.*, Margaret Talbot, *Baghdad on the Plains*, THE NEW REPUBLIC, Aug. 11, 1997, at 18 (describing an immigrant family from Iraq).
19 Cas Wouters, SEX AND MANNERS: FEMALE EMANCIPATION IN THE WEST, 1890–2000 (Sage Publications 2004).
20 Whyte, *supra* note 16, at 71–72.
21 Wouters, *supra* note 19.
22 Whyte, *supra* note 16, at 73.
23 Beth Bailey, *From Front Porch to Back Seat: A History of the Date*, 18 MAG. HIST. 23 (2004). Not only could they do this, but some also had to as more young women were living in apartments with other women in urban centers. No parlors or front porches were available.
24 Margaret Mead described pre-war dating of the 1940 as "competitive game" for popularity and protection. Wouters, *supra* at note 19, at 94.
25 Leon R. Kass, *The End of Courtship*, 126 PUB. INT. 39, 41 (1997).
26 Willard Waller, *The Rating and Dating Complex*, 2 AM. SOC. REV. 727, 730 (1937). Some scholars call into question the timeframe and ubiquity of Waller's described dating system. See Michael Gordon, *Was Waller Ever Right? The Rating and Dating Complex Reconsidered*, 43 J. MARRIAGE & FAM. 67 (1981).
27 Bailey, *supra* note 23, at 24.
28 Bailey, *supra* note 23, at 24–25.
29 Dolf Zillmann, *Mood Management Through Communication Choices*, 31 AM. BEHAV. SCI. 327 (1988).
30 Donald G. Dutton & Arthur P. Aron, *Some Evidence for Heightened Sexual Attraction Under Conditions of High Anxiety*, 30 J. PERS. & SOC. PSYCHOL. 510 (1974). However, other research has demonstrated that negative emotions like fear will not be transferred to positive ones like attraction. Instead, positive emotions are transferred to positive and negative to negative. If that is the case, then perhaps it was the positive patriotic emotions that led to the positive attractions and more marriages. Mark P. Zanna, E. Troy Higgins, & Peter A. Taves, *Is Dissonance Phenomenologically Aversive?*, 12 J. EXP. SOC. PSYCHOL. 530 (1976).
31 See Chapter 4 for a detailed discussion about birth control in the United States.
32 Roe v. Wade, 93 S.Ct. 705 (1973).
33 DONNA FREITAS, THE END OF SEX: HOW HOOKUP CULTURE IS LEAVING A GENERATION UNHAPPY, SEXUALLY UNFULFILLED AND CONFUSED ABOUT INTIMACY (Basic Books 2013).

34 Zhana Vrangalova, *Hooking Up and Psychological Well-being in College Students: Short-term Prospective Links Across Different Hookup Definitions*, 52 J. SEX RES. 485 (2014).

35 *Id.*

36 Hanna Rosin, *Boys on the Side*, THE ATLANTIC, September 2012; Elizabeth Armstrong & Laura Hamilton, *Gendered Sexuality in Adulthood: Double Binds and Flawed Options,* 23 GEN. & SOC'Y. 589, 599 (2009). Interview with college-aged women found women saying that they did not want to invest the time in a serious relationship and preferred doing other things with their time.

37 A Title IX complaint was filed at Yale University alleging a hostile sexual environment for failure to adequately respond to a number of incidents, including the Delta Kappa Epsilon frat chanting, "No means yes! Yes means anal!" Jordi Gasso, *Yale Under Federal Investigation for Possible Title IX Violations*, YALE NEWS (April 2, 2011, 10:32 AM), http://yaledailynews.com.

38 Rosin, *supra* note 36.

39 Segan argues that online dating never was only for geeks except during the early years of the Internet when only the most computer-savvy had Internet access. Sascha Segan, *Love, Internet Style*, OPINIONS, PC MAGAZINE DIGITAL EDITION (February, 2014).

40 Nancy Jo Sales, *Tinder and the Dawn of the "Dating Apocalypse,"* VANITY FAIR CULTURE, August 31, 2015; Some research also suggests that more frequent viewing of pornography is related to having more sexual partners. Scott R. Braithwaite et al., *The Influence of Pornography on Sexual Scripts and Hooking Up Among Emerging Adults in College*, 44 ARCH. SEX BEHAV. 111 (2015). Of course, the availability of pornography can be traced to the Internet.

41 Indeed, litigation has even resulted because of such falsification through online dating (*e.g.*, Carafano v. Metrosplash.com, 339 F.3d 1119 (9th Cir. 2003); Dow v. Sexsearch.com, 502 F. Supp. 2d 719 (N.D. Ohio 2007).

42 Simine Vazire & Matthias R. Mehl, *Knowing Me, Knowing You: The Accuracy and Unique Predictive Validity of Self-ratings and Other-ratings of Daily Behavior*, 95 J. PERS. & SOC. PSYCHOL. 1202 (2008).

43 Emily Pronin, Thomas Gilovich, & Lee Ross, *Objectivity in the Eye of the Beholder: Divergent Perceptions of Bias in Self Versus Other*, 111 PSYCHOL. REV. 781 (2004).

44 *Id.* at 791.

45 DAN SLATER, LOVE IN THE TIME OF ALGORITHMS (Penguin Group 2013).

46 CHRISTIAN RUDDER, DATACLYSM: WHO WE ARE (WHEN WE THINK NO ONE'S LOOKING (Crown 2014).

47 TINDER, www.gotinder.com (last visited May 23, 2016). Ironically, a co-founder of Tinder, Whitney Wolfe, sued the company after she alleged sexual harassment by Justin Mateen. The case settled with neither party admitting wrongdoing. Maya Kosoff, *Report: Outed Tinder Cofounder Settled Her Sexual Harassment Lawsuit Against the Company for 'Just over $1 Million,'* BUSINESS INSIDER (Nov. 4, 12:19 PM), www.businessinsider.com.

48 Austin Carr, *I Found Out my Secret Internal Tinder Rating and Now I Wish I Hadn't*, TECHNOLOGY, FAST COMPANY (Jan. 11, 2016, 6:00 AM), www.fastcompany.com.

49 Karen Dion, Ellen Berscheid, & Elaine Walster, *What Is Beautiful Is Good*. 24 J. PERSON. & SOC. PSYCHOL. 285 (1972).

50 Robert P. Burriss, Lisa L.M. Welling, & David A. Puts, *Men's Attractiveness Predicts their Preferences for Female Facial Femininity When Judging for Short-term, but not Long-term, Partners*. 50 PERSON. & IND. DIFF. 542 (2011).

51 Freitas, *supra* note 33.

52 Anne Campbell, *The Morning After the Night Before: Affective Reactions to One-night Stands Among Mated and Unmated Women and Men*. 19 HUM. NAT. 157 (2008); Elaine M. Eshbaugh & Gary Gute, *Hookups and Sexual Regret Among College Women*, 148 J. SOC. PSYCHOL. 77 (2008).

53 Janice Hiller, *Speculations on the Links Between Feelings, Emotions and Sexual Behavior: Are Vasopressin and Oxytocin Involved?* 19 SEX. & RELAT. THERAPY 393 (2004).

54 William F. Flack, Jr. et al., *Some Types of Hookups May Be Riskier than Others for Campus Sexual Assault*. PSYCHOL. TRAUMA: THEORY, RES., PRAC., AND POL'Y. (2015).

55 Wendy D. Manning, Peggy C. Giordano, & Monica A. Longmore, *Hooking Up: The Relationship Contexts of "Nonrelationship" Sex*, 21 J. ADOLESCENT RES. 459 (2006).

56 Zhana Vrangalova, *Hooking Up and Psychological Well-being in College Students: Short-term Prospective Links Across Different Hookup Definitions*, 52 J. SEX RES. 485 (2015).

57 *Id.* at 487. Vrangalova examined casual sexual relationships across three lengths of relationship—onetime occurrences, longer causal relationships, and nonromantic instances—and, furthermore, across four levels of physical intimacy: prolonged kissing, genital touching, oral sex, and intercourse.

58 GALENA K. RHOADES & SCOTT M. STANLEY, NAT'L MARRIAGE PROJECT REPORT, BEFORE "I DO": WHAT DO PREMARITAL EXPERIENCES HAVE TO DO WITH MARITAL QUALITY AMONG TODAY'S YOUNG ADULTS? 9 (2014).

59 Joanne Sweeny, *Undead Statutes: The Rise, Fall, and Continuing Uses of Adultery and Fornication Criminal Laws*, 46 LOYOLA U. CHICAGO L. J. 127 (2013).

60 City of Ontario v. Quon, 130 S. Ct. 2619 (2010).

61 Alex Stone, *Woman Sues Match.com over Sex Assault*, ABC NEWS (April 14, 2011) http://abcnews.go.com.

62 Packingham v. North Carolina, 137 S. Ct. 368 (2017).

63 Taryn Hillin, *'Ring Cam' Lets You Record a Marriage Proposal Without Lifting a Finger*, HUFFPOST WEDDINGS (July 25, 2014, 6:57 PM), www.huffingtonpost.com. Based on the information provided on the company's website, the Ring Cam project began as an engineering design project at Hope College. Four college students got the idea for it because several of their friends were plan-

ning engagements and no doubt feeling the pressure to make the engagement something memorable. Marketing of the Ring Cam seems to be exclusively for heterosexual marriages with men proposing to women. As its commercial tag lines state, "What if you could keep the face you will never forget when *she* said yes" (emphasis added). RING CAM, www.ringcam.com (last visited May 25, 2016).

64 Couples spend an average of $4,000 on engagement rings. Tara Siegel Bernard, *With Engagement Rings, Love Meets Budget*, N. Y. TIMES (Jan. 31, 2014), www.nytimes.com.

65 *See* Maressa Brown, *16 Best Viral Marriage Proposals of All Time*, CAFEMOM (Feb. 14, 2014, 12:22 PM), http://thestir.cafemom.com; *and see* THE KNOT, HOW HE ASKED, http://howheasked.com (last visited Dec. 22, 2016).

66 JONATHAN HAIDT, THE HAPPINESS HYPOTHESIS: FINDING MODERN TRUTH IN ANCIENT WISDOM (Basic Books, 2006).

67 Robert J. Sternberg, *A Triangular Theory of Love*, 93 PSYCHOL. REV. 119 (1986).

68 *Id.*

69 Erica B. Slotter, Wendi L. Gardner, & Eli J. Finkel, *Who Am I Without You? The Influence of Romantic Breakup on the Self-concept*, 36 PERS. SOC. PSYCHOL. B. 147 (2010).

70 Scott M. Monroe et al., *Life Events and Depression in Adolescence: Relationship Loss as a Prospective Risk Factor for First Onset of Major Depressive Disorder*, 108 J. ABNORM. PSYCHOL. 606 (1999); Gary W. Lewandowski, & Nicole M. Bizzoco, *Addition Through Subtraction: Growth Following the Dissolution of a Low Quality Relationship*, 2 J. POSIT. PSYCHOL. 40 (2007).

71 Theodore W. Cousens, *Law of Damages as Applied to Breach of Promise of Marriage*, 17 CORNELL L. Q. 367 (1932).

72 William B. Eldridge, *Domestic Relations—Breach of Promise Actions*, 21 TENN. L. REV. 451 (1950); Indiana was the first in 1935. IND. CODE ANN. 34-12-2-2(b) (LexisNexis 2016).

73 *But see* Bradley v. Somers, 283 S.C. 365, 366–68, 322 S.E.2d. 665, 666 (S.C. 1984) (upholding the cause of action but noting that with the way society treats marriages today this cause of action is not defensible).

74 *See* Campbell v. Robinson, 398 S.C. 12, 726 S.E.2d. 221 (S.C. Ct. App. 2012).

75 KAYNE WEST, *Gold Digger, on* LATE REGISTRATION (Def Jam 2005).

76 Sanetta Tanaka, *Nothing Says Love Like a Prenup*, THE WALL STREET JOURNAL (Nov. 1, 2013); Kelli B. Grant, *Prenups: Not Just for the 1 Percent*, CNBC (Jan. 20, 2015, 4:12 PM), www.cnbc.com.

77 Robyn Tellefsen, *Millennials are Seeking Prenups—and it Might Just be Worth Considering*, SOFI (Mar. 1, 2017), www.sofi.com; Rachel Rowan, *Getting Married? Consider a Student Loan Prenup*, TUITION.IO (April 23, 2013), www.tuition.io.

78 Peter T. Leeson & Joshua Pierson, *Prenups*, 45 J. LEGAL STUD. 367 (2013).

79 UNIFORM PREMARITAL AGREEMENT ACT § 9 (2012). *See also* Simone v. Simone, 581 A.2d 162 (Pa. 1990).

80 Marriage of Bernard, 204 P.3d 907 (Wash. 2009) (finding agreement "involuntary" when, among other reasons, significantly revised version of the agreement was presented three days before the wedding).
81 Potts v. Potts, 303 S.W.3d 177 (Ct. App. Mo. 2010).
82 Vera Hoorens, *Self-enhancement and Superiority Biases in Social Comparison*, 4 EUR. J. SOC. PSYCHOL. 113 (2011). Also referred to as the Lake Wobegon Effect. D. Koretz, *Arriving at Lake Wobegon: Are Standardized Achievement Tests Exaggerating Advancement and Distorting Educational Instruction?*, 74 J. APPL. PSYCHOL. 411 (1989).
83 Marie Helweg-Larsen & James A. Shepperd, *Do Moderators of the Optimistic Bias Effect Personal or Target Risk Estimates? A Review of the Literature*, 5 PERS. SOC. PSYCHOL. REV. 74 (2001); Neil D. Weinstein, *Unrealistic Optimism About Future Life Events*, 39 J. PERS. SOC. PSYCHOL. 806 (1980); Neil D. Weinstein & William M. Klein, *Resistance of Personal Risk Perceptions to Debiasing Interventions*, 14 HEALTH PSYCHOL. 132 (1995).
84 Bram P. Buunk & Regina J.J.M. van den Eijnden, *Perceived Prevalence, Perceived Superiority, and Relationship Satisfaction: Most Relationship Are Good, but Ours Is the Best*, 23 PERS. SOC. PSYCHOL. B. 219 (1997).
85 Lynn A. Baker & Robert E. Emery, *When Every Relationship Is Above Average: Perceptions and Expectations of Divorce at the Time of Marriage*, 17 L. & HUM. BEHAV. 439 (1993).
86 Sam Margulies, *The Psychology of Prenuptial Agreements*, 31 J. PSYCHIAT. & LAW 415 (2003).
87 Florence Kaslow, *Enter the Prenuptial: A Preclude to Marriage or Remarriage*, 9 BEHAV. SCI. & L. 375 (1991).
88 Although the topic of surnames is not always included in traditional family law texts, it is a particularly relevant topic at the intersection of psychology and law. As this section details, human behavior led to the imposition of legal requirements and the eventual tearing down of those same legal rules.
89 Deborah J. Anthony, *A Spouse by Any Other Name*, 17 WM. & MARY J. WOMEN & L. 187, 191 (2010).
90 Julia C. Lamber, *A Married Woman's Surname: Is Custom Law?*, 1973 WASH. U. L. Q. 779 (1973).
91 Anthony, *supra* note 89, at 187. As Anthony notes, even the English royalty did not have a last name until 1917 when they adopted the name Windsor to distinguish themselves from the Germans during World War I.
92 Elizabeth F. Emens, *Changing Name Changing: Framing Rules and the Future of Marital Names*, 74 U. CHI. L. REV. 761, 772 (2007). *E.g.*, Forbush v. Wallace, 341 F.Supp. 217, 221 (N.D. Ala. 1971); *In re* Kayaloff, 9 F.Supp. 176 (S.D.N.Y. 1934); People *ex rel.* Rago v. Lipsky, 63 N.E.2d. 642 (Ill. App. Ct. 1945).
93 Anthony, *supra* note 89, at 196.
94 For example, in most areas where Spanish is the dominate language, a name contains elements from both the mother's and father's names. Traditionally, indi-

viduals have their given name (or first name), the name their father gained from their grandfather, and the name their mother gained from their grandmother. For example, if Juan Lopez Marcos married Maria Covas Callas, any child could be Mario Lopez Covas. From an English perspective, it appears that in modern-day Spain, the surnames follow the matriarchal line because the last name is from the mother. Gerald Erichsen, *Spanish Surnames*, ABOUT EDUCATION (Dec. 10, 2014), http://spanish.about.com.

95 Forbush v. Wallace, 1972 405 U.S. 970 (1972). This case was a class action lawsuit contesting an Alabama regulation that required married women to have their drivers' licenses issued in their husband's last names. The federal district court upheld the regulation and the Supreme Court upheld that decision with no opinion.

96 Emens, *supra* note 92.

97 *See, e.g.*, OR. REV. STAT. § 106.220 (2015). *See* Priscilla R. MacDougall, *The Right of Women to Name Their Children*, 3 L. & INEQ. 91, 109 (1985); Amanda Black, *How to Change Your Last Name After the Wedding*, THE KNOT, www.theknot.com (last visited May 29, 2016).

98 Claudia Goldin & Maria Shim, *Making a Name: Women's Surnames at Marriage and Beyond*, 18 J. ECON. PERSP. 143 (2004); Michele Hoffnung, *What's in a Name? Marital Name Choice Revisited*, 55 SEX ROLES 817 (2006).

99 Anthony, *supra* note 89.

100 *See, e.g.*, N.D. CENT. CODE § 14-03-20.1 (2015).

101 Kelly Snyder, *All Names Are Not Equal: Choice of Marital Surname Change and Equal Protection*, 30 WASH. U. J.L. & POL'Y 561 (2009).

102 *Id.*; Michael Slade, *Who Wears the Pants? The Difficulties Men Face When Trying to Take Their Spouse's Surname After Marriage*, 53 FAM. CT. REV. 336 (2015).

103 Additionally, it ignores same-sex unions. *See* Slade, *supra* note 102, at 337.

104 *Advice: Addressing & Sending Wedding Invitations*, EMILY POST, http://emilypost.com (last visited on April 5, 2016).

105 Daniel Kahneman, Jack L. Knetsch & Richard H. Thaler, *Experimental Tests of the Endowment Effect and the Coase Theorem*, 98 J. POLIT. ECON. 1325 (1990).

106 Amos Tversky & Daniel Kahneman, *Rational Choice and the Framing of Decisions*, in 56 MULTIPLE CRITERIA DECISION MAKING AND RISK ANALYSIS USING MICROCOMPUTERS 81 (Birsen Karpak & Stanley Zionts, eds., 1989); Sankar Sen & Lauren G. Block, *'Why My Mother Never Threw Anything Out': The Effect of Product Freshness on Consumption*, 36 J. CONSUM. RES. 47 (2009).

107 Emens, *supra* note 92.

108 BEYONCE KNOWLES, *Single Ladies (Put a Ring on It)*, on I AM . . . SASHA FIERCE (Columbia Records, 2008).

109 Wendy Wang & Kim Parker, *Record Share of Americans Have Never Married: As Values, Economics and Gender Patterns Change*, PEW RESEARCH CENTER (Sept. 24, 2014), www.pewsocialtrends.org; Shelly Lundberg & Robert A. Pollak, *The Evolving Role of Marriage: 1950–2010*, 25 FUTURE CHILD. 29 (2015).

110 Wang & Parker, *supra* note 109.

111 THE NAT'L MARRIAGE PROJECT, KAY HYMOWTIZ, JASON S. CARROLL, W. BRADFORD WILCOX, & KELLEEN KAYE, KNOT YET: BENEFITS AND COSTS OF DELAYED MARRIAGE IN AMERICA 23–25 (2013).
112 Marsha Garrison, *Nonmarital Cohabitation: Social Revolution and Legal Regulation*, 42 FAM. L. Q. 309, 331 (2008).
113 Martha L. Fineman, *Law and Changing Patterns of Behavior: Sanctions on Nonmarital Cohabitation*, 1981 WIS. L. REV. 275 (1981). As recently as April 2016, the state of Florida had a ban on cohabitation. FLA. STAT. § 798.02 (2016). Michigan and Mississippi both still have laws criminalizing cohabitation. MICH. COMP. LAWS ANN. § 750.335 (2016); MISS. CODE ANN. § 97-29-1 (2016).
114 Larry Bumpass & Hsien-Hen Lu, *Trends in Cohabitation and Implications for Children's Family Contexts in the United States*, 54 POP. STUD. J. DEMOG. 29 (2000).
115 Garrison, *supra* note 112, at 312–13.
116 Daniel T. Lichter & Zhenchoa Qian, *Serial Cohabitation and the Marital Life Course*, 70 J. MARRIAGE FAM. 861 (2008).
117 Claire M. Kamp Dush, Catherine L. Cohan, & Paul R. Amato, *The Relationship Between Cohabitation and Marital Quality and Stability: Change Across Cohorts?*, 65 J. MARRIAGE FAM. 539 (2003).
118 *See* Thomas DeLeire & Ariel Kalil, *How Do Cohabitating Couples With Children Spend Their Money?*, 67 J. MARRIAGE FAM. 286 (2005); Pamela J. Smock, Wendy D. Manning, & Meredith Porter, *'Everything's There Except Money': How Money Shapes Decisions to Marry Among Cohabitors*, 67 J. MARRIAGE. FAM. 680 (2005); Lichter & Qian, *supra* note 116; Rhoades & Stanley, *supra* note 58, at 10.
119 Jennifer K. Robbennolt & Monica Kirkpatrick Johnson, *Legal Planning for Unmarried Committed Partners: Empirical Lessons for a Preventative and Therapeutic Approach*, 41 ARIZ. L. REV. 417 (1999).
120 Meg Jay, *The Downside of Cohabiting Before Marriage*, N.Y. TIMES (April 14, 2012), www.nytimes.com.
121 Chiung-Ya Tang, Melissa Curran, & Analisa Arroyo, *Cohabitators Reasons for Living Together, Satisfaction with Sacrifices, and Relationship Quality*, 50 MARRIAGE & FAM. REV. 598, 613 (2014).

CHAPTER 3. GETTING, BEING, AND STAYING MARRIED

1 FRANK SINATRA, *Love and Marriage*, on THIS IS SINATRA! (Capitol Records 1955).
2 Rachel B. Tambling & Tatiana Glebova, *Preferences of Individuals in Committed Relationships About Premarital Counseling*, 41 AM. J. FAM. THER. 330, 335 (2013).
3 Louisiana and Arizona require counseling if the couple wants a covenant marriage. LA. REV. STAT. ANN. § 9:275.C.1.b.i. (2017); ARIZ. REV. STAT. § 25–902 (2017). In 2014, there was a ballot initiative in Colorado to require 10 hours of education for a first marriage, 20 for a second, and 30 for a third. However, the ballot initiative did not submit enough signatures to move the ballot forward.

Kate Gibbons, *Colorado Ballot Measure Proposes Education Classes to Marry*, THE DENVER POST (Jan. 19, 2014, 1:03 PM), www.denverpost.com.

4 Florida, Maryland, Minnesota, Oklahoma, and Tennessee provide a discount to their license fee if the couple participates in a Premarital Preparation course. FLA. STAT. § 741.0305(2017), MD. CODE ANN. FAM. LAW § 2–404.1 (2017), MINN. STAT. § 517.08. 1b.b. (2017), OKLA. STAT. ANN. tit. 43 § 5.1 (2017), TENN. CODE ANN. § 36-6-413.b.2 (2017). Georgia waives the fee. GA. CODE ANN. § 19-3-30.1 (2016).

5 Christine E. Murray, *Professional Responses to Government-endorsed Premarital Counseling*, 40 MARRIAGE & FAM REV. 53 (2006).

6 Justin A. Lavner, Benjamin R. Karney, & Thomas N. Bradbury, *Newlyweds' Optimistic Forecasts of their Marriage: For Better or for Worse?*, 27 J FAM. PSYCHOL. 531 (2013).

7 Jason S. Carroll & William J. Doherty, *Evaluating the Effectiveness of Premarital Prevention Programs: A Meta-analytic Review of Outcome Research*, 52 FAM. RELAT. 105, 111 (2004).

8 *Id.* at 112.

9 Christine E. Murray, *The Relative Influence of Client Characteristics on the Process and Outcome of Premarital Counseling: A Survey of Providers*, 26 CONTEMP. FAM. THERAPY 447 (2004).

10 W. Kim Halford et al., *Do Couples at High Risk of Relationship Problems Attend Premarriage Education*, 20 J. FAM. PSYCHOL. 160 (2006).

11 Brian D. Doss et al., *Differential Use of Premarital Education in First and Second Marriage*, 23 J. FAM. PSYCHOL. 268 (2009).

12 Halford, *supra* note 10.

13 Scott M. Stanley et al., *Premarital Education, Marital Quality, and Marital Stability: Findings from a Large, Random Household Survey*, 20 J. FAM. PSYCHOL. 117 (2006).

14 Hannah C. Williamson et al., *Does Premarital Education Decreases or Increases Couples' Later Help-seeking?* 28 J. FAM. PSYCHOL. 112 (2014).

15 Shelby B. Scott et al., *Reasons for Divorce and Recollections of Premarital Intervention: Implications for Improving Relationship Education*, 2 COUPLE & FAM. PSYCHOL.: RES. & PRAC. 131 (2013).

16 *Id.* at 138.

17 Barriers to marriage are addressed in Chapter 2.

18 A few examples include must-have wedding photos (Amy Levin-Epstein, *51 Must-have Wedding Photos You Don't Want to Miss*, THE KNOT, www.theknot.com), must-haves for a traditional wedding (Anne Matea, *The Must-haves of a Traditional Wedding*, WED NET (Sept. 18, 2015), www.angelspringsevents.com), and must-haves in bride emergency kit (Sarah Pierce, *Emergency Prep Kit for Brides and Bridesmaids: 20 Must Haves*, MY WEDDING (Mar. 12, 2014), www.kahnscatering.com).

19 Unif. Marriage & Divorce Act § 206 (2015).

20 Michio Kitahara, *Function of Marriage Ceremony*, 16 ANTHROLOGICA 163 (1974).
21 Dawn H. Currie, *'Here Comes the Bride': The Making of a 'Modern Traditional' Wedding in Western Culture*, 24 J. COMP. FAM. STUD. 403 (1993).
22 *Id.*
23 Matthijs Kalmijn, *Marriage Rituals as Reinforcers of Role Transitions: An Analysis of Weddings in the Netherlands*, 66 J. MARRIAGE & FAM. 582 (2004).
24 Leslie A. Baxter et al., *Empty Ritual: Young-adult Stepchildren's Perception of the Remarriage Ceremony*, 26 J. SOC. & PERS. RELAT. 467 (2009).
25 WENDY LEEDS-HURWITZ, WEDDING AS TEXT: COMMUNICATING CULTURAL IDENTITIES THROUGH RITUAL (Lawrence Erlbaum Associates 2002).
26 NAT'L MARRIAGE PROJECT REPORT, GALENA K. RHOADES & SCOTT M. STANLEY, BEFORE "I DO": WHAT DO PREMARITAL EXPERIENCES HAVE TO DO WITH MARITAL QUALITY AMONG TODAY'S YOUNG ADULTS? 14 (2014).
27 *Id.*
28 Andrew M. Francis-Tan & Hugo M. Mialon, *'A Diamond Is Forever' and Other Fairy Tales: The Relationship Between Wedding Expenses and Marriage Duration*, 53 ECON. INQ. 1919 (2014).
29 MARRIAGE BY PROXY, www.marriagebyproxy.com (last visited June 17, 2016).
30 *Id.*
31 Brittany Caldwell et al., *Nonprobative Photos Rapidly Lead People to Believe Claims About Their Own (and Other People's) Pasts*, 44 MEM. COG. 883 (2016).
32 Linda A. Henkel, *Photograph-induced Memory Errors: When Photographs Make People Claim They Have Done Things They Have Not*, 25 APP. COG. PSYCHOL. 78 (2011).
33 THE SEVEN YEAR HITCH (The Hallmark Channel, 2012).
34 Ginny Carroll, *Marriage by Another Name*, NEWSWEEK, July 24, 1989, at 46.
35 In addition, the couple must be legally able to be married.
36 CYNTHIA GRANT BOWMAN, UNMARRIED COUPLES, LAW, AND PUBLIC POLICY (Oxford University Press 2010).
37 Matthew J. Lindsay, *Reproducing a Fit Citizenry: Dependency, Eugenics, and the Law of Marriage in the United States, 1860–1920*, 23 LAW & SOC. INQUIRY 541 (1998).
38 BRIAN BIX, THE OXFORD INTRODUCTIONS TO U.S. LAW: FAMILY LAW 35 (Oxford University Press 2013).
39 Cynthia G. Bowman, *A Feminist Proposal to Bring Back Common Law Marriage*, 75 OR. L. REV. 709 (1996).
40 *In re* Estate of McClelland, 541 P.2d 780 (Mont. 1975); Coleman v. Graves, 122 N.W.2d 853 (Iowa 1963).
41 *In re* Estate of Dallman, 228 N.W.2d 187 (Iowa 1975).
42 Bowman, *supra* note 39.
43 Bowman, *supra* note 39.
44 Property in this context includes income and items purchased.

45 GRANT S. NELSON ET AL., CONTEMPORARY PROPERTY 376 (West Publishing Co. 4th ed. 2013).

46 *Id.* at 368–75. Community property states include Arizona, California, Idaho, Louisiana, Nevada, New Mexico, Texas, and Washington.

47 *E.g.*, Bradwell v. Illinois, 83 U.S. 130 (1873).

48 Nancy Cott, PUBLIC VOWS: A HISTORY OF MARRIAGE AND A NATION 52—55 (Harvard University Press 2002).

49 Jeremy A. Blumenthal, *"To Be Human": A Psychological Perspective on Property Law*, 83 TUL. L. REV. 609 (2009).

50 *Id.*

51 *Id.*

52 See generally AM. ASS'N OF UNIV. WOMEN, SIMPLE TRUTH GENDER PAY GAP REPORT (2016) (even with considering the different life and career choices between men and women there is still an earning gap).

53 This is referred to as Resource Theory. Robert O. Blood & Donald M. Wolfe, HUSBANDS AND WIVES: THE DYNAMICS OF FAMILY LIVING (Oxford Free Press 1960).

54 Liat Kulik, *Developments in Spousal Power Relations: Are We Moring Toward Equality?*, 47 MARRIAGE & FAM. REV. 419 (2011).

55 Mark A. Small & Pat A. Tetreault, *Social Psychology, 'Marital Rape Exemptions', and Privacy*, 8 BEHAV. SCI. & L. 141 (1990).

56 Jennifer A. Bennice & Patricia A. Resick, *Marital Rape: History, Research, and Practice*, 4 TRAUMA, VIOLENCE & ABUSE 228 (2003).

57 S.C. CODE ANN. § 16-3-615 (2018).

58 Michelle Anderson, *Marital Immunity, Intimate Relationships, and Improper Inferences: A New Law on Sexual Offenses by Intimates*, 54 HASTINGS L. J. 1463 (2003).

59 Kulik, *supra* note 54.

60 *Id.*

61 DAVID FINKELHOR & KERSTI YILO, LICENSE TO RAPE: SEXUAL ABUSE OF WIVES 126 (1985).

62 Anderson, *supra* note 58.

63 I.R.C. §§ 2056, 2523 (2016).

64 *Is it Better for a Married Couple to File Jointly or Separately*, TURBOTAX, https://ttlc.intuit.com (last visited June 19, 2016).

65 Daniel Kahneman & Amos Tversky, *Prospect Theory: An Analysis of Decision Under Risk*, 47 ECONOMETRICA 263 (1979).

66 Edward J. McCaffery & Jonathan Baron, *Thinking About Tax*, 12 PSYCHOLOGY, PUBLIC POLICY & THE LAW, 106 (2006).

67 Sandra Block, *IRS 'Innocent Spouse' Rules Can Be Tough*, USA TODAY (June 24, 2011, 11:23 AM), http://usatoday30.usatoday.com.

68 *Id.*

69 *Innocent Spouse Questions & Answers*, IRS, www.irs.gov (last visited June 19, 2016).
70 Stephanie Hunter McMahon, *What Innocent Relief Says About Wives and The Rest of Us*, 37 HARV. J. L. & GEN. 141 (2014); *see also* Jacqueline Clarke, *(In)Equitable Relief: How Judicial Misconceptions about Domestic Violence Prevent Victims from Attaining Innocent Spouse Relief Under I.R.C. Section 6015(F)*, 22 J. GEN. SOC. POL'Y & L. 825 (2014).
71 J. Abraham Gutting, *The "Price" Is Right: An Overview of Innocent Spouse Relief and the Critical Need for a Uniform Approach to Interpreting the Knowledge Requirement of Internal Revenue Code § 6015*, 2 CHARLESTON L. REV. 751 (2008).
72 Clarke, *supra* note 70.
73 *Health-care Decisions Act Summary*, UNIFORM LAW COMMISSION, www.uniformlaws.org (last visited June 19, 2016).
74 Sara M. Moorman & Robert M. Hauser, *Do Older Adults Know Their Spouses' End-of-life Treatment Preferences*, 31 RES. AGING 463 (2009).
75 Angela Fagerlin et al., *Projection in Surrogate Decisions About Life-sustaining Medical Treatments*, 20 HEALTH PSYCHOL. 166 (2001).
76 Lee D. Ross, Teresa M. Amabile, & Julia L. Steinmetz, *Social Roles, Social Control and Biases in Social Perception*, 35 J. PERS. & SOC. PSYCHOL. 485 (1977).
77 Peter H. Ditto et al., *Advance Directives as Acts of Communication: A Randomized Controlled Trial*, 161 ARCH. INTERN. MED. 421 (2001).
78 Kristen M. Coppola et al., *Accuracy of Primary Care and Hospital-based Physicians' Predictions of Elderly Outpatients' Treatment Preferences with and without Advance Directives*, 161 ARCH. INTERN. MED. 431 (2001).
79 Elden v. Sheldon, 758 P.2d 582, 589 (Cal. 1988).
80 John Hochfelder, *Spouse Awarded $1,000,000 for Loss of Consortium Claim*, NEW YORK INJURY CASES BLOG (Mar. 7, 2009), www.newyorkinjurycasesblog.com.
81 *See* Cookie Stephan & Judy Corder Tully, *The Influence of Physical Attractiveness of a Plaintiff on the Decisions of Simulated Jurors*, 101 J. SOC. PSYCHOL.149 (1977).
82 Christian Pfeifer, *Physical Attractiveness, Employment and Earnings*, 19 APPL. ECON. LETT. 505 (2012).
83 Edward L. Thorndike, *A Constant Error in Psychological Ratings*, 4 J. APPL. PSYCHOL. 25 (1920).
84 MICHAEL J. SAKS & BARBARA A. SPELLMAN, THE PSYCHOLOGICAL FOUNDATIONS OF EVIDENCE LAW 133 (New York University Press 2015).
85 THOMAS A. MAUET & WARREN D. WOLFSON, TRIAL EVIDENCE 256–59 (Wolters Kluwer 6th ed. 2016).
86 *Id.* at 261, 269.
87 *Id.* at 256.
88 Saks & Spellman, *supra* note 84.
89 *Id.*
90 54 S. Ct. 212 (1933).

91 100 S. Ct. 906 (1980).

92 *Id.* at 911.

93 *See* State v. Evans, 287 S.E.2d 922, 923 (W. Va. 1982).

94 Mauet & Wolfson, *supra* note 85, at 258–59.

95 *Id.*

96 Amee A. Shah, *The Parent-child Testimonial Privilege—Has the Time for it Finally Arrived*, 47 CLEV. ST. L. REV. 41 (1999); Dan Markel, Jennifer M. Collins, & Ethan J. Leib, *Criminal Justice and the Challenge of Family Ties*, 2007 U. ILL. L. REV. 1147 (2007).

97 Scott Medintz, J. Chaplin, J. Feldman, & E. McGrit, *Secrets, Lies, and Money*, 34 MONEY 121 (2005); Beth Easterling, David Knox, & Alora Brackett, *Secrets in Romantic Relationships: Does Sexual Orientation Matter?*, 8 J. GLBT FAM. STUD. 196 (2012).

98 Saks and Spellman, *supra* note 84, at 167.

99 *Id.*

100 John M. Gottman & Clifford I. Notarius, *Marital Research in the 20th Century and a Research Agenda for the 21st Century*, 41 FAM. PROCESS 159 (2002).

101 Anna Miller, *Can This Marriage be Saved?*, AM. PSYCHOL. ASS'N: SCIENCE WATCH (Apr. 2013), www.apa.org.

102 *Id.*

103 Alain de Botton, *How Romantic Ideas Destroy Your Chance at Love*, TIME (June 2, 2016), http://time.com.

104 Kim T. Buehlman, John M. Gottman, & Lynn F. Katz, *How a Couple Views Their Past Predicts Their Future: Predicting Divorce from an Oral History Interview*, 5 J. FAM. PSYCHOL. 295 (1992).

105 Justin A. Lavner & Thomas N. Bradbury, *Why Do Even Satisfied Newlyweds Eventually Go on to Divorce?* 26 J. FAM. PSYCHOL. 1 (2012).

106 Marceline Thompson-Hayes & Lynne M. Webb, *Documenting Mutuality: Testing a Dyadic and Communicative Model of Marital Commitment*, 73 SOUTH. COMMUN. J. 143 (2008).

107 Leslie L. Bachand & Sandra L. Caron, *Ties That Bind: A Qualitative Study of Happy Long-term Marriages*, 23 CONTEMP. FAM. THER. 105 (2001).

108 Tommy M. Phillips, Joe D. Wilmoth, & Loren D. Marks, *Challenges and Conflicts . . . Strengths and Supports: A Study of Enduring African American Marriages*, 43 J. BLACK STUD. 936 (2012).

109 Samantha Joel, *Getting Married? Love Science? Here Are Our Ten Research-based Wedding Vows*, SCI. OF RELAT. (Dec. 9, 2013), www.scienceofrelationships.com.

110 *Id. citing* Sandra L. Murray, John G. Holmes, & Dale W. Griffin, *The Benefits of Positive Illusions: Idealization and The Construction of Satisfaction in Close Relationships*, 70 J. PERS. & SOC. PSYCHOL. 79 (1996).

111 Joel, *supra* note 109 *citing* Amie M. Gordon et al., *To Have and To Hold: Gratitude Promotes Relationship Maintenance in Intimate Bonds*, 103 J. PERS. & SOC. PSYCHOL. 257 (2012).

112 EMILE DURKHEIM, SUICIDE (New York: Free Press 1951) (1897).
113 Tim Stanley, *The Changing Face of the American Family*, 62 HIST. TODAY (2012), www.historytoday.com.

CHAPTER 4. BECOMING A PARENT AND "MAKING" A FAMILY

1 Lewis Turner, *Picture Perfect: A Local Photographer's Journey to Parenthood*, FIRST COAST NEWS (May 24, 2016, 9:47 PM), www.firstcoastnews.com.
2 *What is Assisted Reproductive Technology (ART)?*, C.D.C. (Nov. 1, 2014), www.cdc.gov.
3 *Assisted Reproductive Technology (ART)*, NAT'L INST. CHILD HEALTH & HUMAN DEV. (July 2, 2013), www.nichd.nih.gov.
4 Some would argue that surrogacy is the oldest referencing the biblical story of Abram, Sarai, and Sarai's chambermaid, Hagar. The difference with that story and modern surrogacy is that Abram, although encouraged by his wife to do so, had sexual intercourse with Hagar. *Genesis* 11; *See* Ann M. Fisher, *The Journey of Gestational Surrogacy: Religion, Spirituality and Assisted Reproductive Technologies*, 18 INT. J. CHILD SPIRITUA. 235 (2015).
5 W. Ombelet & J. Van Robays, *Artificial Insemination History: Hurdles and Milestones*, 7 FACTS VIEWS VIS. OBGYN 137 (2015).
6 Elizabeth Yuko, *The First Artificial Insemination Was an Ethical Nightmare*, THE ATLANTIC (Jan. 8, 2015), www.theatlantic.com.
7 Kara W. Swanson, *Adultery by Doctor: Artificial Insemination 1890–1945*, 87 CHI.-KENT L. REV. 591 (2012).
8 *Id.*
9 UNIF. PARENTAGE ACT § 703, (amended 2002).
10 MARY LYNDON SHANLEY, MAKING BABIES, MAKING FAMILIES, WHAT MATTERS MOST IN AN AGE OF REPRODUCTIVE TECHNOLOGIES, SURROGACY, ADOPTION, AND SAME-SEX AND UNWED PARENTS 80 (Beacon Press, 2001).
11 Chandrika Narayan, *Kansas Court Says Sperm Donor Must Pay Child Support*, CNN (Jan. 24, 2014, 2:33 AM), www.cnn.com.
12 Naomi R. Cahn, THE NEW KINSHIP: CONSTRUCTING DONOR-CONCEIVED FAMILIES 131 (New York University Press, 2013).
13 Eva M. Durna, & Leo R. Leader, *Attitudes of Parents of Donor Insemination Children to Disclosure and Donor Registries*, 10 REPROD. TECH. 224 (2000).
14 Cahn, *supra* note 12.
15 Diane Beeson, Patricia Jennings, & Wendy Kramer, *A New Path to Grandparenthood: Parents of Sperm and Egg Donors*, 34 J. FAM. ISSUES 1295 (2013).
16 Cahn, *supra* note 12, at 152.
17 Holli Ann Askren & Kathleen Bloom, *Postadoptive Reactions of the Relinquishing Mother: A Review*, 28 J. OB. GYN. & NEONATAL NUR. 395 (1999).
18 Andrea D. Gurmankin et al., *Aspiring Parents, Genotypes and Phenotypes: The Unexamined Myth of the Perfect Baby*, 68 ALB. L. REV. 1097 (2005).

19 *Id.* at 1101.

20 *Id.*

21 Karin Hammarberg et al., *The Experience of Pregnancy: Does Age or Mode of Conception Matter?*, 31 J. REPROD. & INFANT PSYC. 109 (2013). However, it should be noted that this relationship disappeared in multivariate analyses.

22 Paula Kuivasaari-Pirinen et al., *Outcome of Assisted Reproductive Technology (ART) and Subsequent Self-reported Life Satisfaction*, 9 PLOS ONE 1 (2014).

23 537 A.2d 1227 (N.J. 1988).

24 Mike Kelly, *Kelly: 25 Years After Baby M, Surrogacy Questions Remain Unanswered*, NORTHJERSEY.COM (Mar. 30, 2012, 5:18 PM), www.northjersey.com.

25 Johnson v. Calvert, 851 P.2d 776 (Cal. 1993).

26 JERRY MENIKOFF, LAW AND BIOETHICS: AN INTRODUCTION 101 (Georgetown University Press, 2001).

27 Janice C. Ciccarelli & Linda J. Beckman, *Navigating Rough Waters: An Overview of Psychological Aspects of Surrogacy*, 61 J. SOC. ISSUES 21 (2005).

28 Paula Abrams, *The Bad Mother: Stigma, Abortion and Surrogacy*, 43 J. L. MED. & ETHICS 179 (2015).

29 Ciccarelli, *supra* note 27.

30 Susan Golombok et al., *Families Created Through Surrogacy: Mother-child Relationships and Children's Psychological Adjustment at Age 7*, 47 DEV. PSYCHOL. 1579 (2011) *and* Susan Golombok et al., *Children Born Through Reproductive Donation: A Longitudinal Study of Psychological Adjustment*, 54 J. CHILD PSYCHOL. & PSYC. 653 (2013) (hereinafter *Children Born Through Reproductive*).

31 *Children Born Through Reproductive*, *supra* note 30.

32 Darra L. Hofman, *"Mama's Baby, Daddy's Maybe:" A State-by-state Survey of Surrogacy Laws and Their Disparate Gender Impact*, 35 WM. MITCHELL L. REV. 449 (2009).

33 Ciccarelli, *supra* note 27.

34 Adoption issues related to the Adoption and Safe Families Act and Termination of Parental Rights are addressed in Chapter 8.

35 Amanda L. Baden, *"Do You Know Your Real Parents?" and Other Adoption Microaggressions*, 19 ADOPTION QUART 1 (2016).

36 Leslie Doty Hollingsworth, *Who Seeks to Adopt a Child?*, 3 ADOPTION QUART 1 (2008).

37 Stephen B. Presser, *The Historical Background of the American Law of Adoption*, 11 J. FAM. L. 446 (1971).

38 Douglas Henderson, *Challenging the Silence of Mental Health Community on Adoption Issues*, 11 J. SOC. DISTRESS HOMEL. 131, 133–34 (2002).

39 *Id.*

40 Burton Z. Sokoloff, *Antecedents of American Adoption*, 3 FUTURE CHILD. 7 (1993).

41 *See* Joan S. Meier, *Dangerous Liaisons: Social Science and Law in Domestic Violence Cases* (Feb. 2, 2017). Available at SSRN: https://papers.ssrn.com.

42 Maryalene Laponsie, *10 Store with the Best Return Policies*, MONEYTALKS NEWS (Nov. 30, 2015), www.moneytalksnews.com.

43 ROADRUNNERSPORTS, www.roadrunnersports.com (last visited Dec. 15, 2016).

44 For example, the Illinois Families Act provides that "[a] consent to adoption or standby adoption by a parent, including a minor, executed and acknowledged in accordance with the provisions of Section 10 of this Act, or a surrender of a child by a parent, including a minor, to an agency of the purpose of adoption shall be irrevocable unless it have been obtained by fraud or duress . . ." 750 ILL. COMP. STAT. ANN. 50/11(a) (LexisNexis 2016).

45 Elizabeth Samuels, *Legal Representation of Birth Parents and Adoptive Parents*, 9 ADOPTION QUART 73 (2008).

46 Although the story in 1 Kings 3:16–28 about King Solomon saying he would cut a child in half is not about an adoption but, rather, about two women fighting over one living child, judges today refer to this ancient story to symbolize how they feel in adoption revocation cases. *See In re* Sarah K., 487 N.E.2d 241, 241, n.6 (1985) (beginning the opinion "This tragic case pits two couples—each found to be fit as parents—against each other for custody of Sarah K, now two years old."). Other legal scholars also refer to this biblical tale in the context of contested adoptions. *See* Note, *Natural vs. Adoptive Parents: Divided Children and the Wisdom of Solomon*, 57 IOWA L. REV. 171, 180, 193–98 (1971); Kirsten Korn, *The Struggle for the Child: Preserving the Family in Adoption Disputes Between Biological Parents and Third Parties*, 72 N.C.L. REV. 1279 (1994).

47 Timothy D. Wilson & Daniel T. Gilbert, *Affective Forecasting: Knowing What to Want*, 14 AM. PSYCHOL. SOC. 131 (2005).

48 Elizabeth J. Samuels, *Adoption Consents*, 10 ADOPTION QUART. 85 (2006).

49 ARIZ. STAT. REV. § 8–103(C)(4)(2017).

50 IDAHO CODE ANN. § 16–1502. There are two exceptions to this age requirement: first, if the person adopting the child is the spouse of a natural parents and, second, if the adopting person is 25 years or older.

51 MINN. STAT. ANN. §§ 259.22; 259.21.

52 22 VA. ADMIN. CODE § 20-221-70(E) (2016).

53 ALA. CODE § 26–10A-19; ALA. ADMIN. CODE R. 660-5-22-.03(7); ALASKA STAT. § 25.23.020; ALASKA ADMIN. CODE TIT. 7, § 56.650; UTAH ADMIN. CODE R. 512-41-3; FLA. STAT. ANN. § 63.092; FLA. ADMIN CODE ANN. R.65C-16.005.

54 Jonathan James Nobile, *Adoptions Gone Awry: Enhancing Adoption Outcomes Through Post-adoption Services and Federal and State Laws Imposing Criminal Sanctions for Private Internet Rehoming*, 53 FAM. CT. REV. 474, 474–75 (2015).

55 *Id.* at 474–76.

56 *Id.* at 745.

57 *Id.* at 477–78.

58 Diana E. Post, *Adoption in Clinical Psychology: A Review of the Absence, Ramifications, and Recommendations for Change*, 9 J. SOC. DISTRESS HOMEL. 361

(2000); Martha J. Henry, Daniel Pollack & Aaron Lazare, *Teaching Medical Students about Adoption and Foster Care*, 10 ADOPTION QUART. 45 (2007).

59 Juliana M. Tayman, et al., *Adoption as a Diversity Issue in Professional Preparation: Perceptions of Preservice Education Professionals*, 11 ADOPTION QUART. 24 (2008).

60 Nobile, *supra* note 54 at 480–81.

61 Presumably, adoptions with children of a different race than the parents make this conversation inevitable as the child assesses physical differences.

62 Wayne E. Carp, *Adoption and Disclosure of Family Information: A Historical Perspective*, 74 CHILD WELFARE 217 (1995).

63 U.S. DEP'T OF COMMERCE, ADOPTED CHILDREN AND STEPCHILDREN: 2010: POPULATION CHARACTERISTICS 4 (2014), *available at* www.census.gov. *See also* Douglas B. Henderson, *Challenging the Silence of the Mental Health Community on Adoption Issues*, 11 J. SOC. DISTRESS HOMEL. 131, 133 (2002).

64 Katarina Wegar, *Adoption, Family Ideology, and Social Stigma: Bias in Community Attitudes Adoption Research, and Practice*, 49 FAM. RELAT. 363 (2000).

65 Abbie E. Goldberg & Joanna E. Scheib, *Why Donor Insemination and not Adoption? Narratives of Female-partnered and Single Mothers*, 64 FAM. RELAT. 726 (2015); Dylan Turner & Robert D. Nachtigall, *The Experience of Infertility by Low-income Immigrant Latino Couples: Attitudes Toward Adoption*, 13 ADOPTION QUART. 18 (2010).

66 Leslie A. Baxter et al., *Narrating Adoption: Resisting Adoption as "Second Best" in Online Stories of Domestic Adoption Told by Adoptive Parents*, 14 J. FAM. COMMUN. 253, 258–61 (2014).

67 Or biological inability such as lesbian couples or single individuals desiring to be parents without a partner.

68 Baxter, *supra* note 66 at 259–60.

69 Irving G. Leon, *Adoption Losses: Naturally Occurring or Socially Constructed?* 73 CHILD DEV. 652 (2002).

70 Baden, *supra* note 35.

71 *Id.* at 11.

72 *Id.* at 6.

73 Addison Cooper, *Finding Dory Adoption Movie Review*, ADOPTION AT THE MOVIES (June 21, 2016), www.adoptionlcsw.com.

74 *Id.*

75 Kelly Jerome & Kathryn A. Sweeney, *Birth Parents' Portrayals in Children's Adoption Literature*, 35 J. FAM. ISSUES 677 (2014).

76 *Id.* at 691.

77 *Id.* at 695.

78 Including need for love and feelings of loss. Susan L. Kline, Amanda I. Karel, & Karishma Chatterjee, *Covering Adoption: General Depictions in Broadcast News*, 55 FAM. RELAT. 487, 490 (2006).

79 The percentage was 34.3%, with the example provided being aggression. *Id.*

80 *Id.*

81 Marinus H. van IJzendoorn, Femmie Juffer, & Caroline W. Klein Poelhuis, *Adoption and Cognitive Development: A Meta-analytic Comparison of Adopted and Nonadopted Children's IQ and School Performance*, 131 PSYCHOL. BULL. 301 (2005).

82 *Id.*; Femmie Juffer & Marinus H. von IJzendoorn, *Adoptees Do not Lack Self-esteem: A Meta-analysis of Studies on Self-Esteem of Transracial, International, and Domestic Adoptees*, 133 PSYCHOL. BULL. 1067 (2007).

83 Marinus H. von IJzendoorn & Femmie Juffer, *The Emanuel Miller Memorial Lecture 2006: Adoption as Intervention. Meta-analytic Evidence for Massive Catch-up and Plasticity in Psychical, Socio-emotional, and Cognitive Development*, 47 J. CHILD PSYCHOL. & PSYC. 1228 (2006).

84 Burr v. Bd. of Cnty. Comm'rs of Stark Cnty, 491 N.E.2d 1101 (Ohio 1986).

85 *Id.* at 1105–06.

86 *Id.* at 1101.

87 *Id.*

88 Huntington's disease is a fatal genetic disorder that progressively degenerates a person's physical movements and cognitions. MAYO CLINIC, DISEASES AND CONDITIONS: HUNTINGTON'S DISEASE, www.mayoclinic.org (last visited Dec. 20, 2016).

89 491 N.E.2d at 1108.

90 M.H. v. Caritas Family Serv., 475 N.W.2d 94 (Minn. Ct. App. 1991).

91 *Id.* at 96.

92 *Id.* at 97.

93 Madelyn Freundlich & Lisa Peterson, WRONGFUL ADOPTION: LAW, POLICY, & PRACTICE (Child Welfare League of America 1998).

94 Sharon James Williams, Daniel Dubovsky, & Jason Merritt, *Legal and Psychological Implications of Nondisclosure in the Adoption of a Child with Fetal Alcohol Spectrum Disorder*, 39 J. PSYCH. & L. 193 (2011).

95 Jessica Ann Schlee, *Genetic Testing: Technology that is Changing the Adoption Process*, 18 N.Y.L. SCH. J. HUM. RTS. 133 (2001).

96 Palmore v. Sidoti, 426 So. 2d 34 (Fla. Dist. Ct. App. 1982) *overruled by* Palmore v. Sidoti, 466 U.S. 429 (1984).

97 Palmore v. Sidoti, 466 U.S. 429 (1984).

98 NATIONAL ASS'N OF BLACK SOCIAL WORKERS, POSITION STATEMENT ON TRANS-RACIAL ADOPTIONS, (1972), http://c.ymcdn.com.

99 NATIONAL ASS'N OF BLACK SOCIAL WORKERS, NABSW POSITION STATEMENTS, http://nabsw.org (last visited Dec. 20, 2016).

100 J. Toni Oliver, *Adoptions Should Consider Black Children and Black Families*, N.Y. TIMES (Dec. 22, 2016, 10:46 AM), www.nytimes.com.

101 ASS. OF BLACK SOCIAL WORKERS, *Kinship Care* (2003) http://c.ymcdn.com.

102 BRIAN BIX, THE OXFORD INTRODUCTIONS TO U.S. LAW: FAMILY LAW 89 (Oxford University Press 2013).

103 The Multiethnic Placement Act of 1994, Pub. L. 103–382, § 551, 108 Stat. 4056 (1994) (codified as 42 U.S.C. § 5115a (1994)).

104 Inter-Ethnic Placement Act of 1996, 42 U.S.C.S. § 1996b.

105 CHILDREN'S BUREAU, CHILD WELFARE INFORMATION GATEWAY, RACIAL DISPROPORTIONALITY AND DISPARITY IN CHILD WELFARE, ISSUE BRIEF (2016), *available at* www.childwelfare.gov.

106 *Id.*

107 Indian Child Welfare Act of 1978, 95 Pub. L. 608, 92 Stat. 3069 (1978).

108 *Id.* at § 101.

109 *Id.* at § 105.

110 JOANNA L. GROSSMAN & LAWRENCE M. FRIEDMAN, INSIDE THE CASTLE: LAW AND THE FAMILY IN 20TH CENTURY AMERICA (Princeton Univ. Press, 2011).

111 Indian Child Welfare Act § 103.

112 Tara Arnold et al., *Ethnic Socialization, Perceived Discrimination, and Psychological Adjustment Among Transracially Adopted and Nonadopted Ethnic Minority Adults*, 86 AM. J. ORTHOPSYCH. 540 (2016).

113 Miriam Klevan, *Resolving Race: How Adoptive Parents Discuss Choosing the Race of Their Child*, 15 ADOPTION QUART. 88 (2012).

114 PAMELA ANNE QUIROZ, ADOPTION IN A COLOR-BLIND SOCIETY (Rowman & Littlefield Publishers 2007).

115 *Id.*

116 Klevan, *supra* note 113, at 98.

117 *Id.*

118 *Id.*

119 *Id.* at 105

120 Kathryn A. Sweeney, *Race-conscious Adoption Choices, Multiraciality, and Colorblind Racial Ideology*, 62 FAM. RELAT. 42 (2013).

121 *Id.*

122 Josie Crolley-Simic & M. Elizabeth Vonk, *White International Transracial Adoptive Mothers' Reflections on Race*, 16 CHILD FAM. SOC. WORK 169 (2011).

123 Arnold et al., *supra* note 112.

124 Anthony L. Burrow & Gordon E. Finley, *Transracial, Same-race Adoption, and the Need for Multiple Measures of Adolescent Adjustment*, 74 AM. J. ORTHOPSYCH. 577 (2004); Juffer & van IJzendoorn, *supra* note 82.

125 Mylene Boivin & Ghayda Hassan, *Ethnic Identity and Psychological Adjustment in Transracial Adoptees: A Review of the Literature*, 38 ETHNIC RACIAL STUD. 1084 (2015).

126 *Id.*

127 ROUDI NAZARINIA ROY, WALTER R. SCHUMM, & SONYA L. BRITT, TRANSITION TO PARENTHOOD (Springer 2014).

128 Richard Lincoln, *Population and the American Future: The Commission's Final Report*, 4 FAM. PLANN. PERSPECT. 10 (1972).

129 The assumption that men created life and women provided a home for growth was disproved when scientists in 1843 discovered how the sperm fertilizes the egg.
130 Suppression of Trade in, and Circulation of, Obscene Literature and Articles of Immoral Use, 17 STAT. 598, 42 CONG. CH. 258 (1873).
131 CONN. GEN. STAT. §§ 53–32, 54–196 (1958).
132 People v. Sanger, 118 N.E. 637 (N.Y 1918).
133 118 N.E. 637 (N.Y. 1918). The decision is often referred to as the Crane decision named so for the judicial opinion written by Judge Frederick Crane of the New York Court of Appeals.
134 86 F.2d 737 (2d Cir. 1936).
135 JAMES A. MORONE & DAN EHLKE, HEALTH POLITICS AND POLICY (5th ed. 2014).
136 MARGARET SANGER, MOTHERHOOD IN BONDAGE (Ohio State University Press, 2000). According to an information sheet published by Planned Parenthood, contraception available (although illegal) at the time included condoms, chemical spermicides, plugs, sponges, suppositories, and rubber diaphragms. PLANNED PARENTHOOD FED'N OF AM., INC., MARGARET SANGER—20TH CENTURY HERO (2009), *available at* www.plannedparenthood.org.
137 381 U.S. 479 (1965).
138 *Id.* at 482–84.
139 405 U.S. 438 (1972).
140 Div. of Reprod. Health, Nat'l Ctr. For Chronic Disease Prevention and Health Promotion, C.D.C., *Achievements in Public Health, 1900–1999: Family Planning*, 48 MMWR 1073 (1999), *available at* www.cdc.gov.
141 Rachel K. Jones, Jacqueline E. Darroch, & Stanley K. Henshaw, *Contraceptive Use Among U.S. Women Having Abortions in 2000–2001*, 34 PERSPECT. SEX REPROD. HEALTH 294 (2002).
142 Valerie Bader et al., *The Role of Previous Contraception Education and Moral Judgment in Contraceptive Use*, 59 J. MIDWIFERY WOM. HEAL. 447 (2014).
143 Robert Brom, *Birth Control*, Catholic Answers (Aug. 10, 2004), www.catholic.com.
144 Nicholas J. Hill, Mxolisi Siwatu, & Alexander K. Robinson, *'My Religion Picked my Birth Control': The Influence of Religion on Contraceptive Use*, 53 J. RELIG. HEALTH 825 (2014).
145 ROY F. BAUMEISTER, TODD F. HEATHERTON, & DIANNE M. TICE, LOSING CONTROL: HOW AND WHY PEOPLE FAIL AT SELF-REGULATION (Academic Free Press, 1994).
146 George Loewenstein, *Hot-cold Empathy Gaps and Medical Decision Making*, 24 HEALTH PSYCHOL. 49 (2005), George Loewenstein, *Out of Control: Visceral Influences on Behavior*, 65 ORGAN. BEHAV. HUM. DEC. 272 (1996).
147 Ron S. Gold, Michael J. Skinner, & Michael W. Ross, *Unprotected Anal Intercourse in HIV-infected and Non-HIV-infected Gay Men*, 31 J. SEX RES. 59 (1993) (examining similar issues related to unprotected sex of gay men).

148 410 U.S. 113 (1973).

149 JENNA JERMAN, RACHEL K. JONES, TSUYOSHI ONDA, GUTTMACHER INSTITUTE, CHARACTERISTICS OF U.S. ABORTION PATIENTS IN 2014 AND CHANGES SINCE 2008 (May 2016), www.guttmacher.org.

150 MO. REV. STAT. § 199.240 (Supp. 1975).

151 Planned Parenthood v. Danforth, 428 U.S. 52 (1976).

152 505 U.S. 833 (1992).

153 *Id.* at 898.

154 H. W. Smith & Cindy Kronauge, *The Politics of Abortion: Husband Notification Legislation, Self-disclosure, and Marital Bargaining*, 31 SOC. QUART. 585 (1990).

155 Rachel K. Jones, Ann M. Moore, & Lori F. Frohwirth, *Perceptions of Male Knowledge and Support Among U.S. Women Obtaining Abortions*, WOMEN HEALTH ISS. (2010), www.guttmacher.org.

156 GUTTMACHER INSTITUTE, DATA CENTER, https://data.guttmacher.org (last visited July 11, 2016).

157 S.D. CODIFIED LAWS § 34-23A-10.1 (2016).

158 D.G. Foster et al., *A Comparison of Depression and Anxiety Symptoms Trajectories Between Women who Had an Abortion and Women Denied One*, 45 PSYCHOL. MED. 2073 (2015).

159 Jeremy A. Blumenthal, *Emotional Paternalism*, 35 FLA. ST. U. L. REV. 1 (2007).

160 Nancy E. Adler et al., *Psychological Factors in Abortion: A Review*, 47 AM. PSYCHOL. 1194, 1198–99 (1992).

161 *Id.*

162 *Id.* at 1199–1201.

163 Merryn Ekberg, *Maximizing the Benefits and Minimizing the Risks Associated with Prenatal Genetic Testing*, 9 HEALTH RISK & SOC. 67 (2007).

164 Cailin Harris, *Statutory Prohibitions on Wrongful Birth Claims and Their Dangerous Effects on Parents*, 34 B.C.J.L. & SOC. JUST. 365 (2014).

165 *Montana Jury Rules Against Women's Wrongful-birth Suit*, LAWYER HERALD (Feb. 12, 2016, 12:11 AM), www.lawyerherald.com.

166 Kerry T. Cooperman, *The Handicapping Effect of Judicial Opinions in Reproductive Tort Cases: Correcting the Legal Perception of Persons with Disabilities*, 68 MD. L. REV. ENDNOTES 1, 11–14 (2009).

167 *Id.*

168 David T. Lykken, *Parental Licensure*, 56 AM. PSYCHOL. 885, 885 (2001).

169 *Id.* at 886.

170 Richard E. Redding, *The Impossibility of Parental Licensure*, 57 AM. PSYCHOL. 987 (2002). Redding relies on cases such as Stanley v. Illinois, 405 U.S. 645 (1972) in which the Supreme Court held that the right to conceive and to raise is essential. Stanley is not the only case with such a holding; *see also Griswold*, 381 U.S. 479 (1965); *Pierce v. Society of Sisters*, 268 U.S. 510 (1925); *Zablocki v. Redhail*, 434 U.S. 374 (1978).

171 Sandra Scarr, *Toward Voluntary Parenthood*, 68 J. PERS. 615, 618 (2000).

CHAPTER 5. PARENTHOOD AND OTHER CAREGIVING

1 Bob Harrison, *I Didn't Ask to Be a Role Model for my Kids*, THE ONION (Oct. 4, 2006), www.theonion.com.

2 Steve Doughty, *Having Children May not Make Us Happier . . . But it Gives Our Lives More Meaning, Says Research*, DAILYMAIL.COM (April 26, 2016 2:37 PM), www.dailymail.co.uk.

3 Jennifer Glass, Robin W. Simon, & Matthew A. Andersson, *Parenthood and Happiness: Effects of Work-family Reconciliation in 22 OECD Countries*, 122 AM. J. SOCIOL. 886 (2016).

4 See Chapter 7.

5 See Chapter 7.

6 BETTY FRIEDAN, THE FEMININE MYSTIQUE (W. W. Norton & Co. 1963, reprinted 2001).

7 Eve M. Brank & Leroy Scott, *The Historical, Jurisprudential, and Empirical Wisdom of Parental Responsibility Laws*, 6 SOC. ISSUES & POL'Y REV. 26 (2012).

8 Plato, REPUBLIC (C.D.C. Reeve, trans., 3rd ed., Hackett Publishing 2004).

9 MELFORD E. SPIRO, CHILDREN OF THE KIBBUTZ: A STUDY IN CHILD TRAINING AND PERSONALITY (1999).

10 *See* MARGARET ATWOOD, THE HANDMAID'S TALE (Houghton Mifflin Harcourt 1986), LOIS LOWRY, THE GIVER (GIVER QUARTET) (Laurel Leaf 2002), *and* VERONICA ROTH, DIVERGENT (DIVERGENT TRILOGY) (Katherine Tegen Books 2011).

11 See *In re* Gault, 87 S. Ct. 1428 (1967). Developmental research demonstrates differences at the genetic level for immune response when children were institutionalized at a young age versus cared for by biological parents. Oksana Yu Naumova et al., *Differential Patterns of Whole-Genome DNA Methylation in Institutionalized Children and Children Raised by Their Biological Parents*, 24 DEV. PSYCHOPATHOL. 143 (2012).

12 Meyer v. Nebraska, 43 S. Ct. 625 (1923), Pierce v. Soc'y of Sisters, 45 S. Ct. 571 (1925).

13 SECRET CONFESSIONS, www.secret-confessions.com (last visited Oct. 7, 2015).

14 *Archives*, SECRET CONFESSIONS, www.secret-confessions.com (last visited Oct. 7, 2015).

15 *Id.*

16 Ann, *I Hate Being a Mom*, SECRET CONFESSIONS (Feb. 21, 2009), www.secret-confessions.com.

17 The confession in its entirety reads, "I killed my baby son . . . its [*sic*] been three years . . . my husband is in jail for it." Anonymous, *I Killed my Baby*, SECRET CONFESSIONS (Mar. 6, 2009), www.secret-confessions.com.

18 Ann, *supra* note 16. To be clear, there are many comments that are in disagreement, are off topic, or are commenting on other's comments. But there are also many comments like this one from Wendy on September 3, 2015: "I can't

agree with you more. I never wanted kids and with two at 16 and almost 20, I still hate it. I tell people all the time, 'if I could turn the clock back, I would NEVER have kids'. I was talked into it and am still sorry to this day. And my kids are good kids, but all they do is cost me money and even though they love me and tell me, it does absolutely nothing for me. It continues to be a thankless job that gives me nothing. Its sucks. If you don't want kids, listen to your heart and don't feel pressured by anyone, society or your biological clock. I hate it!"

19 I REGRET HAVING CHILDREN: FACEBOOK, www.facebook.com (last visited July, 17, 2016).

20 *About*, I REGRET HAVING CHILDREN, FACEBOOK, www.facebook.com (last visited July 17, 2016).

21 CHEERFULLY CHILDFREE: FACEBOOK, www.facebook.com (last visited Oct. 7, 2015). Cheerfully Childfree has 1,951 likes. Indeed, the "motherhood mandate" is the term used to describe the societal pressure placed on women to become a mother and the underlying judgment if they do not.

22 DANIEL GILBERT, STUMBLING ON HAPPINESS (Vintage, 2007).

23 McLanahan and Adams found that marriage and employment are associated with positive adjustment for women, but parenthood is associated with greater psychological distress. Sara McLanahan & Julie Adams, *Parenthood and Psychological Well-Being*, 5 ANN. REV. IMMUNOL. 237 (1987). Campbell and colleagues found married couples without children report greater happiness than married couples with children. ANGUS CAMPBELL, PHILIP E. CONVERSE, & WILLARD L. RODGERS, THE QUALITY OF AMERICAN LIFE: PERCEPTIONS, EVALUATIONS, AND SATISFACTION (Russell Sage Foundation 1976). In fact, parents provide more positive memories of their experiences with their children than in-the-moment episodic assessments suggest they truly are. Daniel Kahneman, Alan B. Krueger et al., *A Survey Method for Characterizing Daily Life Experience: The Day Reconstruction Method*, 305 SCI. 1776 (2004).

24 Frank Newport & Joy Wilke, *Desire for Children Still Norm in U.S.*, GALLUP (Sept. 25, 2013), www.gallup.com.

25 Jennifer Senior, *All Joy and No Fun: Why Parents Hate Parenting*, N.Y. TIMES, July 4, 2010, http://nymag.com.

26 Kahneman, *supra* note 23.

27 Brian D. Doss et al., *The Effect of the Transition to Parenthood on Relationship Quality: An Eight-year Prospect Study*, 96 J. PERS. SOC. PSYCHOL. 601 (2009).

28 Gilbert, *supra* note 22; Robin Simon, *Twenty Years in the Sociology of Mental Health: The Continued Significance of Gender and Marital Status for Emotional Well-being*, in SOCIOLOGY OF MENTAL HEALTH: SELECTED TOPICS FROM FORTY YEARS, 1970S-2010S 21 (Robert J. Johnson, R. Jay Turner, & Bruce G. Link, eds., Springer 2014). *See also* Jean M. Twenge, W. Keith Campbell, & Craig A. Foster, *Parenthood and Marital Satisfaction: A Meta-analytic Review*, 65 J. MARRIAGE & FAM. 574 (2003).

29 *See generally* David M. Buss & David P. Schmitt, *Sexual Strategies Theory: An Evolutionary Perspective on Human Mating*, 100 PSYCHOL. REV. 204 (1993) (examining distinct evolutionary, psychological mechanisms underlying long and short-term mating strategies for males and females); Sarah R. Hayford & S. Philip Morgan, *Religiosity and Fertility in the United States: The Role of Fertility Intentions*, 86 SOC. FORCES 1163 (2008) (examining the relationship between religiosity and fertility and intended fertility among women); Corinne H. Rocca, Cynthia C. Harper, & Tina R. Raine-Bennett, *Young Women's Perceptions of the Benefits of Childbearing: Associations with Contraceptive Use and Pregnancy*, 45 PERSPECT. SEX REPROD. HEALTH 23 (2013) (examining relationship between perceived benefits of childbearing and contraceptive use).

30 There is some research to the contrary. *See* S. Katherine Nelson et al., *In Defense of Parenthood: Children are Associated with More Joy than Misery*, 24 PSYCHOL. SCI. 3 (2013). The authors employed three studies finding in a national survey, a momentary assessment study, and a day reconstruction effect that parents reported higher general life satisfaction and positive emotions than nonparents. See the following section on cognitive dissonance for a possible explanation of these results.

31 Gilbert, *supra* note 21.

32 *Id.* at 243.

33 *Id.* at 244.

34 MARTIN E. P. SELIGMAN, FLOURISH: A VISIONARY NEW UNDERSTANDING OF HAPPINESS AND WELL-BEING (Atria Books 2012).

35 Zelizer called this "the economically worthless but emotionally priceless child." VIVIANA A. ZELIZER, PRICING THE PRICELESS CHILD: THE CHANGING SOCIAL VALUE OF CHILDREN 3 (Princeton University Press 1994).

36 LEON FESTINGER, A THEORY OF COGNITIVE DISSONANCE (Stanford University Press, 1957).

37 In Leon Festinger's experiment (with Carlsmith in 1959) participants performed a series of boring tasks and then paid $1 or $20 to tell a waiting participant that the experiment was interesting. Those in the $20 condition experienced little to no dissonance, but for those in the $1 condition, the participants experienced dissonance and were only able to overcome the dissonance by believing that the experiment truly was interesting. Leon Festinger & James M. Carlsmith, *Cognitive Consequences of Forced Compliance*, 58 J. ABN. & SOC. PSYCHOL. 203 (1959).

38 Richard P. Eibach & Steven E. Mock, *Idealizing Parenthood to Rationalize Parental Investments*, PSYCH. SCI. 1, 2–3 (2011), http://o-pss.sagepub.com. Parenting costs were manipulated by presenting the participants with the U.S. Department of Agricultural data on how much it monetarily costs an average family to raise a child to age 18. The parental benefit manipulation focused on how adult children provide financial and practical support for their aging parents.

39 In their second study, those participants in the parenting–cost conditions also expressed more relative enjoyment of the time they spent with their children and predicted spending more time with their children. *Id.* at 3–4.

40 *Id.*

41 Bonnie M. Le & Emily A Impett, *The Rewards of Caregiving for Communally Motivated Parents*, 6 SOC. PSYCHOL. & PERS. SCI. 758 (2015).

42 Miron Zuckerman et al., *On the Importance of Self-determination for Intrinsically-motivated Behavior*, 4 PERS. & SOC. PSYCHOL. B. 443 (1978).

43 Ellen J. Langer & Judith Rodin, *The Effects of Choice and Enhanced Personal Responsibility for the Aged: A Field Experiment in an Institutional Setting*, 34 J. PERS. & SOC. PSYCHOL. 191 (1976). Langer and Rodin manipulated a number of other choices for the nursing home residents by giving them a speech about all the decision-making options they have living in the home versus all the activity options available to the residents.

44 William B. Swann & Thane S. Pittman, *Initiating Play Activity of Children: The Moderating Influence of Verbal Cues on Intrinsic Motivation*, 48 CHILD DEV. 1128 (1977).

45 Bruce J. Winick, *On Autonomy: Legal and Psychological Perspectives*, 37 VILL. L. REV. 1705 (1992).

46 Sheena S. Iyengar & Mark R. Lepper, *When Choice Is Demotivating: Can One Desire Too Much of a Good Thing?*, 79 J. PERS. & SOC. PSYCHOL. 995 (2000).

47 *Id.*

48 *Id.* at 998–1000.

49 Barry Schwartz, *Self-determination: The Tyranny of Freedom*, 55 AM. PSYCHOL. 79 (2000).

50 *Id.* at 85; *see also* BARRY SCHWARTZ, THE PARADOX OF CHOICE: WHY LESS IS MORE (Harper Perennial, 2005).

51 Schwartz, *supra* note 49, at 85.

52 Leta Hong Fincher, *China Dropped Its One-child Policy. So Why Aren't Chinese Women Having More Babies?*, N.Y. TIMES (Feb. 20, 2018), www.nytimes.com.

53 RICHARD H. THALER, NUDGE: IMPROVING DECISIONS ABOUT HEALTH, WEALTH, AND HAPPINESS (Penguin Books, 2014).

54 *Id.* at 83–84.

55 Marjorie Maguire Shultz, *Reproductive Technology and Intent-based Parenthood: An Opportunity for Gender Neutrality*, 1990 WIS. L. REV. 297, 304–7 (1990).

56 *Id.* at 304.

57 THE U.S. DEP'T OF AGRIC., CENTER FOR NUTRITION POLICY AND PROMOTION, THE COST OF RAISING A CHILD (August 2013), www.cnpp.usda.gov.

58 *Id.*

59 THE U.S. DEP'T OF AGRIC., CTR. FOR NUTRITION POLICY AND PROMOTION, USDA COST OF RAISING A CHILD CALCULATOR, www.cnpp.usda.gov (last visited Jan. 2, 2017).

60 Bunmi Laditan, FACEBOOK (Sept. 25, 2016) www.facebook.com.

61 U.S. Dep't of Agric., *Parents Projects to Spend $245,340 to Raise a Child Born in 2013, According to USDA Report*, NEWS RELEASE (Aug. 18, 2014) www.usda.gov.

62 *Id.*

63 Jessica Grose, *The Year Having Kids Became a Frivolous Luxury*, SLATE (Dec. 22, 2014, 2:00 PM) www.slate.com.

64 *Id.*

65 For the purposes of this section, we focus on intact biological families without any history of child maltreatment.

66 June Carbone & Naomi Cahn, *Judging Families*, 77 UMKC L. REV. 267 (2008) [hereinafter *Judging Families*]; June Carbone & Naomi Cahn, *The Gender/Class Divide: Reproduction, Privilege, and the Workplace*, 8 FIU L. REV. 287 (2013) [hereinafter *Gender/Class Divide*]; Naomi Cahn & June Carbone, *Growing Inequality and Children*, 23 AM. U.J. GENDER SOC. POL'Y & L. 283 (2015) [hereinafter *Growing Inequality*]; *see also* JUNE CARBONE & NAOMI CAHN, MARRIAGE MARKETS: HOW INEQUALITY IS REMAKING THE AMERICAN FAMILY (Oxford Uni. Press 2014) [hereinafter MARRIAGE MARKETS]; NAOMI CAHN & JUNE CARBONE, RED FAMILIES V. BLUE FAMILIES: LEGAL POLARIZATION AND THE CREATION OF CULTURE (Oxford Uni. Press, reprinted 2011) [hereinafter RED FAMILIES V. BLUE FAMILIES].

67 *Growing Inequality*, *supra* note 66, at 284–84.

68 *Id.* at 284.

69 Raj Chetty et al., *Where Is the Land of Opportunity? The Geography of Intergenerational Mobility in the United States* (NBER Working Paper Series, Working Paper No. 19,843, 2014).

70 *Gender/Class Divide*, *supra* note 66.

71 *Id.* at 295.

72 *Growing Inequality*, *supra* note 66, at 293.

73 *Gender/Class Divide*, *supra* note 66, at 292.

74 *Growing Inequality*, *supra* note 66, at 293.

75 *Judging Families*, *supra* note 66.

76 *Id.* at 277; *see also* RED FAMILIES V. BLUE FAMILIES, *supra* note 66.

77 *Judging Families*, *supra* note 66, at 280.

78 *Id.* at 281.

79 Chris Segrin et al., *Overparenting Is Associated with Child Problems and a Critical Family Environment*, 24 J. CHILD FAM. STUD. 470 (2015).

80 Chris Segrin et al., *The Association Between Overparenting, Parent-child Communication, and Entitlement and Adaptive Traits in Adult Children*, 61 FAM. RELAT. 237 (2012).

81 *Id.*

82 Segrin et al., *supra* note 80.

83 Marc Cutright, *From Helicopter Parent to Valued Partner: Shaping the Parental Relationship for Student Success*, 144 NEW DIR. HIGHER EDUC. 39 (2008).

84 *Id.*

85 Daniel J. van Ingen et al., *Helicopter Parenting: The Effect of an Overbearing Caregiving Style on Peer Attachment and Self-efficacy*, 18 J. COLL. COUNS. 7 (2015).

86 Sherwyn P. Morreale & Constance M. Staley, *Millennials, Teaching and Learning, and the Elephant in the College Classroom*, 65 COMMUN. EDUC. 370 (2016); Jeff Cain, Frank Romanelli, & Kelly M. Smith, *Academic Entitlement in Pharmacy Education*, 76 AM. J. PHARM. EDUC. 189 (2012).

87 Terri LeMoyne & Tom Buchanan, *Does "Hovering" Matter?: Helicopter Parenting and its Effect on Well-being*, 31 SOCIOL. SPECTRUM 399 (2011).

88 Kayla Reed et al., *Helicopter Parenting and Emerging Adult Self-efficacy: Implications for Mental and Physical Health*, 25 J. CHILD FAM. STUD. 3136 (2016).

89 Kelly G. Odenweller, Melanie Booth-Butterfield, & Keith Weber, *Investigating Helicopter Parenting, Family Environments, and Relational Outcomes for Millennials*, 65 COMMUN. STUD. 407 (2014).

90 Karen L. Fingerman et al., *Helicopter Parents and Landing Pad Kids: Intense Parental Support of Grown Children*, 74 J. MARRIAGE FAM. 880 (2012).

91 Edward L. Deci & Richard M. Ryan, INTRINSIC MOTIVATION AND SELF-DETERMINATION IN HUMAN BEHAVIOR (Springer, 1985); Edward L. Deci & Richard M. Ryan, *The "What" and "Why" of Goal Pursuits: Human Needs and the Self-determination of Behavior*, 11 PSYCHOL. INQUIRY 227 (2000); Richard M. Ryan & Edward L. Deci, *Self-determination Theory and the Facilitation of Intrinsic Motivation, Social Development, and Well-being*, 55 AM. PSYCHOL. 68 (2000).

92 Deci & Ryan, *supra* note 91; Edward L. Deci, Richard Koestner, & Richard M. Ryan, *A Meta-Analytic Review of Experiments Examining the Effects of Extrinsic Rewards on Intrinsic Motivation*, 125 PSYCHOL. BULLETIN 627 (1999).

93 Katy Steinmetz, *This Is What "Adulting" Means*, TIME (June 8, 2016), http://time.com.

94 Holly H. Schriffin et al., *Helping or Hovering? The Effects of Helicopter Parenting on College Students' Well-being*, 23 J. CHILD FAM. STUD. 548 (2014).

95 Lenore Skenazy, *Why I Let my 9-year-old Ride the Subway Alone*, THE N.Y. SUN (April 1, 2008), www.nysun.com.

96 Amy Joyce, *What Exactly Is This Whole 'Free-range Kid' Thing*, THE WASHINGTON POST (May 26, 2015), www.washingtonpost.com.

97 Eun Kyung Kim, *Maryland 'Free Range' Parents Cleared of Neglect, Still Plan to Sue CPS, Police*, TODAY (Jun. 22, 2015 12:32 PM), www.today.com.

98 Brian Sullivan, *'Free Range' Parents Encourage Kids to Broaden their Horizons—the Law, not so Much*, A.B.A. J. 1 (2015).

99 *A Mom's Neglect? Not so Fast. Back off, DCFS*, CHICAGO TRIBUNE (Oct. 7, 2015, 5:24 PM), www.chicagotribune.com.

100 Markella B. Rutherford, *The Social Value of Self-esteem*, 48 SOC. 407 (2011).

101 *Id.*

102 David T. Lykken, *Parental Licensure*, 56 AM. PSYCHOL. 885 (2001).

103 Richard E. Redding, *Impossibility of Parental Licensure*, 57 AM. PSYCHOL. 987 (2002).

104 *Id.*

105 RED FAMILIES V. BLUE FAMILIES, *supra* note 66.

106 Dianna Baumrind, *Child Care Practices Anteceding Three Patterns of Preschool Behavior*, 75 GENETIC PSYCHOL. MONOGRAPHS 43 (1967).

107 *Id.*

108 Elenor E. Maccoby & John A. Martin, *Socializing in the Context of the Family: Parent-child Interaction*, in HANDBOOK OF CHILD PSYCHOLOGY: FORMERLY CARMICHAEL'S MANUAL OF CHILD PSYCHOLOGY (Paul H. Mussen, eds. 1983).

109 Laurence Steinberg, *We Know Some Things: Parent-adolescent Relationships in Retrospect and Prospect*, 11 J. RES. ADOLESCNCE 1 (2001).

110 Jia Zhao, Barbara H. Settles, & Xuewen Sheng, *Family-to-work Conflict: Gender, Equity and Workplace Policies*, 42 J. COMP. FAM. STUD. 723 (2011).

111 Family Medical Leave Act of 1993, Pub. L. No. 103–03, 107 Stat. 6 (1993).

112 NAT'L P'SHIP FOR WOMEN & FAMILIES, FACTS ABOUT THE FMLA: WHAT DOES IT DO, WHO USES IT, & HOW, www.nationalpartnership.org.

113 *Id.*

114 *Id.*

115 INTERNAT'L LABOUR OFFICE, MATERNITY AND PATERNITY AT WORK: LAW AND PRACTICE ACROSS THE WORLD (2014), https://fortunedotcom.files.wordpress.com.

116 Claire Zillman, *America Comes in Last Place on Paid Maternity Leave*, FORTUNE (May 15, 2014, 9:15 AM) http://fortune.com.

117 Maya Rossin-Slater, Christopher J. Ruhm, & Jane Waldfogel, *The Effects of California's Paid Family Leave Program on Mothers' Leave-taking and Subsequent Labor Market Outcomes*, 32 J. POL'Y ANAL. MANAG. 224 (2013).

118 *Id.*

119 *Id.*

120 Laurie A. Rudman & Kimberly Fairchild, *Reactions to Counterstereotypic Behavior: The Role of Backlash in Cultural Stereotype Maintenance*, 87 J. PERS. SOC. PSYCHOL. 157 (2004).

121 Laurie A. Rudman & Kris Mescher, *Penalizing Men who Request a Family Leave: Is Flexibility Stigma a Femininity Stigma?*, 69 J. SOC. ISSUES 322 (2013).

122 JUSTINE CALCAGNO, THE 'MOMMY TAX' AND 'DADDY BONUS:' PARENTHOOD AND PERSONAL INCOME IN THE UNITED STATES BETWEEN 1990 AND 2010 (2014) *available at* http://clacls.gc.cuny.edu.

123 Daniel L. Millimet, *The Impact of Children on Wages, Job Tenure, and the Division of Household Labour*, 110 ECON. J. C139 (2000).

124 Susan G. Singley & Kathryn Hynes, *Transitions to Parenthood: Work-family Policies, Gender and the Couple Context*, 19 GENDER SOC. 376 (2005).

125 Naomi Gertsel & Katherine McGonagle, *Job Leaves and the Limits of the Family and Medical Leave Act*, 26 WORK OCCUPATION 510 (1999).

126 Patricia Short Tomlinson & Barbara Irwin, *Qualitative Study of Women's Reports of Family Adaptation Pattern Four Years Following Transition to Parenthood*, 14 ISS. MENTAL HEALTH. NURS. 119 (1993).

127 Judith R. Fuller, *Early Patterns of Maternal Attachment*, 11 HEALTH CARE WOMEN IN. 433 (2009); Regina Sullivan et al., *Infant Bonding and Attachment to the Caregiver: Insights from Basic and Clinical Science*, 38 CLIN. PERINATOL 643 (2011).

128 *See* Christin L. Porter & Hui-Chin Hsu, *First-time Mothers' Perceptions of Efficacy During the Transition to Motherhood: Links to Infant Temperament*, 17 J. FAM. PSYCHOL. 54 (2003); Janet Currie, *Managing Motherhood: Strategies Used by New Mothers to Maintain Perceptions of Wellness*, 30 HEALTH CARE WOMEN INT. 635 (2009); *and* WENDY HIRSH, BEYOND THE CAREER BREAK: A STUDY OF PROFESSIONAL AND MANAGERIAL WOMEN RETURNING TO WORK AFTER HAVING A CHILD (BEBC Distribution, 1992).

129 Jan Winberg, *Mother and Newborn Baby: Mutual Regulation of Physiology and Behavior—A Selective Review*, 47 DEV. PSYCHOBIOL. 217 (2005).

130 Geoffrey M. Hodgson, *The Concept of Routine* (Univ. Hertfordshire Bus. Sch., Working Paper No. AL109AB, 2004); Janelle Ross, *Paul Ryan's Big Speaker Hangup Is Reportedly his Family. For a Male Lawmaker, That's Unusual*, THE WASHINGTON POST (Oct. 12, 2015), www.washingtonpost.com.

131 Kim Parker & Wendy Wang, *Modern Parenthood: Roles of Moms and Dads Converge as They Balance Work and Family*, PEW RESEARCH CTR (Mar. 14, 2013) www.pewsocialtrends.org; Aaron B. Rochlen et al., *'I'm Just Providing for my Family:' A Qualitative Study of Stay-at-home Fathers*, 9 PSYCHOL. MEN MASCULINITY 193 (2008); Aaron B. Rochlen et al., *Predictors of Relationship Satisfaction, Psychological Well-Being, and Life Satisfaction Among Stay-at-home Fathers*, 9 PSYCHOL. MEN MASCULINITY 17 (2008).

132 CHILD WELFARE INFORMATION GATEWAY, INFANT SAFE HAVEN LAWS 2 (Feb. 2013), www.childwelfare.gov.

133 Annette R. Appell, *Safe Havens to Abandon Babies, Part I*, 5 ADOPT. QUART. 59, 61 (2002) [hereinafter Appell Part I].

134 *Id.* at 61; CHILD WELFARE INFORMATION GATE, *supra* note 132. *See* MISS. CODE ANN. § 43-15-201 (2012) (72 hours after birth), IND. CODE ANN. § 31-34-2.5-1 (2012) (30 days after birth), *and* N.D. CENT. CODE § 27-20-02(1)(a) (2015) (defining infant as under 1 year of age).

135 CHILD WELFARE INFORMATION GATE, *supra* note 132, at 2–3. *See* WASH. REV. CODE ANN. § 13.34.350(1)(a) (2016) (defining appropriate location as an emergency room, a fire station, or a health clinic) *and* 23 PA. CONS. STAT. §§ 6504, 6504.1 (2016) (providing for requirements of health care providers and police officers accepting abandoned newborns).

136 CHILD WELFARE INFORMATION GATE, *supra* note 132, at 5. *See* CAL. HEALTH & SAFETY CODE § 1255.7(f)(2016); IOWA CODE § 233.2(4)(2016); *and* TENN. CODE ANN. § 36-1-142(d)(1)(2016).
137 Kevin O'Hanlon, *5 Years Later, Nebraska Patching Cracks Exposed by Safe-haven Debacle*, LINCOLN JOURNAL STAR (Jan. 21, 2013), http://journalstar.com.
138 Nora Gustavsson & Ann E. MacEachron, *Lessons from Nebraska*, 56 SOC. WORK 181 (2011).
139 Erik Eckholm, *Nebraska Revises Child Safe Haven Law*, N.Y. TIMES (Nov. 21, 2008), www.nytimes.com.
140 Joshua Rhett Miller, *Father who Ditched Nine Kids Via Safe Haven Law Has Twins on the Way*, FOX NEWS (June 30, 2009), www.foxnews.com.
141 NEB. REV. STAT. § 29–121 (2008).
142 Eckholm, *supra* note 139.
143 Annette R. Appell, *Safe Havens to Abandon Babies, Part II: The Fit*, 6 ADOPT. QUART. 61 (2002) [Appell Part II].
144 Gustavsson, *supra* note 138.
145 Appell Part I, *supra* note 133, at 61.
146 Appell Part II, *supra* note 143, at 65.
147 Annette R. Appell, *Safe Havens to Abandon Babies, Part III: The Effects*, 6 ADOPT. QUART. 67, 68 (2002) [hereinafter Appell Part III].
148 *Id.* at 68.
149 Carol Sanger, *Infant Safe Haven Laws: Legislating in the Culture of Life*, 106 COLUM. L. REV. 753, 756 (2006).
150 Appell Part III, *supra* note 147, at 68.
151 CLAUDIA F. PARVANTA ET AL., ESSENTIALS OF PUBLIC HEALTH COMMUNICATIONS (Jones & Bartlett Learning 2011).
152 Eve M. Brank, Stephanie C. Kucera, & Stephanie A. Hays, *Parental Responsibility Statutes: An Organization and Policy Implications*, 7 J.L. & FAM. STUD. 1, 6–14 (2005).
153 *Id.* at 19–25.
154 Eve M. Brank & Leroy Scott, *The Historical, Jurisprudential, and Empirical Wisdom of Parental Responsibility Laws*, 6 SOC. ISSUES POL'Y REV. 26, 28–31 (2012).
155 Eve M. Brank & Victoria Weisz, *Paying for the Crimes of their Children: Public Support of Parental Responsibility*, 32 J. CRIM. JUST. 465, 472 (2004); Eve M. Brank, Stephanie A. Hays, & Victoria Weisz, *All Parents Are to Blame (Except This One): Global Versus Specific Attitudes Related to Parental Responsibility Laws*, 36 J. APPLIED SOC. PSYCHOL. 2670, 2678 (2006); Eve M. Brank & Jodi Lane, *Punishing My Parents: Juveniles' Perspectives on Parental Responsibility*, 19 CRIM. JUST. POL'Y REV. 333, 341–344 (2008).
156 Ashley Wellman, Katherine Hazen, & Eve M. Brank, *Parental Blame Frame: An Empirical Examination of the Media's Portrayal of Parents and Their Delinquent Juveniles*, 15 WHITTIER J. CHILD & FAM. ADVOC. 87 (2017).
157 *Id.*

158 Dale A. Ihrie, *Parental Delinquency: Should Parents Be Criminally Liable for Failing to Supervise Their Children*, 74 U. DET. MERCY L. REV. 93 (1996).

159 Amy L. Tomaszewski, *From Columbine to Kazaa: Parental Liability in a New World*, 2005 UNIV. ILL. L. REV. 573 (2005).

160 Brank, et al., *supra* note 152, at 6–9.

161 ALA. CODE § 6-5-380(a) (2016).

162 Brank, et al., *supra* note 152, at 9.

163 *Id.* at 9–10.

164 *Id.* at 9–10; David Whisenant, *Mom Accused of Having 10-year-old Daughter Hold Drugs During Traffic Stop*, WBTV.COM (Oct. 18, 2016, 7:50 AM), www.wbtv.com.

165 Brank, et al., *supra* note 152, at 11–14.

166 NEV. REV. STAT. § 62.212 (1997); Nevada Assembly Bill 39 (1997).

167 Leslie Joan Harris, *Am Empirical Study of Parental Responsibility Laws: Sending Messages, but What Kind and to Whom?*, 5 UTAH L. REV. 5 (2006).

168 G. STANLEY HALL, ADOLESCENCE: ITS PSYCHOLOGY AND ITS RELATIONS TO PHYSIOLOGY, ANTHROPOLOGY, SOCIOLOGY, SEX, CRIME, RELIGION AND EDUCATION (D. Appleton and Co. 1904).

169 Brank, *supra* at note 154, at 45–47.

170 State v. Ephraim, 898 N.E.2d 974, 980 (Ohio Ct. App. 2008).

171 UNITED STATES CENSUS BUREAU: NEWSROOM, 10 PERCENT OF GRANDPARENTS LIVE WITH A GRANDCHILD, CENSUS BUREAU REPORTS, Oct. 22, 2014, www.census.gov.

172 NAT'L CENTER FOR CHRONIC DISEASE PREVENTION AND HEALTH PROMOTION, THE STATE OF AGING & HEALTH IN AMERICA 2013, www.cdc.gov.

173 Grandparent visitation is addressed in Chapter 8.

174 Meredith M. Minkler & Esme Fuller-Thompson, *The Health of Grandparents Raising Grandchildren: Results of a National Study*, 89 AM. J. PUBLIC HEALTH 1384 (1999).

175 Aaron Manns, Karen E. Atler, & Christine A. Fruhauf, *Daily Activities and Experiences of Custodial Grandparents: An Exploratory Study*, 35 PHYSICAL & OCCUPATIONAL THER. IN GERIATRICS 34, 45 (2017).

176 Kathleen Meara, *What's in a Name? Defining and Granting A Legal Status to Grandparents Who Are Informal Primary Caregivers of Their Grandchildren*, 52 FAM. CT. REV. 128 (2014).

177 Roberta G. Sands, Robin S. Goldberg-Glen, & Heajong Shin, *The Voice of Grandchildren of Grandparent Caregivers: A Strengths-Resilience Perspective*, 88 CHILD WELFARE 25, 27 (2009).

178 *Id.*

179 For one example of such financial help, see AARP New York, *Financial Help for Grandparents Raising Grandchildren*, AARP (June 4, 2010) www.aarp.org.

180 Catherine Chase Goodman et al., *Grandmother as Kinship Caregivers: Private Arrangements Compared to Public Child Welfare Oversight*, 26 CHILD. YOUTH SERVICES REV. 287 (2004).

181 Simon Clarke, *A Definition of Paternalism*, 5 CRISPP 81 (2010).

182 Joel Feinberg, *Legal Paternalism*, 1 CAN. J. PHILOS. 105 (1971).

183 John Hospers, *Libertarianism and Legal Paternalism*, 4 J. LIBERTARIAN STUD. 255 (1980).

184 *Id.*

185 Douglas N. Husak, *Paternalism and Autonomy*, 10 ROY I PH S 27 (1981).

186 STATE EDUCATION REFORMS, NATIONAL CENTER FOR EDUCATION STATISTICS, https://nces.ed.gov (last visited May 7, 2018). Some exceptions apply, *see* Wisconsin v. Yoder, 406 U.S. 205 (1972).

187 Twenty-three states mandate the subject matter taught: Arizona (ARIZ. REV. STAT. ANN. § 15–802); California (CAL. EDUC. CODE § 33190 (2018)); Colorado (COLO. REV. STAT. § 22-33-104.5); Connecticut (CON. GEN. STAT. §§ 10–249, 251); Delaware (DEL. CODE ANN. TIT 14 §§ 2703A, 2704); Georgia (GA. CODE ANN. § 20-2-690(c)(4)); Idaho (IDAHO CODE § 33–202); Illinois (105 ILCS §§ 5/26–1, 5/27–1); Kentucky (KY. REV. STAT. ANN. §§159.030(1)(b), 159.040, 159.080); Louisiana (LA. REV. STAT. ANN. § 17:236.1); Maine (Me. Rev. Stat. Ann. tit. 20-A § 5001-A(3)(A)(4)); Maryland (MD. CODE ANN., EDUC. § 7–301(a)(1); MD. REGS. CODE TIT. 13A §§ 10.01.01, 10.01.02, 10.01.03); Massachusetts (MASS. GEN. LAWS CH. 76 § 1); Michigan (MCLA § 380.1561(3)(f)); Minnesota (Minn. Stat. Ann. §§ 120A.22, 120A.24); Missouri (MO. ANN. STAT. § 167.031.2(2)(b)); Montana (MONT. CODE ANN. §§ 20-5-102(2)(e), 20-5-109); Nebraska (NEB. REV. STAT. § 79–1601(4)); Nevada (NEV. REV. STAT. § 392.700(12)); New Hampshire (N.H. Rev. Stat. Ann. § 193-A); New Mexico (N.M. STAT. ANN. § 22-1-2(E)); New York (N.Y. COMP. CODES R. & REGS. TIT. 8, § 100.01(e)(2)); North Dakota (N.D. Cent. Code §§ 15.1-23-04, 15.1-21-01, 15.1-21-02); Ohio (OHIO REV. CODE ANN. § 3301-34-03); Pennsylvania (24 P.S. §§ 13–1327.1(c)-(d)); Rhode Island (R.I. GEN. LAWS § 16-19-2(3)); South Carolina (S.C. CODE § 59-65-45(c)); South Dakota (S.D. CODIFIED LAWS § 13-27-3); Texas (TEX. EDUC. CODE ANN. § 25.086(a)(1)); Vermont (V.S.A. §§ 166b(j), 906); Washington (WASH. REV. CODE §§ 28A.200.010(4)-(5)); Wisconsin (WIS. STAT. ANN. § 118.165(1d)); and Wyoming (WYO. STAT. § 21-4-101(a)(vi)); 29 states set record-keeping requirements: Alabama (ALA. CODE §§ 16-28-5, 16-28-8); California (Cal. Educ. Code §§ 48222, 33190); Colorado (COLO. REV. STAT. § 22-33-204.5); Delaware (DEL. CODE ANN. TIT. 14 §§ 2703A, 2704); Florida (FLA. STAT. § 1002.41(b)); Georgia (GA. CODE ANN. § 20-2-690(c)(8)); Hawaii (HAW. ADMIN. R. § 8-12-15); Indiana (IND. CODE § 20.33.2); Kentucky (KY. REV. STAT. ANN. §§ 159.030(1)(b), 159.040, 159.080); Maine (ME. REV. STAT. ANN. TIT. 20-A § 5001-A(3)(A)(4)); Maryland (MD. CODE ANN. EDUC. § 7–301(a)(1)); Massachusetts (MASS. GEN. LAWS CH. 76 § 1); Minnesota (MINN. STAT. ANN. §§ 120A-22, 120A.24); Missouri (MO. ANN. STAT. § 167.031.2(2)(b)); Montana (MONT. CODE ANN. § 20-5-102(2)(e), 20-5-109); New Hampshire (N.H. REV. STAT. ANN. § 193-A); New Mexico (N.M. STAT. ANN. § 22-1-2.1(B)); New York (N.Y. COMP. CODES R. & REGS. TIT. 8, § 100.10(g)); North Carolina (GEN STAT. §§115C-548,

115C-549, 115C-556, & 115C-557); North Dakota (N.D. CENT. CODE § 15.1-23-05); Oregon (OR. REV. STAT. § 339.030(1)(e)); Pennsylvania (24 P.S. §§ 13–1327.1(e)(1), (2)); Rhode Island (R.I. GEN. LAWS § 16-19-2(2)); South Carolina (S.C. CODE § 59-65-40-(A)(4)); South Dakota (S.D. CODIFIED LAWS § 13-27-3); Tennessee (TENN. CODE ANN. § 49-6-3050); Virginia (VA. CODE ANN. § 22.1–271.4); Washington (WASH. REV. CODE §§ 28A.200.020(1); 28A.200.020(1)(b)); West Virginia (W. VA. CODE §§ 18-8-1(c)(1); 18-5-45). Twenty-seven states require a certain number of hours or days: Alabama (ALA. CODE § 16-28-5); Colorado (COLO. REV. STAT. § 22-33-204.5); Georgia (GA. CODE ANN. § 20-2-690(c)(5)); Indiana (IND. CODE § 20.33.2); Kansas (KAN. STAT. ANN. § 72–1111(a)(2)); Kentucky (KY. REV. STAT. ANN. §§ 159.030(1)(b), 159.040, 159.080); Louisiana (LA. REV. STAT. ANN. § 17:236); Massachusetts (MASS. GEN. LAWS CH. 76 § 1); Mississippi (MISS. CODE ANN. §§ 37-13-91(2)(e), 37-13-91(2)(i)); Missouri (MO. ANN. STAT. § 167.031.2(2)(a)); Montana (MONT. CODE ANN. § 20-5-102(2)(e), 20-5-109); Nebraska (NEB. REV. STAT. § 79–1601); New Mexico (N.M. STAT. ANN. § 22-12-2(B)); New York (N.Y. COMP. CODES R. & REGS. TIT. 8, § 100.10(f) (1, 2)); North Carolina (GEN STAT. § 115C-556); North Dakota (N.D. CENT. CODE § 15.1-23-04); Ohio (OHIO REV. CODE ANN. § 3301-34-03); Oklahoma (OKLA. STAT. TIT. 70, § 10–105(A); Pennsylvania (24 P.S. §§ 13–1327.1(c)); Rhode Island (R.I. GEN. LAWS § 16-19-2(1)); South Carolina (S.C. CODE § 59-65-40 (A)(2)); South Dakota (S.D. CODIFIED LAWS § 13-27-3); Tennessee (TENN. CODE ANN. § 49-6-3050); Virginia (VA. CODE ANN. § 22.1–254(A)); Washington (WASH. REV. CODE §§ 28A.200.020(1), 28A.200.010(5)); West Virginia (W. VA. CODE § 18-8-1(c)(1)); Wisconsin (WIS. STAT. ANN. § 118.165(1c)).

188 JOHN TAYLOR GATTO & ZACHARY SLAYBACK, DUMBING US DOWN: THE HIDDEN CURRICULUM OF COMPULSORY SCHOOLING (New Society Publishers, 2017).

189 Gary B. Melton, *The Clashing Symbols: Prelude to Child and Family Policy*, 42 AM. PSYCHOL. 345 (1987).

CHAPTER 6. DISSOLUTION OF MARRIAGE

1 McGuire v. McGuire, 157 Neb. 226 (1953).

2 *Id.* at 238.

3 Sanford N. Katz, FAMILY LAW IN AMERICA 77 (Oxford University Press, 2nd ed. 2014).

4 DIVORCE AND AFTER (Paul Bohannan ed., Doubleday, 1970).

5 Steve Duck, *A Topography of Relationship Disengagement and Dissolution*, 4 PERSONAL RELAT. 1 (1982).

6 Stephanie S. Rollie & Steve Duck, *Divorce and Dissolution of Romantic Relationships: Stage Models and Their Limitations*, in HANDBOOK OF DIVORCE AND RELATIONSHIP DISSOLUTION 223–240 (Mark A. Fine, eds., 2013).

7 Steve Duck, *How Do You Tell Someone You're Letting Go*, 18 PSYCHOL. 210 (2005).

8 Rollie & Duck, *supra* note 6, at 233.

9 *Id.*
10 Timothy D. Wilson & Daniel T. Gilbert, *Affective Forecasting: Knowing What to Want*, 14 AM. PSYCHOL. SOC. 131 (2005).
11 *See* Daniel T. Gilbert et al., *Immune Neglect: A Source of Durability Bias in Affective Forecasting*, 75 J. PERS. & SOC. PSYCHOL. 617 (1998); Timothy D. Wilson & Daniel T. Gilbert, *The Impact Bias Is Alive and Well*, 105 J. PERS. & SOC. PSYCHOL. 740 (2013).
12 *In re* Burrus, 136 U.S. 586 (1890).
13 Santosky v. Kramer, 455 U.S. 745, 770 (1982).
14 Although the Uniform Marriage and Divorce Act (UMDA) provides uniform standards for a number of topics related to marriage and divorce, states have not widely adopted it.
15 Joseph L. Steinberg, *Notes and Comments: The Law Office as a Social Laboratory*, 13 J. SEX & MARITAL THER. 142, 142 (1987).
16 NAT'L CTR. FOR HEALTH STATISTICS, CTR. DISEASE CONTROL AND PREVENTION, MARRIAGE AND DIVORCE (Mar. 17, 2017), www.cdc.gov.
17 BRIAN BIX, THE OXFORD INTRODUCTIONS TO U.S. LAW: FAMILY LAW 127 (Oxford University Press 2013).
18 JOANNA L. GROSSMAN & LAWRENCE M. FRIEDMAN, INSIDE THE CASTLE: LAW AND THE FAMILY IN 20TH CENTURY AMERICA (Princeton Univ. Press 2011).
19 *Id.*
20 *Id.*
21 Note, *Collusive and Consensual Divorce and the New York Anomaly*, 36 COLUM. L. REV. 1121 (1936).
22 HARRY KRAUSE & DAVID MEYER, FAMILY LAW IN A NUTSHELL (Thomson West, 5th ed. 2007).
23 Grossman & Friedman, *supra* note 18.
24 Robert K. Merton, *The Unanticipated Consequences of Purposive Social Action*, 1 AM. SOCIOL. REV. 894 (1936).
25 Rankin v. Rankin, 124 A.2d 639, 644 (Pa. 1956).
26 TRISHA ZELLER, FAMILY LAW AND PRACTICE § 4 (Arnold H. Rutkin, eds., Matthew Bender & Co., Inc. 2017).
27 Grossman & Friedman, *supra* note 18.
28 Stanley F. Mazur-Hart, *Changing from Fault to No-fault Divorce: An Interrupted Time Series Analysis*, 7 J. APPL. SOC. PSYCHOL. 300 (1977).
29 B. G. Gunter & Doyle P. Johnson, *Divorce Filing as Role Behavior: Effect of No-fault Law on Divorce Filing Patterns*, 40 J. MARRIAGE &. FAM. 571 (1978); *and* Ruth B. Dixon & Lenore J. Weitzman, *When Husbands File for Divorce*, 44 J. MARRIAGE & FAM. 103 (1982).
30 Dixon, *supra* note 29.
31 Thomas B. Marvell, *Divorce Rates and the Fault Requirement*, 23 LAW & SOC. REV. 543 (1989).

32 Gerald C. Wright & Dorothy M. Stetson, *The Impact of No-fault Divorce Law Reform on Divorce in Americans States*, 40 J. MARRIAGE & FAM. 575 (1978).

33 D. KELLY WEISBERG & SUSAN FRELICH APPLETON, MODERN FAMILY LAW (Aspen Publishers, 4th ed. 2010).

34 Superior Court of California, County of Sacramento, ONE DAY DIVORCE PROGRAM www.saccourt.ca.gov (last visited June 5, 2017).

35 Marianne Wyder, Patrick Ward, & Diego De Leo, *Separation as a Suicide Risk Factor*, 116 J. AFFECTIVE DISORDERS 208 (2009).

36 See, e.g, Jennifer E. McIntosh, Bruce M. Smyth, & Margaret Kelaher, *Overnight Care Patterns Following Parental Separation: Associations with Emotion Regulation in Infants and Young Children*, 19 J. FAM. STUD. 224 (2013).

37 David Knox & Ugo Corte, '*Work it Out/See a Counselor': Advice from Spouses in the Separation Process*, 48 J. DIVORCE & REMARRIAGE 79 (2008).

38 W. Kim Halford & Susie Sweeper, *Trajectories of Adjustment to Couple Relationship Separation*, 52 FAM. PROCESS 228 (2013).

39 David A. Sbarra et al., *Expressive Writing Can Impede Emotional Recovery Following Marital Separation*, 1 CLIN. PSYCHOL. SCI. 120 (2013).

40 Susie Sweeper & Kim Halford, *Assessing Adult Adjustment to Relationship Separation: The Psychological Adjustment to Separation Test (PAST)*, 20 J. FAM. PSYCHOL. 632 (2006).

41 Wyder, *supra* note 35.

42 Kairi Kolves, Naoko Ide, & Diego De Leo, *Suicidal Ideation and Behaviour in the Aftermath of Marital Separation: Gender Differences*, 120 J. AFFECTIVE DISORDERS 48 (2010); Kairi Kolves, Naoko Ide, & Diego De Leo, *Fluctuations of Suicidality in the Aftermath of a Marital Separation: 6-month Follow-up Observations*, 142 J. AFFECTIVE DISORDERS 256 (2012).

43 Halford & Sweeper, *supra* note 38. Of course, without true experimentation, causality cannot be confirmed. See Sheree J. Gibb, David M. Fergusson, & L. John Horwood, *Relationship Separation and Mental Health Problems: Findings from a 30-year Longitudinal Study*, 45 AUSTL. & N.Z. J. PSYCHIATRY 163 (2011).

44 David A. Sbarra, Hillary L. Smith, & Matthias R. Mehl, *When Leaving Your Ex, Love Yourself: Observational Ratings of Self-compassion Predict the Course of Emotional Recovery Following Marital Separation*, 23 PSYCHOL. SCI. 261 (2012).

45 *Id.*

46 *Id.*

47 Karen Hasselmo et al., *Psychological Distress Following Marital Separation Interacts with a Polymorphism in the Serotonin Transporter Gene to Predict Cardiac Vagal Control in the Laboratory*, 52 PSYCHOPHYSIOLOGY 736 (2015). In particular, short allele carriers.

48 Elena Moore, *Delaying Divorce: Pitfalls of Restrictive Divorce Requirements*, 37 J. FAM. ISSUES 2265 (2015).

49 *Id.* at 2278–81.

50 Jill D. Duba & Richard F. Ponton, *Catholic Annulment, and Opportunity for Healing and Growing: Providing Support in Counseling*, 31 J. PSYCHOL. & CHRISTIANITY 242 (2012).
51 John L. Young & Ezra E. H. Griffith, *Psychiatric Consultation in Catholic Annulment Proceedings*, 36 HOSPITAL & CMTY PSYCHIATRY 346 (1985).
52 John L. Young & Ezra E. H. Griffith, *Understanding Due Discretion of Judgment in Catholic Marriage Courts*, 19 BULL. AM. ACAD. PSYCHIATRY L. 109 (1991).
53 John L. Young & Ezra E. H. Griffith, *Experts in Church Courts: A Role not Sacred*, 13 BULL. AM. ACAD. PSYCHIATRY L. 359 (1985).
54 McGuire, 157 Neb. 226 (1953).
55 Richard H. Chused, *Married Women's Property Law: 1800–1850*, 71 GEO. L.J. 1359, 1396 (1983); NANCY COTT, PUBLIC VOWS: A HISTORY OF MARRIAGE AND THE NATION 52–55 (Harvard Univ. Press 2002).
56 James R. Ratner, *Community Property, Right to Survivorship, and Separate Property Contributions to Marital Assets: An Interplay*, 41 ARIZ. L. REV. 993 (1999).
57 Jeremy A. Blumenthal, *'To Be Human': A Psychological Perspective on Property Law*, 83 TULANE L. REV. 1 (2009).
58 Some research suggests this effect extends to items owned by a person close to them such as an intimate partner. See Weihua Zhao, Tingyong Feng, & Rebecca Kazinka, *The Extensibility of the Endowment Effect to Others Is Mediated by Degree of Intimacy*, 17 ASIAN J. SOC. PSYCHOL. 296 (2014).
59 *See infra* Chapter 1 *and* Carey K. Morewedge & Colleen E. Giblin, *Explanations of the Endowment Effect: An Integrative Review*, 19 TRENDS COG. SCI. 339 (2015).
60 Michal A. Strahilevitz & George Loewenstein, *The Effect of Ownership History on the Valuation of Objects*, 25 J. CONSUMER RELATIONS 276 (1998).
61 Timthy M. Flemming et al., *The Endowment Effect in Orangutans*, 25 INT'L J. COMP. PSYCHOL. 285 (2012).
62 Alice Wieland et al., *Gender Differences in the Endowment Effect: Women Pay Less, But Won't Accept Less*, 9 JUDGMENT & DECISION MAKING 558 (2014).
63 Sara Loughran Dommer & Vanitha Swaminathan, *Explaining the Endowment Effect Through Ownership: The Role of Identity, Gender, and Self-threat*, 39 J. CONSUMER RESEARCH 1034 (2013).
64 Luis F. Martinez, Marcel Zeelenberg, & John B. Risman, *Regret, Disappointment and the Endowment Effect*, 32 J. ECON. PSYCHOL. 962 (2011).
65 Joann Peck & Suzanne B. Shu, *The Effect of Mere Touch on Perceived Ownership*, 36 J. CONSUMER RES. 000 (2009).
66 This has become a growing field with the increase in online shopping. S. Adam Brasel & James Gips, *Tablets, Touchscreens, and Touchpads: How Varying Touch Interfaces Trigger Psychological Ownership and Endowment*, 24 J. CONSUMER PSYCHOL. 226 (2014).
67 Peck & Shu, *supra* note 65.
68 Joann Peck, Victor A. Barger, & Andrea Webb, *In Search of a Surrogate for Touch: The Effect of Haptic Imagery on Perceived Ownership*, 23 J. CONSUMER PSYCHOL. 189 (2013).

69 *Id.*

70 Arthur B. LaFrance, *Child Custody and Relocation: A Constitutional Perspective*, 34 U. LOUISVILLE J. FAM. L. 1 (1995).

71 Chris Guthrie, Jeffrey J. Rachlinski, & Andrew J. Wistrich, *Inside the Judicial Mind*, 86 CORNELL L. REV. 777 (2001).

72 Their remaining two studies used a different vignette about a boy finding a tree branch and focused on how he had used the branch and his future intentions with the branch.

73 Sarah Malcolm, Margaret A. Defeyter, & Ori Friedman, *Children and Adults Use Gender and Age Stereotypes in Ownership Judgments*, 15 J. COG. & DEVELOP. 123 (2014).

74 UNIFORM MARRIAGE AND DIVORCE ACT § 308 (1996); AMERICAN LAW INSTITUTE, PRINCIPLES OF THE LAW OF FAMILY DISSOLUTION: ANALYSIS AND RECOMMENDATIONS § 5.04 (2002).

75 Orr v. Orr, 440 U.S. 268 (1979).

76 *Id.* at 279.

77 *Id.* at 280.

78 CYNTHIA LEE STARNES, THE MARRIAGE BUYOUT: THE TROUBLED TRAJECTORY OF U.S. ALIMONY LAW (N.Y. Univ. Press 2014).

79 John C. Sheldon & Nancy Diesel Mills, *In Search of a Theory of Alimony*, 45 ME. L. REV. 283 (1993). Although there is some talk that regulations like child support may be necessary, see Victoria M. Ho & Jennifer J. Cohen, *An Update on Florida Alimony Case Law: Are Alimony Guidelines a Part of our Future*, 77 FLA. BAR J. 79 (2003).

80 Grossman & Friedman, *supra* note 18.

81 Sheldon & Mills, *supra* note 79.

82 Starnes, *supra* note 78, at 4.

83 Jennifer L. McCoy, *Spousal Support Disorder: An Overview of Problems in Current Alimony Law*, 33 FLA. ST. U. L. REV. 501 (2005).

84 L. J. Jackson, *Alimony Arithmetic: More States Are Looking at Formulas to Regulate Spousal Support*, 98 A.B.A. J. 15 (2012).

85 FLA. STAT. §61. 08(1) (2017).

86 *Id.* § 61.01(2).

87 *Id.* § 61.08(2)(f).

88 Marcia Canavan & Eva Kolstad, *Does the Use of Social Media Evidence in Family Law Litigation Matter?*, 15 WHITTIER J. CHILD & FAM. ADVOC. 49 (2016).

89 N.C. GEN. STAT. § 50–16.3A(b)(1) (2017).

90 *Id.* § 50–16.3A(d).

91 GA. CODE ANN. § 19-6-1(b) (2010).

92 Cynthia Lee Starnes, *One More Time: Alimony, Intuition, and the Remarriage-termination Rule*, 81 IND. L.J. 971 (2006).

93 Elisabeth M. Landes, *Economics of Alimony*, 7 J. LEGAL STUD. 35 (1978); Sharon S. Oster, *A Note on the Determinants of Alimony*, 49 J. MARRIAGE & FAM. L. 81 (1987).

94 TENN. CODE ANN. § 36-5-121(i)(1) (2017).
95 Guthrie et al., *supra* note 71.
96 *Id.*
97 Jackson, *supra* note 84.
98 Catherine Groves Peele, *Social and Psychological Effects of the Availability and the Granting of Alimony on the Spouses*, 6 LAW & CONTEMP. PROBS. 283 (1939).
99 Judith G. McMullen, *Alimony: What Social Science and Popular Culture Tell Us About Women, Guilt, and Spousal Support After Divorce*, 19 DUKE J. GENDER L. & POL'Y 41 (2011).
100 Tahany M. Gadalla, *Impact of Marital Dissolution on Men's and Women's Incomes: A Longitudinal Study*, 50 J. DIVORCE & REMARRIAGE 55 (2009).
101 See Chapter 1.
102 *In re Marriage of* Meeghan, 13 Cal. Rptr. 2d 799 (Cal. App. 4th Dist. 1992).
103 Colleen Marie Halloran, *Comment: Petitioning A Court to Modify Alimony When a Client Retires*, 28 U. BALT. L. REV. 193,226–227 (1998).
104 Constance L. Shehan et al., *Alimony: An Anomaly in Family Social Science*, 51 FAM. RELATIONS 308 (2002).
105 *Id.*
106 Robert F. Kelly & Greer Litton Fox, *Determinations of Alimony awards: An Empirical Test of Current Theories and a Reflection on Public Policy*, 44 SYRACUSE L. REV. 641 (1993).
107 *Id.*
108 Thomas D. Vu, *Going to Court as a Last Resort: Establishing a Duty for Attorneys in Divorce Proceedings to Discuss Alternative Dispute Resolution with Their Clients*, 47 FAM. CT. REV. 586 (2009).
109 Kathryn D. Rettig & Carla M. Dahl, *Impact of Procedural Factors on Perceived Justice in Divorce Settlements*, 6 SOC. JUST. RES. 301 (1993).
110 Gregory Firestone & Janet Weinstein, *In the Best Interests of Children: A Proposal to Transform the Adversarial System*, 42 FAM. CT. REV. 203 (2004).
111 Jeffery Zimmerman, *Divorce: Using Psychologists' Skills for Transformation and Conflict Reduction*, 72 J. CLIN. PSYCHOL. 423 (2016).
112 A. Rodney Nurse & Peggy Thompson, *Collaborative Divorce: A Family-centered Process*, in THE WILEY-BLACKWELL HANDBOOK OF FAMILY PSYCHOLOGY 475 (James H Bray & Mark Stanton, eds. 2009).
113 Marina Tolou-Shams, *Collaborative Divorce: An Oxymoron?*, 31 BROWN UNIV. CHILD & ADOLESCENT BEHAV. LETTER 1 (2015).
114 Susan J. Gamache, *Family Peacemaking with an Interdisciplinary Team: A Therapist's Perspective*, 53 FAM. CT. REV. 378 (2015).
115 Maria Alba-Fisch, *Collaborative Divorce: An Effort to Reduce the Damage of Divorce*, 75 J. CLIN. PSYCHOL. 444, 445 (2016).
116 *Id.* at 446–449.
117 Lauren Behrman, *It Takes a Village—Taming High Conflict with the "2 PC Model,"* 75 J. CLIN. PSYCHOL. 469 (2016).

118 Alba-Fisch, *supra* note 115, at 444.
119 Dori Cohen, *Making Alternative Dispute Resolution (ADR) Less Alternative: The Need for ADR as Both a Mandatory Continuing Legal Education Requirement and a Bar Exam Topic*, 44 FAM. CT. REV. 640 (2006).
120 Marsha Kline Pruett, Glendessa M. Insabella, & Katherine Gustafson, *The Collaborative Divorce Project: A Court-based Intervention for Separating Parent with Young Children*, 43 FAM. CT. REV. 38 (2005).
121 Penelope Eileen Bryan, *'Collaborative Divorce' Meaningful Reform or Another Quick Fix?* 5 PSYCHOL. PUB. POL'Y & L. 1001 (1999).
122 *Id.*
123 Joan Dworkin & William London, *What Is a Fair Agreement*, 7 MEDIATION Q. 3 (1989).
124 Yishai Boyarin, *Court-connected ADR—A Time of Crisis, A Time of Change*, 50 FAM CT. REV. 377 (2012) [hereinafter *Court-connected ADR*].
125 Jay Folberg, *A Mediation Overview: History and Dimension of Practice*, 1 MEDIATION Q. 3, 5–6 (1983) (describing divorce mediation efforts beginning in the 1960s and gaining momentum in the 1970s); JOAN B. KELLY, CARL ZLATCHIN, & JOEL SHAWN, DIVORCE MEDIATION: PROCESS, PROSPECTS, AND PROFESSIONAL ISSUES IN PSYCHOLOGY, PSYCHIATRY, AND THE LAW: A CLINICAL AND FORENSIC HANDBOOK 243, 245 (C.P. Ewing Ed., 1985).
126 Yishai Boyarin, *Court-connected ADR—A Time of Crisis, A Time of Change*, 95 MARQ. L. REV. 993 (2012) [hereinafter *Time of Change*].
127 *Id.*
128 Lin Adrian & Solfrid Mykland, *Creativity in Court-connected Mediation: Myth or Reality?*, 30 NEGOTIATION J. 421 (2014).
129 Janet Walker, *Family Mediation: The Rhetoric, the Reality and the Evidence*, 47 VITENSKAP OG PSYKOLOGI 676 (2010).
130 Ilan G. Gewurz, *(Re)Designing Mediation to Address the Nuances of Power Imbalance*, 19 CONFLICT RESOLUTION Q. 135 (2001).
131 Robert E. Emery & Melissa M. Wyer, *Divorce Mediation*, 42 AM. PSYCHOL. 472 (1987).
132 Robert E. Emery & Melissa M. Wyer, *Child Custody Mediation and Litigation: An Experimental Evaluation of the Experience of Parents*, 55 J. CONSULT. & CLIN. PSYCHOL. 179, 185 (1987).
133 The researchers randomly assigned whether the parents would be asked whether they would like to participate in mediation. The majority asked did participate.
134 *Id.*
135 *Id.*
136 Robert E. Emery, Sheila G. Matthews, & Melissa M. Wyer, *Child Custody Mediation and Litigation: Further Evidence on the Differing Views of Mothers and Fathers*, 59 J. CONSULT. & CLIN. PSYCHOL. 410 (1991).
137 *Id.* at 414–418.
138 Katherine M. Kitzmann & Robert E. Emery, *Child and Family Coping One Year After Mediated and Litigated Child Custody Disputes*, 8 J. FAM. PSYCHOL. 150 (1994).

139 Kathleen A. Camara & Gary Resnick, *Styles of Conflict Resolution and Cooperation Between Divorced Parents: Effects on Child Behavior and Adjustment*, 59 AM. J. ORTHOPSYCHIATRY 560 (1989).

140 MUZAFER SHERIF, EXPERIMENTAL STUDY OF POSITIVE AND NEGATIVE INTERGROUP ATTITUDES BETWEEN EXPERIMENTALLY PRODUCED GROUPS: ROBBERS CAVE STUDY (1954).

141 Norman G. Poythress et al., *Procedural Justice Judgments of Alternative Procedures for Resolving Medical Malpractice Claims*, 23 J. APPLIED SOC. PSYCHOL. 1639 (1993).

142 Krause & Meyer, *supra* note 22, at 239.

143 Tim Stanley, *The Changing Face of the American Family*, 62 HIST. TODAY (2012), www.historytoday.com.

144 REBECCA TRAISTER, ALL THE SINGLE LADIES: UNMARRIED WOMEN AND THE RISE OF AN INDEPENDENT NATION 159 (2016).

CHAPTER 7. CHILD CUSTODY, VISITATION, AND SUPPORT

1 WIKIHOW, www.wikihow.com (last visited June 9, 2017).

2 *wikiHow to Win a Custody Battle*, WIKIHOW, www.wikihow.com (last visited June 9, 2017).

3 Joseph L. Steinberg, *Notes and Comments: The Law Office as a Social Laboratory*, 13 J. SEX & MARITAL THER. 142 (1987).

4 *See generally* MARY ANN MASON, FROM FATHER'S PROPERTY TO CHILDREN'S RIGHTS: THE HISTORY OF CHILD CUSTODY IN THE UNITED STATES (1994) (discussing the history of child custody norms under the Common Law in the colonial era).

5 Jamil S. Zainaldin, *The Emergence of a Modern American Family Law: Child Custody, Adoption, and the Courts, 1769–1851*, 73 NW. U. L. REV. 1038 (1979); Nickols v. Giles, 2 Root 461 (Conn. 1796).

6 DOROTHY A. MAYS, WOMEN IN EARLY AMERICA: STRUGGLE, SURVIVAL, AND FREEDOM IN A NEW WORLD 72 (ABC Clio, Inc. 2004).

7 Orr v. Orr, 440 U.S. 268, 278–79 (1978).

8 Laura E. Santilli & Michael C. Roberts, *Custody Decisions in Alabama Before and After the Abolition of the Tender Years Doctrine*, 14 L. & HUM. BEHAV. 123 (1990); Devine v. Devine, 398 So. 2d. 686 (Ala. 1981).

9 Santilli & Roberts, *supra* note 8.

10 Palmore v. Sidoti, 466 U.S. 429 (1984).

11 Eileen P. Huff, *The Children of Homosexual Parents: The Voices the Courts Have Yet to Hear*, 9 AM. U. J. GENDER SOC. POL'Y & L. 695 (2001).

12 *Id.* at 433.

13 Timothy J. Biblarz & Evren Savci, *Lesbian, Gay, Bisexual, and Transgender Families*, 72 J. MARRIAGE & FAM. 480 (2010); Nanette Gartrell & Henny Bos, *U.S. National Longitudinal Lesbian Family Study: Psychological Adjustment of 17-year-old Adolescents*, 126 PEDIATRICS 28 (2010).

14 According to Eastman, there are 12 states that use this terminology. Christina M. Eastman, *Statutory Regulation of Legal Parentage in Cases of Artificial Insemination by Donor: A New Frontier of Gender Discrimination*, 41 MCGEORGE L. REV. 371, 378–80 (2010).
15 Wisconsin v. Yoder, 406 U.S. 205 (1972).
16 Pater v. Pater, 588 N.E.2d 794 (Ohio 1992).
17 *In re* Sampson, 317 N.Y.S.2d 641 (N.Y. Fam. Ct. 1970).
18 Warren D. Camp, *Child Custody Disputes in Families of Muslim Tradition*, 49 FAM. CT. REV. 582 (2011).
19 Kristine Uhlman & Elisa Kisselburg, *Islamic Shari'a Contracts: Pre-nuptial and Custody Protections*, 10 J. CHILD CUSTODY 359, 365–66 (2013).
20 *Id.* at 366.
21 *Id.* at 367.
22 Camp, *supra* note 871.
23 GARY B. MELTON, JOHN PETRILA, NORMAN G. POYTHRESS, & CHRISTOPHER SLOBOGIN, PSYCHOLOGICAL EVALUATIONS FOR THE COURTS: A HANDBOOK FOR MENTAL HEALTH PROFESSIONALS AND LAWYERS (Guilford Press 2007).
24 Karen S. Adam & Stacey N. Brady, *Fifty Years of Judging in Family Law: The Cleavers Have Left the Building*, 51 FAM. CT. REV. 28 (2013).
25 CHILD WELFARE INFO. GATEWAY, CHILDREN'S BUREAU, U.S. DEP'T OF HEALTH & HUMAN SERV., DETERMINING THE BEST INTERESTS OF THE CHILD: SUMMARY OF STATE LAWS (2010).
26 Glenn H. Miller, *The Psychological Best Interest of the Child Is Not the Legal Best Interest*, 30 J. AM. ACAD. PSYCHIATRY L. 196 (2002).
27 Melton, et al., *supra* note 23.
28 Leigh D. Hagan & Ann C. Hagan, *Custody Evaluations without Psychological Testing: Prudent Practice or Fatal Flaw?*, 36 J. PSYCHIATRY & L. 27 (2008).
29 A.P.A., *Guidelines for Child Custody Evaluations in Family Law Proceedings*, 65 AM. PSYCHOL. 863 (2010).
30 *Id.* at 864.
31 James N. Bow & Francella A. Quinnell, *A Critical Review of Child Custody Evaluation Reports*, 40 FAM. CT. REV. 164 (2002).
32 *Id.* at 167.
33 *Id.*
34 *Id.* at 171.
35 James N. Bow, Michael C. Gottlieb, & Gould-Saltman, *Attorneys' Beliefs and Opinions About Child Custody Evaluations*, 49 FAM. CT. REV. 301 (2013).
36 Linda Nielsen, *Woozles: Their Role in Custody Law Reform, Parenting Plans, and Family Court*, 20 PSYCHOL. PUB. POL'Y & L. 164 (2014).
37 *Id.*
38 *Id.* at 2.
39 *Id.* at 3.

40 Ira Daniel Turkat, *Harmful Effects of Child-custody Evaluations on Children*, 52 CT. REV. 152 (2016) [hereinafter *Harmful Effects*]; Jonathan W. Gould & Allan Posthuma, *The Unsubstantiated Claims of Turkat's Harmful Effects of Child-custody Evaluations on Children*, 52 CT. REV. 160 (2016); *and* Ira Daniel Turkat, *Child Dead and Parent Charged with Murder After Psychologist Recommends Said Parent to Court: Turkat Responds to Gould and Posthuma's Custody-evaluation Fallacies*, 52 CT. REV. 170 (2016) [hereinafter *Turkat Responds*].

41 *Harmful Effects*, *supra* note 40.

42 *Id.* at 155.

43 Gould & Posthuma, *supra* note 40.

44 It should be noted that Turkat only asked about the negative impacts of a child custody evaluation and not any potential positive effects.

45 *Id.*

46 Karen Saywitz, Lorinda B. Camparo, & Anna Romanoff, *Interviewing Children in Custody Cases: Implications of Research and Policy for Practice*, 28 BEHAV. SCI. & L. 542 (2010).

47 *Id.* at 549–556.

48 Judith Cashmore & Patrick Parkinson, *The Use and Abuse of Social Science Research Evidence in Children's Cases*, 20 PSYCHOL. PUB. POL'Y & L. 239 (2014).

49 Robert H. Mnookin, *Child-custody Adjudication: Judicial Functions in the Face of Indeterminacy*, 30 L. & CONTEMP. PROBS. 225, 289 (1975).

50 Inge Bretherton et al., *'If I Could Tell the Judge Something About Attachment . . .' Perspectives on Attachment Theory in the Family Law Courtroom*, 49 FAM. CT. REV. 539 (2011).

51 John A. Zervopoulos, *Drafting the Parenting Evaluation Court Order: A Conceptual and Practical Approach*, 28 BEHAV. SCI. & L. 480 (2010).

52 J. Herbie DiFonzo, *From the Rule of One to Shared Parenting: Custody Presumptions in Law and Policy*, 52 FAM. CT. REV. 213 (2014).

53 *Id.*

54 Julie E. Artis & Andrew V. Krebs, *Family Law and Social Change: Judicial Views of Joint Custody, 1998–2011*, 40 L. & SOC. INQUIRY 723 (2015).

55 Amos Tversky & Daniel Kahneman, *Rational Choice and the Framing of Decisions*, 59 J. BUS. S251 (1986); Richard H. Thaler et al., *The Effect of Myopia and Loss Aversion on Risk Taking: An Experimental Test*, 112 Q. J. ECON, VOL. 647 (1997).

56 Andre P. Derdeyn, *Child Custody: A Reflection of Cultural Change*, 7 J. CLIN. CHILD PSYCHOL. 169 (1978); Andre P. Derdeyn & Elizabeth Scott, *Joint Custody: A Critical Analysis and Appraisal*, 54 AM. J. ORTHOPSYCHIAT. 199 (1984).

57 Lita Linzer Schwartz, *Joint Custody: Is it Right for All Children?*, 1 J. FAM. PSYCHOL. 120 (1987).

58 Marjorie Lindner Gunnoe & Sanford L. Braver, *The Effects of Joint Legal Custody on Mothers, Fathers, and Children Controlling for Factors that Predispose a Sole Maternal Versus Joint Legal Award*, 25 L. & HUM. BEHAV. 25 (2001).

59 Peter Jaffe, *A Presumption Against Shared Parenting for Family Court Litigants*, 52 FAM. CT. REV. 187 (2014).
60 David L. Chambers, *Rethinking the Substantive Rules for Custody Disputes in Divorce*, 83 MICH. L. REV. 477 (1984).
61 Ariana Prazen et al., *Joint Physical Custody and Neighborhood Friendships in Middle Childhood*, 81 SOCIOLOG. INQUIRY 247 (2011).
62 Richard A. Warshak, *Social Science and Parenting Plans for Young Children: A Consensus Report*, PSYCHOL. PUB. POL'Y & L. 46 (2014). *But see* Jennifer E. McIntosh et al., *Responding to Concerns About a Study of Infant Overnight Care Postseparation, With Comments on Consensus: Reply to Warshak (2014)*, 21 PSYCHOL. PUB. POL'Y & L. 111 (2015).
63 Amandine Baude, Jessica Pearson, & Sylvie Drapeau, *Child Adjustment in Joint Physical Custody Versus Sole Custody: A Meta-analytic Review*, 57 J. DIVORCE & REMARRIAGE 338 (2016); Robert Bauserman, *Child Adjustment in Joint-custody Versus Sole-custody Arrangements: A Meta-analytic Review*, 16 J. FAM. PSYCHOL. 91 (2002).
64 Edward Kruk, *'Bird's Nest' Co-parenting Arrangements: When Parents Rotate in and out of the Family Home*, PSYCHOLOGY TODAY (Jul. 16, 2013), www.psychologytoday.com.
65 Prazen, et al., *supra* note 61.
66 Vanessa A. K. Hurwtiz, *Bird's Nest Parenting: Parent's Perceptions of Their Nesting Process*, PROQUEST DISSERTATIONS PUBLISHING (2016).
67 *Id.*
68 WIKIHOW TO IMPLEMENT A BIRD'S NEST CUSTODY ARRANGEMENT, WIKIHOW, www.wikihow.com (last visited June 11, 2017).
69 Hurwitz, *supra* note 66.
70 Phoebe C. Ellsworth & Robert J. Levy, *Legislative Reform of Child Custody Adjudication: An Effort to Rely on Social Science Data in Formulating Legal Policies*, 4 L. & SOC'Y REV. 167 (1969).
71 Bruce Sales, Rachel Manber, & Linda Rohman, *Social Science Research and Child-custody Decision Making*, 1 APPLIED & PREVENTIVE PSYCHOL. 23 (1992).
72 Social Security Act, 42 U.S.C.S. § 667 (2017).
73 18 U.S.C.S. § 228 (2017).
74 Nat'l Conference of State Legislature, *Child Support Guideline Models by State* (June 9, 2016) www.ncsl.org.
75 *Deion Sanders Must Pay $10,500/Month*, FOXSPORTS (May 15, 2012, 1:00 AM) www.foxsports.com.
76 Bureau of Labor Statistics, *Usual Weekly Earnings of Wage and Salary Workers First Quarter 2017*, NEWS RELEASE (April 18, 2017, 10:00 AM) www.bls.gov.
77 Jennifer M. Threlfall & Patricia L. Kohl, *Addressing Child Support in Fatherhood Programs: Perspectives of Fathers and Service Providers*, 64 FAM. RELAT. 291 (2015).

78 Judith A. Seltzer, Nora Cate Schaeffer, & Hong-Wen Charng, *Family Ties After Divorce: The Relationship Between Visiting and Paying Child Support*, 51 J. MARRIAGE & FAM. 1013–1032 (1989).
79 Joyce A. Arditti & Timothy Z. Keith, *Visitation Frequency, Child Support Payment, and the Father-child Relationship Postdivorce*, 55 J. MARRIAGE & FAM. 699 (1993).
80 Sanford L. Braver et al., *A Longitudinal Study of Noncustodial Parents: Parents Without Children*, 7 J. FAM. PSYCHOL. 9 (1993).
81 Arditti & Keith, *supra* note 79.
82 Paul R. Amato & Bruce Keith, *Parental Divorce and the Well-being of Children: A Meta-analysis*, 110 PSYCHOL. BULL. 26 (1991); Paul R. Amato, *Children of Divorce in the 1990s: An Update of Amato and Keith (1991) Meta-analysis*, 15 J. FAM. PSYCHOL. 355 (2001) [hereinafter *Update of Amato and Keith (1991)*]; Paul R. Amato, *The Impact of Family Formation Change on the Cognitive, Social, and Emotional Well-being of the Next Generation*, 15 FUTURE OF CHILD. 75 (2005) [hereinafter *Family Formation Change*].
83 Gene V. Glass, *Primary, Secondary, and Meta-analysis of Research*, 5 EDUC. RESEARCHER 3 (1976).
84 Amato & Keith, *supra* note 82, at 28.
85 *Update of Amato and Keith (1991)*, *supra* note 82.
86 *Id.*
87 Tamara A. Fackrell, Alan J. Hawkins, & Nicole M. Kay, *How Effective Are Court-affiliated Divorcing Parents Education Programs? A Meta-analytic Study*, 49 FAM. CT. REV. 107 (2011).
88 PARENTEDUCATION & FAMILY STABILIZATION COURSE, *Welcome to FloridaParentingClass.com*, www.floridaparentingclass.com/ (last visited June 12, 2017).
89 PARENTEDUCATION & FAMILY STABILIZATION COURSE, *Parenting Course Overview*, www.floridaparentingclass.com (last visited June 12, 2017).
90 Fackrell, et al., *supra* note 87.
91 *Id.* at 112.
92 Jesse L. Boring et al., *Children of Divorce-coping with Divorce: A Randomized Control Trial of an Online Prevention Program for Youth Experiencing Parental Divorce*, 83 J. CONSULTING & CLIN. PSYCHOL. 999 (2015).
93 Caroline Christopher et al., *Long-term Effects of a Parenting Preventive Intervention on Young Adults' Painful Feelings About Divorce*, 31 J. FAM. PSYCHOL. 799 (2017), http://psycnet.apa.org.
94 Eleni Vousoura et al., *Parental Divorce, Familial Risk for Depression, and Psychopathology in Offspring: A Three-generation Study*, 21 J. CHILD FAM. STUD. 718 (2012).
95 Sherryl H. Goodman et al., *Dimensions of Marital Conflict and Children's Social Problem-solving Skills*, 13 FAM. PSYCHOL. 33 (1999).
96 Maike Luhman et al., *Subjective Well-being and Adaptation to Life Events: A Meta-analysis*, 102 J. PERSON. & SOC. PSYCHOL. 592 (2012).

97 *Id.*

98 Elizabeth Kramrei et al., *Post-divorce Adjustment and Social Relationships*, 46 J. DIVORCE & REMARRIAGE 145 (2007).

99 Ross A. Thompson et al., *Grandparents' Visitation Rights: Legalizing the Ties that Bind*, 44 AM. PSYCHOL. 1217 (1989).

100 WASH. REV. CODE § 26.10.160(3); Troxel v. Granville, 530 U.S. 57, 65, 67 (2000).

101 530 U.S. 57 (2000).

102 *Id.* at 67.

103 JOANNA L. GROSSMAN & LAWRENCE M. FRIEDMAN, INSIDE THE CASTLE: LAW AND THE FAMILY IN 20TH CENTURY AMERICA 1 (Princeton University Press, 2011).

104 Jean Giles-Sims & Charles Lockhart, *Grandparents' Visitation Rights*, 44 J. DIVORCE & REMARRIAGE 1 (2006).

105 Theodore J. Stein, *Court-ordered Grandparent Visitation: Welcome Event or Unwarranted Intrusion into Family Life?*, 81 SOC. SERVICE REV. 229 (2007).

106 *Id.*

107 Tammy L. Henderson, *Grandparent Visitation Rights: Successful Acquisition of Court-ordered Visitation*, 26 J. FAM. ISSUES 107 (2005).

108 *Id.* at 115.

109 *Id.* at 117.

110 FEDERAL JUDICIAL CENTER, DEMOGRAPHY OF ARTICLE III JUDGES, 1789–2015, www.fjc.gov (last visited May 2, 2018).

111 *Who we Elect: The Demographics of State Legislatures*, NAT'L CONFERENCE OF STATE LEGISLATURES, www.ncsl.org (last visited June 12, 2017).

112 Eric Kotloff, *All Dogs Go to Heaven . . . Or Divorce Court: New Jersey Unleashes a Subjective Value Consideration to Resolve Pet Custody Litigation in Houseman v. Dare*, 55 VILL. L. REV. 447 (2010).

113 *Pet Custody Disputes on the Ride Find Nation's Top Matrimonial Lawyers—Survey Reveals More Couples Clawing Through Divorce*, AM. ACA. MATRIMONIAL LAWYERS (Feb. 12, 2017), www.aaml.org.

114 *Id.*

115 Ann Hartwell Britton, *Bones of Contention: Custody of Family Pets*, 20 J. AM. ACA. MATRIMONIAL LAW. 1 (2006).

116 *Id.* at 6.

117 Ann Margaret Carrozza, *A Love Contract to Help Pets Deal with Breakup*, HUFFPOST (June 30, 2015, 3:40 PM), www.huffingtonpost.com.

118 Britton, *supra* note 115.

119 Carrozza, *supra* note 117.

120 Christopher Mele, *When Couples Divorce, Who Gets to Keep the Dog? (Or Cat)*, N.Y. TIMES (Mar. 23, 2017), www.nytimes.com.

121 ALASKA STAT. § 25.24.230(a)(6)(2016).

122 Froma Walsh, *Human-animal Bonds II: The Role of Pets in Family Systems and Family Therapy*, 48 FAM. PROC. 4, 481 (2009); Deborah L. Wells, *The Effects*

of Animals of Human Health and Well-being, 65 J. SOC. ISSUES 3, 523 (2009); Carol M. Cockran, *An Extension of Me*, 23 SOC'Y & ANIMALS 231 (2015); Juliane Kaminski & Marie Nitzchner, *Do Dogs Get the Point? A Review of Dog-human Communication Ability*, 44 LEARNING & MOTIVATION 294 (2013).

123 Gregg Herman & Randy K. Otto, *Introduction to the Special Issues on Families, Divorce, Custody and Parenting*, 28 BEHAV. SCI. & L. 461, 461 (2010).

124 LENORE WALKER, OUR BROKEN FAMILY COURT SYSTEM 7–26 (Ithaca Press 2012).

CHAPTER 8. INTIMATE PARTNER VIOLENCE, CHILD MALTREATMENT, AND ELDER MALTREATMENT

1 DAVE PELZER, A CHILD CALLED 'IT' 31, 35 (HCI 1995).

2 JEANNETTE WALLS, THE GLASS CASTLE: A MEMIOR (Scribner 2006).

3 Geraldine Bedell, *Child Abuse as Entertainment*, THE GUARDIAN (Sept. 2, 2001, 6:33 PM), www.theguardian.com.

4 AMAZON PRIME, "Child Abuse" www.amazon.com (last visited June 13, 2017).

5 ELIZABETH PLECK, DOMESTIC TYRANNY: THE MAKING OF AMERICAN SOCIAL POLICY AGAINST FAMILY VIOLENCE FROM COLONIAL TIMES TO THE PRESENT (Univ. Illinois Press 2004).

6 Matthew J. Breiding, J. Chen, & Michele C. Black, *Intimate Partner Violence in the United States*, NAT'L CTR. FOR INJURY PREVENTION & CONTROL, CDC (2010), www.cdc.gov.

7 *Id.*

8 *See, e.g.*, Victor Wu, Harold Huff, & Mohit Bhandari, *Pattern of Physical Injury Associated with Intimate Partner Violence in Women Presenting to the Emergency Department: A Systematic Review and Meta-analysis*, 11 TRAUMA VIOLENCE & ABUSE 71 (2010); Sarah E. Evans, Corrie Davies, & David DiLillo, *Exposure to Domestic Violence: A Meta-analysis of Child and Adolescent Outcomes*, 13 AGGRESSION & VIOLENT BEHAV. 131 (2008); *and* David A. Wolfe et al., *The Effects of Children's Exposure to Domestic Violence: A Meta-analysis and Critique*, 6 CLIN. CHILD & FAM. PSYCHOL. REV. 171 (2003).

9 Dana L. Radatz & Emily M. Wright, *Integrating the Principles of Effective Intervention into Batterer Intervention Programming: The Case for Moving Toward More Evidence-based Programming*, 17 TRAUMA VIOLENCE & ABUSE 72 (2016); Edward W. Gondolf, *The Weak Evidence for Batterer Program Alternatives*, 16 AGGRESSION & VIOLENT BEHAV. 347 (2011).

10 LENORE E.A. WALKER, BATTERED WOMAN SYNDROME (Springer Publishing Co., 4th ed. 2017).

11 PROBLEM SOLVING COURTS: SOCIAL SCIENCE AND LEGAL PERSPECTIVES (Richard L. Wiener & Eve M. Brank eds., Springer Press 2013).

12 Greg Berman & John Feinblatt, *Problem-solving Courts: A Brief Primer*, 23 L. & POL'Y 125 (2001).

13 Robyn Mazur & Liberty Aldrich, *What Makes a Domestic Violence Court Work? Lessons from New York*, 42 JUDGES' J. 5 (2003).

14 Rekha Mirchandani, *What's so Special about Specialized Courts? The States and Social Change in Salt Lake City's Domestic Violence Court*, 39 L. & SOC'Y REV. 380 (2005).

15 Angela R. Gover, John M. MacDonald, & Geoffery P. Alpert, *Combating Domestic Violence: Findings from an Evaluation of a Local Domestic Violence Court*, 3 CRIM. & PUB. POL'Y 109 (2003).

16 Rekha Mirchandani, *'Hitting Is Not Manly' Domestic Violence Court and the Re-imagination of the Patriarchal State*, 20 GEN. & SOC'Y 781 (2006).

17 *Id.*

18 Angela R. Gover, Eve M. Brank & John M. MacDonald, *A Specialized Domestic Violence Court in South Carolina: An Example of Procedural Justice for Victims and Defendants*, 13 VIOLENCE AGAINST WOMEN 603 (2007).

19 Mark E. Oliver, *A Meta-analysis of Predictors of Offender Treatment Attrition and its Relationship to Recidivism*, 79 J. CONSULTING & CLIN. PSYCHOL. 6 (2011); Lisa M. Jewell & J. Stephen Wormith, *Variables Associated with Attrition from Domestic Violence Treatment Programs Targeting Male Batters: A Meta-analysis*, 37 CRIM. JUST. & BEHAV. 1086 (2010).

20 CHILD WELFARE INFORMATION GATEWAY, CHILDREN'S BUREAU, U.S. DEPART. OF HEALTH & HUM. SERV., MANDATORY REPORTERS OF CHILD ABUSE AND NEGLECT: STATE STATUTES CURRENT THROUGH AUGUST 2015 (2015), *available at* www.childwelfare.gov.

21 Debra Cassens Weiss, *Child Abuse Reporting Law Is Often Trumped by Lawyer's Duty of Confidentiality, Ethics Opinion Says*, A.B.A. JOURNAL (Sept. 11, 2015 9:09 AM) www.abajournal.com.

22 Marije Stoltenberg et al., *The Prevalence of Child Maltreatment Across the Globe: Review of a Series of Meta-analyses*, 24 CHILD ABUSE REV. 37 (2015).

23 Lilian Katz, *The Right of the Child to Develop and Learn in Quality Environments*, 35 INT'L J. EARLY CHILD. 13 (2003).

24 ERIC A. SHELMAN & STEPHEN LAZORITZ, THE MARY ELLEN WILSON CHILD ABUSE CASE AND THE BEGINNING OF CHILDREN'S RIGHTS IN 19TH CENTURY AMERICA 11 (McFarland & Co., Inc. 2005).

25 Henry C. Kempe et al., *The Battered-child Syndrome*, 181 JAMA 17, 17 (1962).

26 Child Abuse Prevention and Treatment Act of 1974, 42 U.S.C. §§ 5101–5106 (2006).

27 Stoltenberg, *supra* note 22.

28 NAT'L CTR. FOR INJURY PREVENTION & CONTROL, DIV. OF VIOLENCE PREVENTION, *Child Abuse Prevention*, www.cdc.gov (last visited June 14, 2017).

29 Judith C. Baer & Colleen Daly Martinez, *Child Maltreatment and Insecure Attachment: A Meta-analysis*, 24 J. REPRO. & INFANT PSYCHOL. 187 (2006).

30 Marjolaine Masson et al., *Neuropsychological Profile of Children, Adolescents and Adults Experiencing Maltreatment: A Meta-analysis*, 29 CLIN. NEUROPSYCHOL. 573 (2015).

31 Lena Lim, Joaquim Radua, & Katya Rubia, *Gray Matter Abnormalities in Childhood Maltreatment: A Voxel-wise Meta-analysis*, 171 AM. J. PSYCHIATRY 854 (2014).

32 Tyler C. Hein & Christopher S. Monk, *Research Review: Neural Response to Threat in Children, Adolescents, and Adults After Child Maltreatment—A Quantitative Meta-analysis*, 58 J. CHILD PSYCHOL. & PSYCHIATRY 222 (2017).

33 Cathy Spatz Widom, *Child Abuse, Neglect, and Adult Behavior: Research Design and Findings on Criminality, Violence, and Child Abuse*, 59 AM. J. ORTHOPSYCHIATRY 355 (1989); CATHY SPATZ WIDOM, NAT'L INST. OF JUSTICE: RESEARCH IN BRIEF, THE CYCLE OF VIOLENCE (1992).

34 Allan V. Horowitz, et al., *The Impact of Childhood Abuse and Neglect on Adult Mental Health: A Prospective Study*, 42 J. HEALTH & SOC. BEH. 184 (2001).

35 Xiangming Fang et al., *The Economic Burden of Child Maltreatment in the United States and Implications for Prevention*, 36 CHILD ABUSE & NEGLECT 156 (2012).

36 *Id.*

37 *See, e.g.*, CHILDREN AS VICTIMS, WITNESSES, AND OFFENDERS: PSYCHOLOGICAL SCIENCE AND THE LAW (Bette L. Bottoms, Cynthia J. Najdowski, & Gail S. Goodman, eds., Guildford Press 2009) *and* CHILDREN, SOCIAL SCIENCE, AND THE LAW (Bette L. Bottoms, Margaret Bull Kovera, & Bradley D. MacAuliff, eds., Cambridge University Press 2002).

38 *See, e.g.*, ALA. CODE § 13A-3–24(1) (2017), ALASKA STAT. § 11.81.430(a)(1) (2016).

39 Murray A. Straus, BEATING THE DEVIL OUT OF THEM: CORPORAL PUNISHMENT IN AMERICAN FAMILIES 4 (Lexington Books 1994).

40 George W. Holden, *Perspectives on the Effects of Corporal Punishment: Common of Gershoff (2002)*, 128 PSYCHOL. BULL. 590 (2002).

41 Christopher Ferguson, *Spanking, Corporal Punishment and Negative Long-term Outcomes: A Meta-analytic Review of Longitudinal Studies*, 33 CLIN. PSYCHOL. REV. 196, 197 (2013).

42 Elizabeth Thompson Gershoff, *Corporal Punishment by Parents and Associated Child Behaviors and Experiences: A Meta-analytic and Theoretical Review*, 128 PSYCHOL. BULL. 539 (2002).

43 *Id.*

44 Diana Baumrind, Robert E. Larzelere, & Philip A. Cowan, *Ordinary Physical Punishment: Is it Harmful? Comment on Gershoff (2002)*, 128 PSYCHOL. BULL. 580 (2002).

45 Ferguson, *supra* note 41.

46 APA DIV. 7 & DIV. 37, THE TASK FORCE ON PHYSICAL PUNISHMENT OF CHILDREN, PHYSICAL PUNISHMENT OF CHILDREN: A SUMMARY OF RESEARCH AND ITS IMPLICATIONS FOR PARENTING, POLICY, AND PRACTICE (2016).

47 Paolla Magioni Santini & Lucia C. A. Williams, *Parenting Programs to Prevent Corporal Punishment: A Systematic Review*, 26 PAIDEIA 121 (2016).

48 31 schools have banned corporal punishment according to E. T. Gershoff & S. A. Font, *Corporal Punishment in U.S. Public Schools: Prevalence, Disparities in Use, and Status in State and Federal Policy*, 30 SRCD SOC. POL. REP. 1 (2016).
49 A Task Force of Divisions 7 and 37 of the American Psychological Association (APA) has recently called for APA to pass a resolution opposing physical punishment of children by parents and follow such resolution with public education concerning the topic. APA Div. 7 & Div. 37, *supra* note 46.
50 Julie Crandall, *Poll: Most Approve of Spanking Kids*, ABC NEWS (Nov. 8, 2016) http://abcnews.go.com.
51 GLOBAL INITIATIVE TO END ALL CORPORAL PUNISHMENT OF CHILDREN, *States Which Have Prohibited All Corporal Punishment*, www.endcorporalpunishment.org (last visited May 7, 2018).
52 Holden, *supra* note 40.
53 Cara B. Ebbeling, Dorota B. Pawlak, & David S. Ludwig, *Childhood Obesity: Public-health Crisis, Common Sense Cure*, 360 LANCET 473 (2002).
54 Jenny Reichert & Monica K. Miller, *Assessment of Mock Jurors' Attributions and Decisions in Child Abuse Cases: Protecting the Wellbeing of Obese Children*, in PSYCHOLOGY, LAW, AND THE WELLBEING OF CHILDREN 210 (Monica K. Miller, Jared Chamberlain, & Twila Wingrove eds., Oxford University Press 2014).
55 Keeley J. Pratt & Annette G. Greer, *Debating Parental Responsibility for Childhood Obesity: Ethical and Legal Considerations*, 7 BARIATRIC NURSING & SURGICAL PATIENT CARE 146 (2012).
56 Layson L. Lusk & Brenna Ellison, *Who Is to Blame for the Ride in Obesity*, 68 APPETITE 14 (2013).
57 *Id.* at 17.
58 Deena Patel, *Super-sized Kids: Using the Law in Combat Morbid Obesity in Children*, 43 FAM. CT. REV. 164, 164 (2005).
59 Reichert & Miller, *supra* note 54.
60 Eve M. Brank, Edie Greene, & Katherine Hochevar, *Holding Parents Responsible: Is Vicarious Responsibility the Public's Answer to Juvenile Crime?*, 17 PSYCHOL. PUB. POL'Y & L. 507 (2011).
61 Frank R. Ezzo, Thomas M. Evans, & Meghan McGovern-Kondik, *Termination of Parental Rights: Integration of Theory, Practice, and Demographics*, 22 AM. J. FORENSIC PSYCHOL. 29 (2014).
62 Santosky v. Kramer, 455 U.S. 745 (1982).
63 BENJAMIN D. GARBER, DEVELOPMENTAL PSYCHOLOGY FOR FAMILY LAW PROFESSIONALS: THEORY, APPLICATION, AND THE BEST INTERESTS OF THE CHILD (Springer Publishing Co. 2010).
64 Adoption and Safe Families Act of 1997 § 103, 42 U.S.C. § 1305 (1997).
65 Lenore M. McWey, Tammy L. Henderson, & Susan N. Tice, *Mental Health Issues and the Foster Care System: An Examination of the Impact of the Adoption and Safe Families Act*, 32 J. MARITAL & FAM. THERAPY 195 (2006).
66 Garber, *supra* note 63.

67 U.S. DEP'T OF HEALTH & HUMAN SERVICES, ADMIN. FOR CHILDREN & FAMILIES, THE AFCARS REPORT 23 (2016), www.acf.hhs.gov.
68 Mark E. Courtney, et al., *Midwest Evaluation of the Adult Functioning of Former Foster Youth: Outcomes of Age 26* (Chapin Hill 2011).
69 See *infra* Chapter 7.
70 American Psychological Association, *Guidelines for Psychological Evaluations in Child Protection Matters*, www.apa.org.
71 *Id.*
72 Eve M. Brank et al., *Parental Compliance: Its Role in Termination of Parental Rights Cases*, 80 NEB. L. REV. 335 (2001).
73 *Id.* at 347.
74 Karen Zilberstein, *Parenting in Families of Low Socioeconomic Status: A Review with Implications for Child Welfare Practice*, 54 FAM. CT. REV. 221 (2016).
75 Andrea S. Meyer et al., *Substance Using Parents, Foster Care and Termination of Parental Rights: The Importance of Risk Factors for Legal Outcomes*, 32 CHILD. & YOUTH SERV. REV. 639 (2010).
76 Mark S. Lachs & Karl A. Pillemer, *Elder Abuse*, 373 NEW ENGLAND J. MEDICINE 1947 (2015).
77 As noted in the introduction to this chapter, Amazon.com listed 30,899 books using the search term "child abuse." "Elder abuse" garnered only 735 results.
78 Carolyn L. Dessin, *Financial Abuse of the Elderly: Is the Solution a Problem?*, 34 MCGEORGE L. REV. 267 (2003).
79 Child financial abuse is so infrequent it is included as "Other/Unknown" child abuse by the Children's Bureau of the Administration for Children and Families. THE CHILDREN'S BUREAU, ADMIN. FOR CHILDREN AND FAMILIES, U.S. DEP'T OF HEALTH AND HUMAN SERV., CHILD MALTREATMENT 2016 (2017), www.acf.hhs.gov.
80 Peterson v. State, 765 So. 2d 861 (Fla. Dist. Ct. App. 2000).
81 *Id.* at 864.
82 People v. Simester, 678 N.E.2d 710 (Ill. App. Ct. 1997).
83 *Id.* at 712–13.
84 Sieniarecki v. Florida, 756 So. 2d 68 (Fla. 2000).
85 Lindsey E. Wylie & Eve M. Brank, *Assuming Elder Care Responsibility: Am I a Caregiver?*, 6 J. EMPIRICAL LEGAL STUD. 899 (2009).
86 *Id.*
87 Neal J. Roese & Kathleen D. Vohs, *Hindsight Bias*, 7 PERSP. SCI. 411 (2012); Aileen Oeberst & Ingke Goeckenjan, *When Being Wise After the Event Results in Injustice Evidence for Hindsight Bias in Judges' Negligence Assessments,* 22 PSYCHOL. PUB. POL'Y L. 271 (2016).
88 Jennifer Brown-Cranstoun, *Kringen v. Boslough and Saint Vincent Hospital: A New Trend for Healthcare Professionals who Treat Victims of Domestic Violence?*, 33 J. HEALTH L. 629, 629–31 (2000). At least five states currently mandate that physicians report their suspicion of intimate partner abuse to a law enforcement

agency, even over the protests of the victim. CAL. PENAL CODE § 11160 (West 2011); COLO. REV. STAT. ANN. § 12-36-135 (West 2010); KY. REV. STAT. ANN. § 209.030 (West 2011); N.H. REV. STAT. ANN. § 631:6 (West 2011); R.I. GEN. LAWS § 23–17.8–2 (West 2011). *See generally* James T. R. Jones, *Kentucky Tort Liability for Failure to Report Family Violence*, 26 N. KY. L. REV. 43, 57 (1999); Mia M. McFarlane, *Mandatory Reporting of Domestic Violence: An Inappropriate Response for New York Health Care Professionals*, 17 BUFF. PUB. INT. L.J. 1, 21 (1999).

89 Eve M. Brank, Lindsey E. Wylie, & Joseph A. Hamm, *Potential for Self-reporting of older Adult Maltreatment: An Empirical Examination*, 19 ELDER L. J. 351 (2012).

90 CONN. GEN. STAT. ANN. § 176–450 (West 2011) (defining "elderly person" as "any resident of Connecticut who is sixty years of age or older"); LA. REV. STAT. ANN. § 46:61 (West 2011) (noting that "elderly abuse" constitutes "abuse of any person sixty years of age or older and shall include the abuse of any infirm person residing in a state licensed facility").

91 Janine Robben, *Keeping an Eye Out for Elders: Tough Times Call for Knowing the Signs of Abuse or Neglect*, 69 OR. ST. B. BULL. 19, 27 (2009) (discussing the role of attorneys in spotting the different types of older adult maltreatment).

92 Brank, Wylie, & Hamm, *supra* note 89.

93 *See* ALASKA STAT. § 47.24.010 (2017); Colo. Rev. Stat. § 26–3.1–102 (2017); 320 ILL. COMP. STAT. 20/4 (2014); MD. CODE ANN. FAM. LAW § 14–302 (Lexis-Nexis 2018); OHIO REV. CODE ANN. §§ 5101.60(K), 61 (LexisNexis 2018); WYO. STAT. ANN. § 35-20-103 (2018).

94 Brank, Wylie, & Hamm, *supra* note 89.

95 Eve M. Brank, *Elder Research: Filling an Important Gap in Psychology and Law*, 25 BEH. SCI. & L., 701 (2007).

96 Catherine J. Ross, *Choosing a Text for the Family Law Curriculum of the Twenty-first Century*, 44 FAM. CT. REV. 584 (2006).

CONCLUSION

1 Mary E. O'Connell & J. Herbie DiFonzo, *The Family Law Education Reform Project Final Report*, 44 FAM. CT. REV. 524 (2006).

2 *Id.*

3 *Id.*

4 *Id.*

5 *Supra* note 1.

6 *Id.*

7 Catherine J. Ross, *Choosing a Text for the Family Law Curriculum of the Twenty-first Century*, FAM. CT. REV. 584 (2006).

8 *Id.*

9 International Child Abduction Remedies Act, 42 U.S. C. §§11601–22610 (2006).

10 Carl E. Schneider & Lee E. Teitelbaum, *Life's Golden Tree: Empirical Scholarship and American Law*, 2006 UTAH L. REV. 53, 90–91 (2006).

INDEX

ABOUT THE AUTHOR

Eve M. Brank is a Professor of Psychology, Courtesy Professor of Law, and Director of the Center on Children, Families, and the Law at the University of Nebraska, Lincoln.

Made in the USA
Las Vegas, NV
21 June 2021